THE MOMENT

THE MOMENT

Standing Up to Bill Cosby, Speaking Up for Women

ANDREA CONSTAND

VIKING

VIKING

an imprint of Penguin Canada, a division of Penguin Random House Canada Limited

Canada • USA • UK • Ireland • Australia • New Zealand • India • South Africa • China

First published 2021

Copyright © 2021 by Andrea Constand

All rights reserved. Without limiting the rights under copyright reserved above, no part of this publication may be reproduced, stored in or introduced into a retrieval system, or transmitted in any form or by any means (electronic, mechanical, photocopying, recording or otherwise), without the prior written permission of both the copyright owner and the above publisher of this book.

www.penguinrandomhouse.ca

Library and Archives Canada Cataloguing in Publication

Title: The moment : standing up to Bill Cosby, speaking up for women / Andrea Constand.
Names: Constand, Andrea, 1973- author.
Identifiers: Canadiana (print) 2021009334X | Canadiana (ebook) 20210093617
| ISBN 9780735240476 (hardcover) | ISBN 9780735240483 (EPUB)
Subjects: LCSH: Constand, Andrea, 1973- | LCSH: Sexual abuse victims—Canada—Biography. |
LCSH: Rape victims—Canada—Biography. | LCSH: Constand, Andrea, 1973-—Trials, litigation, etc.
| LCSH: Cosby, Bill, 1937-—Trials, litigation, etc. | LCSH: Sex crimes—United States. | LCSH: Trials
(Sex crimes)—United States. | LCSH: Sexual harassment of women. | LCSH: MeToo movement.
Classification: LCC HV6592 .C66 2021 | DDC 364.15/3092—dc23

Book design by Kate Sinclair
Cover design by Kate Sinclair
Cover image © Mark Makela / Stringer / Getty Images

Manufactured in Canada

10 9 8 7 6 5 4 3 2 1

Penguin
Random House
VIKING CANADA

To Great Uncle Salvo and to my nonna,
Erminia D'Acquisto Morace, who embodied
Salvo's legacy. Their presence in my life gave me
the hope, faith and courage to tell my story.

"One must resign oneself to the will of God at
the cost of whatever pain or whatever sacrifice."

Salvo D'Acquisto

CONTENTS

PUBLISHER'S NOTE

In writing this book, Andrea Constand worked with an editor and fact-checker. Material about other accusers as well as all trials and legal actions was independently sourced through criminal trial transcripts, press reports, and other published accounts. All excerpts from police records or legal depositions were quoted from the publicly available records and transcripts of the two criminal trials. A partial list of sources appears on page 231.

On June 30, 2021, just as this book was on its way to the printer, the Supreme Court of Pennsylvania overturned the 2018 conviction of Bill Cosby on a procedural issue. The decision hinged on a promise by the District Attorney not to prosecute Mr. Cosby if he would agree to sit for a deposition in Ms. Constand's civil case against him. The DA never informed Ms. Constand and her attorneys of any conversations between the former prosecutor and Mr. Cosby or his then criminal counsel, nor was there any written agreement memorializing it. Mr. Cosby's testimony in the deposition later became key evidence in the criminal trial when the DA's successors pressed charges against him. The Court ruled that the original promise was binding on any successors to the DA, and therefore they should not have brought a criminal case against him. The decision did not challenge any of the facts disclosed in the deposition or during the trial. Andrea Constand and her attorneys issued a statement in reaction to this decision, which you may read on page 227.

TIMELINE OF EVENTS

Pre-2004

Winter 2001   I am named director of operations for women's basketball at Temple University in Philadelphia, Pennsylvania.

Fall 2002   I meet Bill Cosby, an alumnus and supporter of the men's and women's basketball programs, at Temple.

2004

Early January   Bill Cosby drugs and assaults me at his Elkins Park, Pennsylvania, home.

March 31   I leave Temple University to return to Toronto and enrol in a massage therapy course.

2005

January 13   After I disclose my assault, my mother calls the Durham Regional Police to file a complaint. Three officers come to the house to take my statement.

January 19   A detective from the Cheltenham Township Police Department in Pennsylvania calls to discuss my statement, which was forwarded to him by the Durham Regional Police.

January 21   News of my allegation against Cosby appears in the press.

January 22   I travel to Philadelphia to be interviewed by the Cheltenham Township police.

January 26   In the New York City offices of his lawyers, Bill Cosby is also interviewed by the Cheltenham Township police.

February 8   Tamara Green makes an allegation of assault by Cosby after my story breaks.

February 9   Cheltenham detectives come to Toronto to interview me a second time.

| February 17 | Bruce Castor, the Montgomery County district attorney, announces that he will not bring charges against Bill Cosby. |
| March 8 | My lawyers launch a civil suit against Cosby. Cosby is deposed September 28, 2005. |

2006

| June 9 | Barbara Bowman makes a public accusation of sexual assault by Cosby. |
| November 8 | My civil suit against Cosby is settled. As part of the settlement, I sign a strict non-disclosure agreement. At the same time, I settle my defamation suit against his lawyer, Marty Singer, and the *National Enquirer*. |

2014

| October 16 | A video of comedian Hannibal Buress calling Bill Cosby a rapist goes viral. |
| November | Several accusers go public with accusations against Cosby in this month: Joan Tarhis, Linda Joy Traitz, Janice Dickinson, Therese Serignese. |

2015

March	Lise-Lotte Lublin asks Nevada legislators to rescind the statute of limitations on sexual assault.
April 23	Janice Baker-Kinney publicly discloses her allegation of sexual assault by Cosby.
April 30	Lili Bernard goes public with her accusation of sexual assault by Cosby.
July 6	The Associated Press obtains portions of Cosby's deposition from my civil suit. In it, he admits to giving a woman Quaaludes and then having sex with her.
July 19	The *New York Times* publishes a summary of the entire deposition.

November 4	Kevin Steele beats Bruce Castor to become the district attorney of Montgomery County. During the campaign, he was critical of Castor's failure to prosecute Cosby.
December 30	Bill Cosby is charged with three counts of aggravated indecent assault against me.

2016

May 24	A Montgomery County district court judge rules that the DA's criminal case against Cosby can move forward. Judge Steven T. O'Neill is assigned to the case.

2017

January 21	I attend the Women's March in Washington, DC. Many other Cosby accusers are also there.
June 5	The first criminal trial of Bill Cosby begins.
June 17	After more than fifty hours of deliberations, the jury declares itself hopelessly deadlocked. The case ends in a mistrial.

2018

April 9	Bill Cosby's second criminal trial begins.
April 26	Cosby is found guilty of all three counts of aggravated indecent assault.
September 25	Judge O'Neill sentences Cosby to three to ten years in prison and designates him a sexually violent predator. He's immediately taken to State Correctional Institution–Phoenix, a state prison in Montgomery County, Pennsylvania.

2020

December 1	Bill Cosby's appeal is heard. He maintains his innocence and has never shown remorse for his actions.

2021

June 30	The Supreme Court of Pennsylvania overturns Bill Cosby's criminal conviction on a procedural issue. Cosby is released from prison the same day.

PEOPLE

Prosecutors

 Bruce Castor, district attorney of Montgomery County (2000–2008)

 Risa Vetri Ferman, district attorney of Montgomery County (2008–2016)

 Kevin Steele, district attorney of Montgomery County (2016–present), lead prosecutor in both criminal trials of Bill Cosby

 Kristen Feden, assistant district attorney of Montgomery County, prosecutor in both criminal trials

 Stewart Ryan, assistant district attorney of Montgomery County, prosecutor in both criminal trials

Cosby Defence Attorneys

 Marty Singer, defence counsel in civil suit (2005)

 Brian McMonagle, lead defence counsel in first criminal trial (2017)

 Angela Agrusa, defence counsel in first criminal trial

 Tom Mesereau, lead defence counsel in second criminal trial (2018)

 Kathleen Bliss, defence counsel in second criminal trial

 Joseph P. Green, Jr., lead defence counsel in sentencing hearing (2018)

My Team

 Dolores Troiani and *Bebe Kivitz*, lawyers for the 2005 civil suit and my personal legal representatives for both criminal trials

 Angela Rose and *Delaney Henderson*, representatives from PAVE (Promoting Awareness/Victim Empowerment), a non-profit organization that works to prevent sexual violence through social advocacy and education

 Erin Slight, counsellor with Montgomery County Victims Services

 Kiersten McDonald, investigator with the Montgomery County Detective Bureau (and Turks's handler)

 Turks, Montgomery County therapy dog

Others

Elizabeth McHugh, judge in the 2016 preliminary hearing; ruled that
the case could proceed to trial

Steven T. O'Neill, judge for both criminal trials

Gloria Allred, legal representative for a number of the other
Cosby complainants

Detectives

David Mason, Durham Regional Police; witness in both trials

Richard Schaffer, Cheltenham Township Police Department;
witness in both trials

Jim Reape, Cheltenham Township Police Department; witness in
both trials

Mike Shade, Cheltenham Township Police Department; assigned
to reopened case in 2015

Prior Bad Act Witness, First Trial

Kelley Johnson (identified only as "Kacey" prior to the trial)

Prior Bad Act Witnesses, Second Trial

Janice Baker-Kinney, Janice Dickinson, Chelan Lasha,
Lise-Lotte Lublin, Heidi Thomas

Jane Doe Witnesses, Civil Trial

Virginia Bennet, Barbara Bowman, Denise Ferrari, Beth Ferrier,
Kelley Johnson, Donna Motsinger, Patte O'Connor, Kristina Ruehli,
Therese Serignese, Patricia Steuer, Jennifer "Kaya" Thompson

The twelfth Jane Doe witness wishes to remain anonymous.

Other Cosby Accusers

Pamela Abeyta, Jewel Allison, Donna Barrett, Lili Bernard, Linda Brown, Shawn Brown, Autumn Burns, Sarita Butterfield, Lisa Christie, Lachele Covington, Dottye, Joyce Emmons, Carla Ferrigno, Charlotte Fox, Chloe Goins, Tamara Green, Helen Gumpel, Helen Hayes, Renita Chaney Hill, Colleen Hughes, Michelle Hurd, Judith (Judy) Huth, Beverly Johnson, Lisa Jones, Charlotte Kemp, Linda Kirkpatrick, Cindra Ladd, Angela Leslie, PJ Masten, Sammie Mays, Katherine (Kathy) McKee, Louisa Moritz, Cynthia Myers (witnessed Cosby's assaults on unnamed others), *Rebecca Lynn Neal, Stacey Pinkerton, Linda Ridgeway Whitedeer, Margie Shapiro, Dona Speir, Jena T., Joan Tarshis, Marcella Tate, Eden Tirl, Linda Joy Traitz, Victoria Valentino, Sharon Van Ert, Sunni Welles*

Four other women came forward using the pseudonyms *"Elizabeth," "Lisa," "Sandy,"* and *"Katy."*

CHAPTER 1

A MOMENT LOST

I was perched on the corner of my bed at my parents' cozy cottage-style house in Pickering, Ontario, as a chilly mid-February day faded outside. This place had been my refuge for almost a year now—ever since I'd returned from Philadelphia and my many years far from home. I was holding my cellphone to my ear, listening carefully. I'd known this conversation was coming, but there was part of me that wasn't quite ready to have it.

A few hours earlier, I had been out running errands with my sister when my mother phoned. "Dolores is going to give you a call," she said. This was Dolores Troiani—she and Bebe Kivitz were my lawyers. Diana and I cut short our trip so I could be in the house when the call came.

When we pulled into our quiet street, I knew that whatever my lawyers were going to tell me was big news. The road in front of our house was lined with vans and cars emblazoned with the logos of TV stations and newspapers. Reporters had been harassing my parents and me for weeks now. They called our home phone non-stop; they turned up on our doorstep at all times of the day and night. Sometimes they showed up en masse, like troops camped right outside our front door. That was the scene this day. Clearly something major had just happened.

Diana and I hadn't been in the house long before my cell rang.

"Andrea"—Dolores's tone was kind but measured and matter-of-fact—"we're sorry to tell you this, but the DA isn't going to move forward with the case. There won't be any charges."

I wasn't surprised. Not really.

My lawyers and I had sensed that the case we were attempting to pursue wasn't looking good. It was yet another sharp blow in what had already been, without a doubt, the most difficult year of my life.

A little more than twelve months earlier, everything had been different. I was a happy, confident thirty-year-old with a great job as the director of operations for the women's basketball team at Temple University in Philadelphia. My work at Temple was a natural fit. Sports had always been my passion. I was an active child, and athletics had helped me channel my considerable energy and have fun at the same time. By high school, I was a star basketball player, and in my final year, I was lucky enough to see dozens of university scholarships flood in. In the end, I headed to the University of Arizona to play college ball. It turned out to be a wonderful choice, not just because I enjoyed the team and the school so much, but also because my paternal grandparents decided to retire to Tucson when they learned that I was a bit homesick. I saw them almost every day and was delighted to have my family close by once more.

At the end of my time at university, I had hoped for a spot on the fledgling WNBA roster, but when that didn't materialize, I wasn't disappointed for long. After a wonderful year spent teaching basketball skills to middle-school children in North Hollywood, California, I made the Canadian team for the 1997 World University Games in Italy. While there, I was recruited by Sicily's professional women's basketball team, and I played for two seasons before returning to Canada. I worked for Nike in Toronto for a short while before taking the Temple position, then spent almost three years in Philly. But in early 2004, I was ready to shift my path again. I was planning to move back to Canada to rejoin my large extended family and my old friends, and to pursue a career in the healing arts, as both my mother and my father had done.

I had a good future before me. I knew who I was and I liked who I was. I was at the top of my game, certain that the groundwork laid by my education and my athletic training had prepared me for whatever challenges were ahead.

But I was wrong. Very wrong.

Nothing could have prepared me for an early January evening spent at the home of a man I considered a friend.

That was the night that Bill Cosby raped me.

I was introduced to Bill Cosby in the autumn of 2002, more than a year after I'd started my job at Temple. He was an alumnus of the university, as well as a trustee, a significant donor, and an enthusiastic supporter of the women's basketball program. The first time I met him, he was part of a small group of Temple employees and team supporters who were being given a tour of our newly renovated locker room.

I knew who he was, of course, but I had never watched *The Cosby Show* and had no real idea how big a celebrity he was. He'd been an extremely successful stand-up comedian, and in 1965, he was the first African American to land a starring role in a weekly TV show, the drama *I Spy*. It was a potent symbol of a changing America. (In the previous year, the Civil Rights Act had been signed into law. The Selma March, in which Black protestors were brutalized by police, happened the same year as *I Spy* hit the airwaves.)

Cosby's star power continued to build with a number of his own TV shows—including the popular children's animated series *Fat Albert and the Cosby Kids*—before *The Cosby Show* debuted in 1984. The family-friendly sitcom, in which Cosby played an obstetrician and father of five, was a huge success during its eight-year run, earning him the nickname America's Dad. Cosby was also a big hit with marketers—his wholesome image and goofy charm made him the perfect spokesman for Jell-O and Coca-Cola, among other brands. By the mid-eighties, in fact, he'd become the highest-paid entertainer in the world, according to *Forbes* magazine.

Even as he was conquering the world of stage and screen, Cosby earned a doctorate in education, and he often gave public lectures about the importance of parenting, family, education, personal responsibility, ambition, and self-actualization.

I suppose it's a testament to how little television I consumed as a child that Bill Cosby and most of his achievements had largely escaped my notice. And so I credited the attention he garnered at Temple—his calls had to be returned immediately, his interest in our new locker room was promptly met with an offer to tour the facility—to the fact that he was a major financial supporter of the university.

Yet despite his obvious importance, Bill Cosby struck me as a down-to-earth and affable guy. During the tour of the locker room, he was surrounded by Temple employees and other supporters, but he appeared to have come alone—or at least without an entourage. He was dressed casually. He joked and bantered—and whenever he spoke, his warmly resonant voice was met with a chorus of chuckles. At one point while we were discussing some of the new athletic equipment, he turned and asked if anyone had a sore back. He had the perfect treatment, he said, and he looked over at me. "Here, I'll show you." He told me to stand with my back to his and my arms bent. Once we were back to back, he slipped his arms through mine and attempted to hoist me up. I could tell he was staggering as he did this, and the room erupted in laughter. Since I couldn't see him, I'm not exactly sure what the joke was—perhaps he was making out that I was too tall for the stretching manoeuvre to work—but whatever it was, it seemed all in good fun. A silly moment with a man who obviously loved to entertain.

After that day, I rarely saw him on campus, but he would often call the office to chat about the team and the overall program. As the head of operations, I was often the one fielding the calls. Sometimes he would ring with a specific question, but usually our conversation would slip into a more general discussion of the men's or women's college basketball season, or the NBA, or other sports. We were both huge sports fans. We also began to talk about other shared areas of interest, like healthy eating and homeopathic remedies. Eventually, Mr. Cosby—everyone around the office called him that or Mr. C.—began to ask me a few questions about myself. When he heard that I had been a communications major and had once considered getting into broadcasting, he offered to help, which I thought was kind. He arranged for me to talk to a few media industry executives, suggested I take acting lessons, and advised me to get a headshot for job applications.

While he never invited me to call him Bill or talked to me about his personal life, I became increasingly comfortable with Mr. C. He loved to tease me about my Canadian accent and would work "eh" and "out and about" into his sentences whenever possible. And he always found a way to make me laugh, sometimes simply by speaking to me in what I thought of as his Jell-O Pudding Pop voice. He also loved to offer me advice. When I was on the road with the team, he'd suggest restaurants I should try or sights I should see. He had, after all, been just about everywhere in the States. He also seemed genuinely interested in my family. When he heard that I would be returning to Toronto for Christmas, he asked a number of questions about them and about our family traditions. Later, he offered me tickets so my parents could see him perform at an upcoming Toronto show. And during our phone calls he'd often inquire about my folks, especially my mother. "How's Mom doing?" he'd say. I was touched by his thoughtfulness.

As the months unfolded, he extended a number of invitations. I went to a couple of large dinner parties at his home in the affluent Philadelphia suburb of Elkins Park. I attended a blues concert in New York with a group he'd put together. And I travelled to a First Nations reservation in Connecticut where he was performing at a casino. By the time a year or so had passed, I considered him a friend and a grandfatherly mentor. But there were a few strange moments that should perhaps have given me more pause than they did.

About six months after we met, Mr. C. and I were talking on the phone when, out of nowhere, he asked me if I owned any cashmere sweaters.

"I have nice wool sweaters," I said.

"Ah, you can't afford cashmere," he responded. "You're poor."

I told him that I had a great job with a good paycheque, and I certainly didn't consider myself poor. Nevertheless, a few days later there was a package at my apartment door: three beautiful crewneck cashmere sweaters in light grey, burgundy, and charcoal.

There was no note in the package, but I knew who it was from. I tried to figure out why he'd sent it. It was close to my birthday, so I wondered if I had mentioned that to him. Or maybe this was just something wealthy people did—random acts of generosity.

When he next called, I thanked him for the gift but pointed out how excessive it was. "Now I'm going to have to hit the campus store big time," I said. "Get you five Temple hats or something." He chuckled.

And then there were the conversations about my hair. Mr. Cosby seemed remarkably interested in it. At one point, he asked if I ever used any products to smooth it out. When I said I didn't, he suggested I try something. Another time, he asked if I had ever straightened my hair. And when he was encouraging me to get professional headshots to submit for broadcasting jobs, he returned to the idea of blowing out my crazy curls. "You need a really good hair dryer," he said. He arranged for one to be sent to me.

There were a few odd moments when we saw each other in person as well. The first time I went to his house, Mr. Cosby had invited me there to talk about my career over dinner. I was surprised to find that I would actually be dining alone, however, and I chatted with his personal chef until Mr. Cosby came in at the end of my meal. At that point, we moved to a living room area to sit in front of a fire. As we talked, he briefly put his hand on my thigh. The move didn't offend me or make me feel anxious—I took it simply as a gesture of affection.

Several months later, there was a weirder incident.

I had once again been asked to his house to talk about preparing myself for a future in sports broadcasting. After I arrived, Cosby sat down next to me on the couch and handed me a glass of brandy. Then he reached over and tried to undo the button on my pants. As he fumbled with my zipper, I leaned over and motioned that I wasn't interested. It seemed that I had made myself clear—Cosby stopped what he was doing, and we didn't speak of it again. When I left, he casually handed me a bottle of perfume. I assumed it was a sample he'd been given. I told him I didn't wear perfume, but that I'd give it to my mother or sister. He didn't seem to mind.

Despite the now-evident signs that Cosby saw me as something other than a friend, I never thought at the time that he had any romantic interest in me. He was a married man, only slightly younger than my own grandfather. And he had called me once when I was visiting my then-girlfriend, Sheri, in North Carolina. When he found out that he had interrupted a social moment, he offered to send Sheri and me out for dinner. So I thought he understood the nature of our relationship (although I now realize that he may have thought I meant "girlfriend" in a platonic sense). For all these reasons, I brushed aside the attempt to unbutton my pants as a clumsy error in judgment. I didn't give it any more thought. It certainly wasn't on my mind when he invited me for dinner again some months later, in early January 2004.

In the previous weeks, I had made a decision to leave my position at Temple to move back to Canada and, I hoped, a future in massage therapy. I had let Mr. Cosby know about my plans and explained that despite his encouragement, I knew broadcasting wasn't right for me. He wanted me to come over to talk to him about that. Although I had already made up my mind about my career, I was struggling with how best to deliver the news to my boss, Dawn Staley. I had such enormous respect for her that the thought of disappointing her was keeping me up at night. I wanted to talk to someone who knew her, so I headed for Bill Cosby's place in search of advice from my trusted mentor, a man who had expressed such interest in me and my career for the last eighteen months.

We sat at the kitchen table while I told Cosby how stressed I was about announcing my resignation to Coach Staley. After some time, I excused myself to go to the washroom and Mr. Cosby disappeared. When we both got back to the kitchen, he held his open hand out towards me. In his palm were three blue pills. "These are your friends," he said. "They'll help take the edge off."

Since we had talked so much about my reluctance to take pharmaceuticals and my interest in holistic remedies, I thought the pills must be herbal. I asked if I should put them under my tongue. Cosby said I should swallow them with water. "Just put them down," he said. And so I did.

We sat back at the table and continued to talk, but before long, I was seeing double. Then my mouth became cottony and my words began to slur. Panic and confusion seized me. Cosby said he thought I needed to relax, and he guided me out of the kitchen. My legs were rubbery, and I felt weak. When we got to another room, he helped me onto a sofa, putting a pillow under my head as I lay on my side.

Those feelings were the only sensations breaking through my growing fog. Before I knew it, they receded too, and the world became black.

I don't know how long I lay there, but when I awoke, Bill Cosby was lying behind me, one hand on my breasts. The fingers of his other hand were moving forcefully in and out of my vagina. Next he took my own hand, put it on his penis, and masturbated himself.

My inability to control my own body was utterly terrifying. At six feet, I'm the opposite of petite, and I have always been physically strong. I had never before, even as a child, felt physically intimidated by anyone or anything. I was an athlete, able to take care of myself on the court and off. But now I had no control over my limbs. I couldn't keep my eyes open. My mind was screaming, "No, no, no!" But I couldn't move my lips or make any sounds at all. I had literally lost my voice. And all the while, the most awful, unimaginable things were happening to me.

The next thing I remember was waking up alone. I was able now to pull myself off the couch. As I stood, I realized my bra was up around my neck and my pants were undone. I tugged my clothes back in place and looked at my watch. It was after four in the morning. I had been at Bill Cosby's house for eight or nine hours, but I'd been unconscious for nearly all that time. I walked unsteadily towards the front door. When I passed the doorway between the kitchen and the dining room, Cosby was standing there in a bathrobe and slippers. "There's a blueberry muffin and tea on the table," he said.

I drove home, got in the shower, brushed my teeth, and dressed for work. I had a good cry in the shower, but I tried to move through the rest of the day as if nothing had happened. And I made the same effort the next day. And the next. But the following months were excruciating.

Crushing shame and confusion made me withdraw from friends and family. I threw myself into work. Fortunately, it was a busy time for the team, and the road trips provided a much-needed distraction from my own agonizing thoughts. But there were still days spent in the office—days when Cosby would call to inquire about things. The prospect of seeing him filled me with dread; the sound of his voice was like a knife to my gut. And each time he crossed my path or crept into my mind, I was filled with questions that spun in an endless, tortuous loop: "Why? Why did you do it? And *how* did you do it? What did you give me?" I was so tormented by those thoughts that at one point I forced myself to join a group of people who were dining with him at a Chinese restaurant so that I could confront him at the end of the evening. He insisted I drive to his house to talk. In the doorway leading to his kitchen, I asked what he had given me that night. He was evasive. "I don't know what you are talking about," he said. I left then, knowing I would get no truth from him.

I hoped that once I got to the comfort and love of my parents' home, I would be able to put both the questions and that ugly chapter of my life behind me. But even surrounded by the people I trusted most in the world and enrolled in a new and exciting massage therapy program, I felt the anguish cling to me like a second skin.

I used the demands of my schoolwork to beg off social events and family time. My friends seemed to accept that I was consumed by my studies, but everyone in my family noticed how quiet and withdrawn I had become. I turned down invitations to spend time at my sister's home with the nieces I adored, and I left the house only for classes. At meal-times, I pushed the food around on my plate, my once extraordinary appetite a thing of the past. At night, I struggled to sleep and often woke up screaming. In the mornings, I would appear at the breakfast table, sweaty and exhausted.

As the months passed, I grew thin and wan, and I continued to be plagued by nightmares. In one, I watched another woman be sexually assaulted and knew that it was all my fault. I began to worry that others were being attacked because I had not come forward. A year after my assault, I had a nightmare that made it clear I simply couldn't continue the way I was.

In my dream, I was struggling in a vast body of dark water. My arms and legs were weak and unable to hold me afloat. I kept sinking beneath the surface. I was drowning. Then a huge wooden ship appeared not far away. When I managed to reach it, I noticed that its sides were covered with grey barnacles. I reached out, hoping I could use them to haul myself on board. But as my hand closed around the crusty shells, I realized that the barnacles weren't going to save me. Instead, they would attach themselves to me, and I would grow heavier and heavier, until I sank to the bottom of the sea like a shipwreck. This was not the way to save myself.

I woke up sobbing.

I have never been much of a crier, so all the tears I had shed over the past year truly frightened me. I could understand why people reach for the numbing effects of alcohol and drugs. I wanted so badly to stop crying—to stop *feeling*—that I began to wonder if I might end up with some kind of addiction, like so many other traumatized people. I couldn't let that happen. I needed help.

I knew my mom was on her way to her job as a medical assistant in a rheumatology practice, but I grabbed my phone and called her anyway. As soon as she picked up, I blurted out what had happened to me that dreadful night a year earlier. It was a wonder she didn't drive off the road. Mom told me that she had to hang up but would call me back as soon as she got to the office. When she did, I explained what had happened in more detail. Then my mother called my sister, Diana, and her husband, Stuart, who's a detective constable with the Toronto Police Service. He advised Mom to contact police immediately, which she did with my blessing. Later that evening, three Durham Regional police officers came over to the house to take my statement. They then contacted the authorities in Philadelphia, who referred them to officials in Montgomery County, where Cosby's Elkins Park home was located. Several days later, I went down to Pennsylvania to be interviewed by the Cheltenham Township police and the Montgomery County assistant district attorney.

On February 17, 2005, only four weeks after I'd made my complaint, Bruce Castor, the district attorney for Montgomery County, announced there wasn't enough evidence to proceed with criminal charges. His decision wasn't a complete surprise. He'd already been quoted in the media saying that my year-long delay in making my accusation was one of the factors that "weigh[ed] toward Mr. Cosby."

Nevertheless, my family and I were crushed.

Less than three weeks after that, on March 8, my lawyers and I filed a civil suit against Bill Cosby. That suit, like the attempt to file charges, was a harrowing experience. Telling my story to police and the DA had ripped open my still-raw wounds. Being interrogated by Cosby's sneering lawyers during the civil trial, with my assaulter across the table, was torture. And both the attempted criminal case and the civil suit sheared away my family's privacy and allowed Cosby's spokespeople to put their own spin on my story.

When news of my accusations had first hit the press, on January 21, 2005, Cosby's lawyers and spokespeople called my claims "utterly preposterous" and "categorically false." The year-long delay in reporting, one of Cosby's lawyers said, was "pointedly bizarre." He also said my accusations simply amounted to "inappropriate touching." Much of the media coverage followed the lawyers' lead by avoiding terms like "sexual assault" (even when repeating some of the graphic details) and instead describing the incident as "fondling" or "groping."

In early newspaper articles, I was identified only as an acquaintance of Cosby's and a former Temple employee who now lived in the Toronto area. But a few days after the first stories broke, my father, in an understandable but naive effort to defend my legal actions, did an interview with a Toronto newspaper and allowed the reporter to use our names. This made us easy to find (and elicited a rebuke from my lawyer, Dolores).

A few days later, a man appeared at our front door. He was holding a large bouquet of flowers. Thinking he must be a delivery person, my mother opened the door.

"Mrs. Constand," the man began, "I just wanted to check in to see how you and your family are doing."

By this time I was at the door too, trying to figure out who this fellow might be. One of my mother's co-workers? One of my dad's patients? A former neighbour I didn't remember? My mother looked just as confused as I felt.

The man continued his sympathetic chit-chat. "This must be such a difficult time," he said, then asked if he might step in.

He looked cold, and there was an icy breeze coming through the door. My mother nodded and then closed the door behind him.

My parents' house was tiny. Once the man was past the threshold, he was essentially in our living room. I sat down on the couch, and he followed suit. He was asking how I felt about Bill Cosby's denials. "It must be hard to hear."

"I know what he did. He knows what he did," I said. "Everything will come to light, and the truth will be known."

As he started to ask more detailed questions about the case, my confusion began to lift. This wasn't anyone we knew. My mother was obviously having the same thought. She moved in front of him and thanked him for the flowers and his concern. We had things to do that afternoon, she told the stranger. It was time for him to leave.

As the door closed behind him, my mother and I looked at each other. I could see she felt as uneasy as I did. Sure enough, a day or two later, friends began to call about a story they had seen splashed across the pages of the US tabloid the *National Enquirer*. It quoted the exact words I had said to the man in our living room.

After that unnerving incident, my parents and I were on high alert. We stopped answering the doorbell and the telephone. We looked around with suspicion whenever we left the house. We even found ourselves checking the rear-view mirror when we drove, afraid that reporters were waiting to catch us in an unguarded moment.

The February 1 *National Enquirer* article didn't name me, but most other media stories after my father's interview did. And there were many. In early February, a story appeared on the American tabloid TV show *Celebrity Justice*. Citing "sources connected with Bill Cosby," the show claimed that before I contacted the police, my mother had asked Cosby to "make things right with money." The source (later identified as Cosby's lawyer Marty Singer) called this "a classic shakedown." *Celebrity Justice* followed that up with a story on their website headlined "Cosby's Attorney Claims Accuser After Cash." Singer was quoted again, this time saying, "These people contacted Mr. Cosby with the intention of requesting money from Mr. Cosby. It's very obvious." Then on March 2, after the Montgomery County DA had closed the case, Cosby gave an interview to the *National Enquirer*. "I'm not going to give in to people who try to exploit me because of my celebrity status," he said. "Sometimes you try to help people and it backfires on you and then they try to take advantage of you."

Both stories were covered by countless papers and media outlets when they first appeared, and then regurgitated when we launched our civil suit. In fact, in the coming years, so often when my name was mentioned in relationship to Cosby, those untruths would be repeated, leaving my family's reputation in tatters.

Despite all the difficulties my family and I endured after I reported my assault, there was eventually some positive news. In November 2006, we settled the civil case successfully, and Cosby's lawyers offered us vastly more money than the $150,000 we had asked for. That settlement provided a kind of satisfaction, a certain validation. And it meant that I would have the means to pay for therapy and any other help I needed to get on with my life. But it didn't erase that hollow sensation I'd felt that bleak February afternoon when I'd heard there would be no criminal charges. Because it wasn't money I was after.

I wanted to be heard. I wanted to be believed. I wanted justice. But it was clear none of that was going to happen. No one wanted to hear *my* story. No one wanted to believe *me*.

It was not the moment.

What I could never imagine then was that eleven years later, the world would shift ever so slightly on its axis. Conversations would begin to change, thousands of women's voices would be raised, and the deafening hum of denial and complacency would quiet enough for some of those voices to be heard.

And I would have another chance. I would be able to tell my story and seek true justice on behalf of dozens of women. There *would* be a moment—a powerful, transformative moment.

And I would be there.

CHAPTER 2

THE CALL

The settlement in my civil case against Bill Cosby turned out to be both a blessing and a curse. It included a strict non-disclosure agreement, now commonly known as an NDA. I could share nothing of what had happened between Cosby and me with anyone. When I told my mother that he had drugged and assaulted me, I thought I was finally shedding the big secret in my life. When I went to the authorities to reveal what Bill Cosby had done to me, I assumed that the pain of public disclosure would be somewhat relieved by the act of claiming my story. When I filed suit against him in civil court, I thought I would be heard and would be empowered by that honesty. But the NDA meant that I returned home with an even bigger secret than the one I had left Philadelphia with in the first place. If I said even a single word to *anyone* about the most defining event in my life, I could be sued.

It was suffocating to shut away what was now an essential part of my past. I couldn't be truly open with anyone, except my immediate family. Being so guarded with others—having to watch what I said and shared— left me feeling profoundly alone. Even if I'd been able to describe what I had experienced, I doubt I would have. After all, who could I confide in? That night in Bill Cosby's Elkins Park home had shaken my trust in people.

If someone who was like a grandfather to me could do such a thing, what were others capable of? I wanted to believe in the goodness of people, but I wasn't sure how.

I was also acutely aware that the secret might have consequences outside my own life. During the initial criminal case, other women had come forward with experiences similar to mine—although most of those complainants who shared their stories with the media or the authorities while the case was being investigated were not interviewed by the police or the DA at the time. Twelve of them would eventually become anonymous Jane Doe witnesses in my civil suit. The stories of some, like Tamara Green, Beth Ferrier, and Barbara Bowman, had made it to the press in 2005 and 2006.

Tamara was the first woman to go public after my story broke. A trial lawyer now living in Southern California, she was a model with hopes of a singing career when she met Bill Cosby through a mutual friend thirty years earlier. She alleged that one day she joined Cosby and a number of his friends for lunch. She wasn't feeling well, and he offered her some cold medicine. When she accepted, he left the table and returned with a couple of pills, which Tamara swallowed. To her surprise, she started to feel so drowsy she could barely keep herself from passing out in her salad. Cosby offered to drive her home. When they got to her place, he took her inside, put her on her bed, and proceeded to undress her. Tamara claimed she knew she had been drugged—the pills certainly weren't cold medicine—and she sensed what was about to happen. With her last remaining strength, she grabbed a lamp off her bedside table and hurled it at her bedroom window, hoping the crash would get the attention of her neighbours. Unfortunately, the glass didn't break and she passed out. When she awoke many hours later, she found two hundred-dollar bills on her bedside table. She got dressed and left her house, hoping but failing to locate Cosby and confront him.

The next day she bumped into him at her brother's hospital bedside. Her brother was dying of cystic fibrosis, and he and her mother were thrilled to be visited by the famous comedian. Not wanting to burst their bubble, Tamara decided to keep quiet about what had happened. But she never forgot the assault, and three decades later, she decided to get in touch with my lawyers and the DA in order to support my criminal case. When she realized it wasn't going to proceed, she took her story to Nicole Weisensee Egan at the *Philadelphia Daily News*.

Beth Ferrier was a twenty-four-year-old model from Denver when she met Bill Cosby during New York Fashion Week in 1984. Her agent had set up the meeting with the star and a few others. Cosby, who was then in his very first season of *The Cosby Show*, had offered to help Beth further her modelling career. Although they were both married, according to Beth, by the end of the week they had begun an affair. After several months, Beth ended their long-distance relationship. But when Cosby was next in Denver, he convinced her to come see him at the club where he was performing. She alleged that backstage in his dressing room, he gave her a drink, and she soon passed out. She woke up hours later in her car, with her bra undone and her clothes in disarray. Her agent called her the next day to say that Cosby had forgiven her for drinking too much. But the agent hadn't. Beth was fired.

Barbara Bowman was also a model when her agent (the same one who'd represented Beth Ferrier) introduced her to Cosby in 1985. He mentored the eighteen-year-old and introduced her to his co-stars on his popular show. Barbara alleged that after he'd gained her trust, he drugged and raped her on several different occasions before she finally escaped his orbit.

The statutes of limitations had expired for all these women to bring lawsuits in their own name, so being a witness in this civil trial or going public about what happened to them was their only chance to have a voice now that people were finally starting to listen to women who had survived sexual assault. I didn't speak to them, or hear their testimony, but I read about their stories along with everyone else who followed the news. Those reports all contained allegations that were similar to what I had experienced with Cosby.

At the time, the fact that other women were accusing Bill Cosby of sexual assault made me feel less alone and more confident that I had done the right thing. But the very existence of these women also raised troubling questions that wouldn't go away. If I wasn't the first, what were the chances I was the *last*? While the financial settlement was a huge amount of money by my standards, it was a modest sum compared to Cosby's enormous wealth. Even if money *could* work as a deterrent to his behaviour, it didn't seem likely that the cheque Cosby wrote me was large enough to give him much pause. And that left me wondering, Were other women being drugged and attacked as I quietly went on with my life?

Unfortunately, there was nothing I could do about that. For the next several years, weekly appointments with a psychotherapist helped me tame the feelings of guilt, shame, mistrust, and isolation—and muted the questions that had kept me up at night. I also worked hard at putting my life back together. I bought a small condo in downtown Toronto, near a big park in a neighbourhood filled with energy and life. It felt good to be part of a vibrant community, even if I couldn't always engage with it in the way I would have liked. I also followed through with my plans to work in healthcare. After my courses were finished, I started my own therapeutic massage practice. While my initial focus was on helping clients reduce the effects of accumulated stress, I began to train in medical massage so that I could work with cancer patients struggling with the side effects of chemotherapy and radiation. My client list quickly grew to include those who were battling Parkinson's, arthritis, diabetes, and other illnesses. I was delighted to find that the "healing" part of the healing arts worked in both directions: the more I was able to help others, the better I felt myself.

Eventually, I was able to leave psychotherapy, but I continued to focus on building my emotional strength and developing a deep and rich spiritual life that kept me balanced, fulfilled, and able to nurture hope. And of course, I worked at keeping my body healthy. Although my basketball days were done, I threw myself into cycling, hiking, and yoga, finding comfort in my physical strength once again.

Perhaps most importantly, as soon as I had my own place, I got a dog. Maddy is a shy but intelligent Standard Poodle. Her affection and loyalty were such a balm that I opened my door to a second Poodle less than a year later. Cassie is loving and open, as clumsy as Maddy is nimble. These two buddies took me for daily walks and kept me company when I was unable to engage in a "normal" social life, and they've been an unending source of joy.

I knew that I would never be the same person I was before the assault, but I was gradually discovering a new me. My wounds were healing, my gaze was shifting to the future, and I was beginning to let people in again. About seven years after I returned to Canada, I even met a wonderful woman, Kristin, and began the first romantic relationship I had had since my Temple days. Indeed, by the time a decade had passed, I seemed to have found my groove once more. That is, until a viral video moved the earth under my feet again.

It was October 2014, a crisp fall evening. The sun had set hours earlier, and the street noise had hushed to a quiet hum. I made sure Cassie was settled onto her dog pillow outside my bedroom door, and then I slipped under the covers. Maddy jumped onto the bed and stretched out beside me. I took my phone from my bedside table to check for messages and briefly scroll through Facebook before I called it a day. One of my FB friends had posted a video along with the words "Hey, everybody. Check this out!" I took the cue and clicked Play. I wasn't prepared for what I would see and hear next.

In the grainy video, comedian Hannibal Buress was standing onstage in what looked to be a small nightclub. And he was ranting about Bill Cosby, complaining that he had been lecturing Black people about how to behave. Then Buress said, "Yeah, but you rape women, Bill Cosby, so turn the crazy down a couple of notches." I gasped. I hadn't heard anyone mention the accusations against Cosby in about eight years. Buress continued his routine, talking about how he had said this same thing in a number of shows and people never believed him. "You leave here and google 'Bill Cosby rape,'" Buress told his audience. "That shit has more results than 'Hannibal Buress.'"

It was as if a small earthquake had hit. The floor seemed to tremble beneath me. What would people find if they googled "Bill Cosby rape"?

I thought. And then the answer: They would find Barbara Bowman. They would find Beth Ferrier. They would find Tamara Green. They would find *me*. I thought back to those months in 2005, when my family members had been afraid to pick up the phone or open the front door. The blasts of shouted questions and the barrage of camera flashes. The reluctance to leave home without scouting for reporters first. That feeling of being the fox in a hunt.

I closed my phone and put it by my bedside, then took a deep breath. So what? I said to myself. That's all in the past.

In 2005, when word got out about the charges I'd made and the accusations of other women, the attention had been excruciatingly intense. But it had been relatively brief too, like a wave washing across writing in the sand. After another burst of attention following the civil settlement, the same erasure seemed to happen.

Buress's routine was referring to ancient history, I reminded myself. No one really cared back then, and there was no reason to believe anyone would care now. Those who had seen the video would have forgotten it come morning. The room was still. I snapped off my bedside lamp and pulled the covers up to my chin. Maddy sighed, and I closed my eyes and felt my heartbeat slow. I drifted off to sleep, my past shoved back into the recesses of my mind. Nothing to worry about.

But I was wrong about that.

When I woke up the next morning, I made a point of *not* checking Facebook. But then I got a text from a friend about the Buress video. Over the next few days, my cellphone buzzed and chirped with alarming frequency. The notes from family and friends were all the same: "Have you seen this?" and "Are you okay?" The video was clearly making the rounds.

As the days unfolded, the rumbling sensation I had felt when I first heard Buress's words returned. Media outlets were picking up the story of his viral video. A number of them reviewed the allegations that had been printed in the past and asked why no one had much cared about that news at the time. Some of the accusers asked the same: Tamara Green and

Barbara Bowman wrote op-ed pieces wanting to know why people hadn't believed their stories.

A number of pundits and writers have since weighed in on why Hannibal Buress's remarks about Cosby drew the attention they did. After all, there was some good reporting done in 2005 and 2006. Nicole Weisensee Egan, a dedicated and dogged journalist who was working at the *Philadelphia Daily News* in those years, had put out article after article that seriously and respectfully covered not only my story but those of the other women who had talked about their traumatic experiences with Cosby. She had even penned detailed, thoughtful pieces for national outlets like *People* magazine. And yet, most of that coverage stayed right where it started. Unlike Cosby's defamatory quotations in the *National Enquirer* and Marty Singer's falsehoods on *Celebrity Justice*, few of Nicki's stories were picked up by wire services or other media. Cosby and his reputation as a beloved father figure and family man, therefore, remained largely untarnished as he continued his speaking tours, interviews, and comedy specials. In the years since I'd told my story, he had received numerous awards and accolades from educational institutions and other organizations.

I don't know whether it was because Buress is a man, or because he is a fellow Black comedian, or because he was so blunt, or because of the expanded reach of social media, but Cosby and his people could not contain the scandal. It was becoming clear that at this moment, the story was not going to be washed away.

In the following weeks, as the retrospective on the Cosby accusations gained traction, more women came forward with their own stories of abuse by the man the press still referred to as America's Dad. Some were the anonymous Jane Doe witnesses who had shared their stories with the court in my civil case back in 2005. Some were women no one had heard from before. In December 2014, famed women's rights lawyer Gloria Allred announced that she was representing three of them. (At the same time, she demanded that Cosby provide a $100 million fund to compensate survivors who had no recourse to legal action because of the statute of limitations.) As the months progressed, her Cosby client list would grow and grow.

By the time spring had come and gone, dozens of women had revealed their painful experiences with the comedian. In the end, Bill Cosby's accusers would total more than sixty women.

As each new story broke, I was knocked back by a strange combination of shock and recognition. These were the stories of teenagers and mature women alike. They were models, actresses, waitresses, athletes, university students, flight attendants, writers, massage therapists. Two were just fifteen years old at the time of their assaults. A couple of women acknowledged that they had initially engaged in a consensual sexual relationship with Mr. Cosby. Many told of being invited to meet with him to discuss their careers. Many also said that Cosby got close to them by expressing concern for their families or talking with their mothers. But the vast majority of their stories ended the same way. At some point, they were given a drink or a pill that Cosby said would help them relax. After this, they fell into a stupor or were rendered unconscious. Some were awake for long enough to be aware that Cosby was having sex with them, but they could not speak to say no or physically resist in any way. Others remembered nothing but awoke to find themselves half undressed or fully naked. Many noted that Mr. Cosby had appeared in his robe to send them on their way.

Listening to these accounts often brought me to tears. It was shattering to hear haunting echoes of my past—echoes that forced me to relive my experiences and to imagine the unbearable pain these women had carried with them all this time. At least I had managed to share my secret after only a year had passed.

It was just as painful to hear so many of Cosby's celebrity friends rally around him and dismiss the women's claims. In January 2015, his *Cosby Show* co-star Phylicia Rashad went so far as to suggest we were part of some organized plan to bring down a powerful Black man. "Forget these women," she said to a writer for an entertainment website. "What you're seeing is the destruction of a legacy. And I think it's orchestrated. I don't know why or who's doing it, but it's the legacy."

Another bizarre conspiracy theory asserted that powerful people were behind a campaign to smear Cosby with false sexual assault accusations as retribution for his attempt to buy NBC in the nineties. Many of Cosby's friends and fans called us "bitches," including comedian Damon Wayans, who added that we were all "unrapeable" and just looking for a payout. "It's a money hustle," he said.

As each heartbreaking story or nasty response was published, I could say nothing. It was ironic. It seemed as if many people were finally ready to listen—and perhaps even to believe me—but I was unable to speak out. In fact, as reporters published these disturbing new accounts, some realized that they didn't know how *my* story had ended. They wanted to know what had actually happened with my civil case, and why it had just seemed to go away.

My lawyer, Dolores Troiani, turned down all the interview requests that came my way, but she did let me know each time there was a development that she thought might have an emotional impact. So by the summer of 2015, I knew that the Associated Press had petitioned a judge to release the deposition Bill Cosby made during my civil trial. They were arguing that since Cosby had set himself up as a moral spokesman—giving the sorts of lectures about personal and social responsibility that Hannibal Buress had found so smug and provocative—it was the public's right to know if he was indeed, as Buress had asserted, a hypocrite.

I knew exactly what was in that deposition, of course—I had heard the words as they left Mr. Cosby's mouth, and they had become etched in my soul. The eight months since the Buress video had been packed with revelations, shock, and mud-slinging as Cosby, his representatives, his accusers, and the public wrestled to control the narrative. But the deposition was going to blow the whole thing wide open; I was certain of it.

On a warm day in early July, as I scrolled through my phone while on a walk in the park with my pups, I learned that a judge had released portions of the deposition. It wasn't long before the Associated Press was reporting on Mr. Cosby's matter-of-fact admission that he had given Quaaludes to women and then had sex with them (at the prompting of his lawyer, he amended that to just one woman). Not long after the AP story broke, the *New York Times* managed to get a copy of the entire deposition, and on July 19, they published a piece titled "Bill Cosby, in Deposition, Said Drugs and Fame Helped Him Seduce Women." The article noted that "he presented himself in the deposition as an unapologetic, cavalier playboy, someone who used a combination of fame, apparent concern and powerful sedatives in a calculated pursuit of young women," and referred to the "casual indifference" with which he described his predatory exploits.

I was right about how the release of this document would turn up the heat. A day after the AP story was published, I walked into the waiting room at the massage therapy clinic where I worked to find a man I didn't recognize. As soon as he saw me, he jumped out of his chair and approached. "Are you Andrea?" he said. When I replied that I was, he asked if we could step outside to talk. He wasn't carrying a notebook or a recorder that I could see, but I knew he was a reporter. I had no desire to talk with him, and even if I had, there wasn't much I could say, but I didn't want to appear rude. I went outside to explain that. Before I could get much out, however, he was telling me that he had covered Cosby in the past and thought he knew another victim. He opened his computer to show me a picture of her. I told him that I didn't want to talk about Cosby. "It doesn't define me," I explained. "I have a whole other life and I'm happy." I let him know that I understood he had a story to do, but I couldn't be much help. Besides, it seemed that the story was a force that was unfolding on its own. We chatted a bit about a new elementary school curriculum to teach kids about consent, then he and the photographer (who had been waiting outside) got in their car and left.

Once back in my office, I began to have regrets. I didn't like the way the reporter had invaded my privacy and my workspace, or the way he had played on my sympathy with the story of the other victim. I felt that he had taken advantage of my politeness, and that I had been coaxed into saying more than I wanted to say. I decided that I should call him. When I got hold of him, I explained that I wanted our entire conversation to be off the record. (I didn't know then that an off-the-record conversation has to be signalled from the beginning.) Then I apologized for not giving him much of a story.

I needn't have bothered.

The very next day, his article came out, under the headline "Bill Cosby Sex Case: Toronto Woman Speaks to Sun." The reporter painted a very flattering picture of me, but he printed pretty much everything I had said. I felt my anxiety ratchet up several notches.

Cosby's lawyers were not about to let this non-story go unaddressed. They immediately filed a motion to have me sanctioned, claiming the article was evidence that I had broken our confidentiality agreement. I knew this accusation was frivolous and would go nowhere, but still my heart sank. After nine years of relative peace, I was being dragged back into legal battles and public humiliation.

The deposition returned the spotlight to me, but it also ignited a new debate in the media. Various lawyers, analysts, and talking heads hashed over what might come of all the accusations. Many of the newly revealed stories, as well as the formerly shared ones, appeared to be beyond the statute of limitations, though time limits varied from state to state. What recourse was there, they asked, if all these alleged crimes were too old to prosecute?

I tried not to glance at the papers or tune into the news. But there was no way to escape all of it. Even if I kept my television off and my computer closed, well-meaning family members and friends would call or message me to let me know about the latest developments and find out how I was doing.

That awful night was consuming my life again.

Within just a few weeks of the Buress video, I had felt it necessary to get back into therapy. But even with that support, the stress began eating away at me and threatening the new world I'd built for myself. Despite what I had told the *Sun* reporter about being happy, I soon found myself reluctant to leave my condo when I didn't have to. I still walked the dogs each day, but my long bike rides and vigorous hikes had become less and less frequent. I was having to make a conscious effort to stay in control of my actions and emotions. More than once, at dinner with a family member or friend, I realized that I had somehow downed three glasses of wine instead of my usual one.

At work, I struggled to stay in the moment. I had always believed that an important part of therapeutic massage was maintaining a deep mental concentration on the connection my hands were making with the patient's muscles and tissues. In fact, I was usually so focused on the process that I could later recall each move and every moment of a sixty-minute massage. Yet as the year progressed, I left more and more sessions sure that while my treatment had been thorough and effective, my mind had been far, far away—lost somewhere in the painful past or the uncertain future. I wasn't doing my job the way I wanted or needed to do it.

It wasn't just my health and my work that were set back by the Cosby maelstrom. After four years of a happy, loving relationship, I was having trouble trusting my partner, Kristin. I knew that it had little to do with her, but I just couldn't convince myself that people were not going to hurt me again. And since I couldn't tell who would inflict that pain, I didn't feel I could afford to have another person close to me. It wasn't fair, but I ended our relationship.

Less than a year after the Buress video broke, I had become yet another version of myself. I was certainly not the young athlete who had walked into the offices at Temple University, comfortable in my own skin and trusting the world. And I was not the Andrea who had gone to the police, wanting to be heard and determined to right a wrong. Nor was I the person who had barrelled forward with a civil suit, hoping for a measure of affirmation when it became clear that justice was out of reach.

It was a more cautious, more vulnerable, more world-weary Andrea who got the call that would change everything.

That call was from my lawyer, Dolores Troiani.

It came on a day in early fall 2015. I was home, puttering about with my dogs and getting myself ready for an afternoon shift at the massage clinic. When I answered my cell, Dolores told me that Risa Vetri Ferman's assistant, Kevin Steele, had been in touch with her. Ferman had taken over from Bruce Castor as the DA for Montgomery County, Pennsylvania. "They think there may be something still within the statute of limitations that they can look at," Dolores explained. "But they need to know whether you would be willing to cooperate with them if there is something they can act on."

I thanked her for the call but told her I needed to think about it. I'd ring her in a few days to let her know my thoughts. Then I hung up and called my mother.

As I explained the situation to my mom, I realized that I had been expecting this—that the prospect of an overture from the DA had been hanging over my head for almost a year. Each victim to speak out so far had recounted events that happened years before my attack. And I was the only one who'd had any sort of successful case against Cosby—even if it was only a civil one.

I had no real idea of what the DA was thinking, but my experience with the civil case had demonstrated just how ruthless defence lawyers can be. Cosby's had tried to smear my name in the press by casting me as a gold digger and a liar. They had gone after my family as well. And they weren't alone—Cosby's legions of fans considered me public enemy number one.

I had no illusions. If the new DA determined there was a criminal case to be made and decided to take it to trial, I would have to defend myself every bit as much as Bill Cosby. My family and I would be put through hell again. But this time, with international attention and public interest raging across social media, the intensity—and the cruelty—was likely to be fifty times worse. Did I have what it would take to survive that sort of trauma? Did I have this kind of fight left in me? I was already frayed and fragile. Tired. Confused. Frightened.

And what about my family? Was it fair to drag them through all this?

Not too many families can say that they have a bona fide hero in their past—someone whose virtue and bravery and sacrifice have inspired his descendants and thousands of his fellow citizens. But my family has such a figure. I had heard his story ever since I was a child. I carried a medallion emblazoned with his image in my wallet. When times were tough, I even prayed to him, asking for guidance.

And now, thinking of this extraordinary man, I realized that my decision had already been made.

CHAPTER 3

THE RIGHT THING

We had all gathered at my aunt Pia's for Christmas afternoon. The small house was buzzing with noise and excitement. The aroma of lasagna and seafood filled the air—an Italian Canadian feast was going to start very soon. My young cousins, my sister, and I were talking about what toys Santa had left us under the tree that morning and darting between the living room and the kitchen in search of treats. Then someone noticed that the door to Nonna's room was open just a crack.

A number of years before, my grandmother (my mother's mother) had moved in with my aunt and her family. Her bedroom on the main floor of the house was her only private space, and it was off limits to us kids. Since we had never seen inside it, the room was tantalizingly mysterious. The open door beckoned, and my sister, my cousins, and I gathered outside and peered in. It was dark, and we couldn't make out much. Eventually one of us decided to be bold and step into the room itself.

Once I was standing in the middle of the room with everyone else, taking it all in, I was disappointed. My nonna's bedroom was simple, modest. Pushed against one wall was a daybed with a plain lightweight blanket. There was a small area rug covering the floor and a tall chest of drawers. That was it. But then someone noticed the top of the dresser. I was only about eight or nine, and I had to go up on my toes to see what was on top. I could make out a big fat candle, a framed black-and-white picture of a young man in uniform, and a small piece of folded paper sitting next to the candle.

"What's all that?" one of us asked.

Just then, my mother popped her head into the room. "You're not supposed to be in here, kids," she said.

I pointed at the dresser. "What's up there, Mom? Who's that in the picture?"

My mother walked over to the dresser and took the piece of paper from the top. My sister, my cousins, and I crowded around her to look at it. It was a small leaflet with the same picture of the young man in uniform.

"This is my uncle Salvo," my mother said. And then she told us his story.

Salvo was born in 1920, in Naples, the eldest of eight children, only four of whom would survive infancy and childhood. When he was nineteen, he joined the Carabinieri, a branch of the Italian armed forces that usually provides domestic policing. Just prior to the outbreak of the Second World War, however, Salvo was dispatched to Libya. He spent three years in North Africa, remaining there after being wounded in the leg and returning only when he contracted malaria. In 1942 he enrolled in officers' training school, and then was assigned to Palidoro, a small rural fishing village just northwest of Rome. That's where Salvo was when Benito Mussolini was removed from office and arrested by the Carabinieri on July 25, 1943. Shortly after that, the Italian government signed an armistice with the Allied forces, and the Carabinieri in southern Italy threw their support behind the anti-Fascist Italian liberation movement. Because of that, they were considered enemy forces by the German occupiers who marched into the Palidoro area in mid-September 1943.

On September 22, German soldiers were inspecting their arms supplies at the camp they had set up when a portion of the munitions exploded, killing two soldiers and injuring two more. The German command suspected that locals had booby-trapped their supplies and demanded that the Carabinieri help identify the guilty parties. At the time, Salvo was the temporary head of the Carabinieri in the area, and after undertaking an investigation, he reported to the German commanders that there had been no local involvement and the explosion must have been some kind of accident. The Germans did not accept that explanation, and proceeded to round up twenty-two villagers and bring them to the Torre di Palidoro, an ancient fortification outside the village. They then brought Salvo to join the prisoners.

At the tower, the German soldiers interrogated Salvo and the rest of the accused. All proclaimed their innocence. Salvo tried in vain to convince the Germans that no one had engineered the explosion. The soldiers ridiculed his defence of the villagers and beat him mercilessly. Then they produced shovels and instructed the prisoners to begin digging a pit, which would serve as their final resting place when it was finished. By the time the mass grave had been completed, it was clear that the Germans meant to follow through on their threats. That's when Salvo stepped forward to protect the others. He lied, saying that he was responsible for the explosion, and that he had acted alone. He demanded that the innocent villagers be released. The Germans had what they wanted. A firing squad was assembled, and Salvo was executed on the spot. He never reached his twenty-third birthday.

In the quiet of Nonna's bedroom, my sister, my cousins, and I sat on the daybed and listened to this fantastic tale. My mother told us that her uncle, my grandmother's brother, was considered a national hero in Italy and a martyr by the Catholic Church. He had been the subject of books and films. His face had been featured on postage stamps. Monuments in his honour had been erected in several locations throughout Italy. Celebrations and memorials were held every year in his name. The Church had even started the process of beatification—when it was completed, Salvo would be recognized as a saint.

Once I was aware of Salvo's story, I began to understand how much his death had affected my nonna. She was just thirteen when her older brother was shot, and life was not easy in post-war Naples. But Nonna and her family were lucky—they were middle class and many of them had access to good jobs. After the war, at the age of fifteen, Nonna married my grandfather, who worked for Alitalia airlines. It would not have been uncommon in those days for a fifteen-year-old girl to marry, but I suspect that Nonna's early marriage had little to do with family expectations. Rather, I think the death of her brother and the devastation of war made her eager to wed, have children, and dedicate herself to family life as soon as possible. Nonna and Nonno had several children, and in 1959, my grandfather, now a regional sales manager for the airline, was transferred to Montreal to head up the Alitalia office there. (My mother was eight years old when they immigrated.)

My grandparents and their six children lived in Montreal for several years before being transferred to Toronto. Three years later, Nonno was diagnosed with lung cancer. He died nine months after that. My mother, the third child, was fourteen years old. The youngest was just seven.

My mother's family had never been rich, but they had led a comfortable middle-class life in Canada. With Nonno's death, however, my grandmother and the children struggled to maintain their financial security, and the two oldest children had to go to work to help support the family.

In the eighties and nineties, during the initial stages of the beatification process for Salvo D'Acquisto, my grandmother travelled to Rome to join the processions and even had an audience with Pope John Paul II at the Vatican. She was a quiet, self-effacing person, but when it came to Salvo, she was enormously proud. The older she got, the more she relied on his memory and her devotion to him to give her strength.

It's hard to capture how deeply Salvo's story affected my daily life. But it did. His sacrifice was like a soft note that hummed throughout my little world. I would sometimes forget about it, but it was always there. Every Christmas, my sister, my cousins, and I would seek out the little altar in Nonna's bedroom and gaze at the picture of a man who had given up so much to do what was right. And when life got tough or we were faced with trouble, we would pray to Salvo for guidance. That said, my own prayers to Salvo were fairly generic. I never had any particular hardships to pray about because my life seemed to be unfolding in a perfectly satisfactory way.

When I was interviewed by a psychiatrist as part of my legal proceedings in 2015, one of the first questions he asked was, "How would you describe your childhood?" I didn't hesitate. "Happy," I replied. I didn't say another word. That summed it up perfectly.

The psychologist looked back at me blankly, as if surprised at my response. Perhaps he didn't hear that answer very often. Perhaps he was expecting it to be followed by a "but" and a list of less positive adjectives. He pressed me with more questions, but nothing I said did anything to weaken that initial reply.

Having heard so many other people's stories, I realize how lucky I was to have such positive memories. My rosy youth was not, of course, the result of wealth. We were a family of modest means. My dad's parents had emigrated from Greece in 1953, when my father was just seven years old. Soon after arriving, my grandfather got a lease on a small restaurant in the Yonge and Eglinton neighbourhood of Toronto, near the subway. It was a typical diner—serving up bacon and eggs, sandwiches, and a few Greek staples to subway and bus drivers and other working-class folk. My yiayia (grandmother) and pappou (grandfather) rose at four in the morning to slice potatoes and prepare for the breakfast rush, then locked up the diner long after the sun went down. Their children were raised largely in the kitchen of the greasy spoon. As soon as each one was old enough to be of help, he or she was introduced to the dish sink or the floor mop, and eventually allowed to chop vegetables and man the deep fryer or the grill.

My father, their youngest child, was still working at the restaurant in his early twenties. That's when his parents hired a young Italian girl, Gianna, to wait tables. Before long, my mother and father were married and had a baby, my sister, Diana, on the way. While my grandparents continued to work punishing hours in the diner, my parents moved on to other jobs. My mother eventually became a secretary and my father worked as a security guard before going back to school to become a massage therapist.

While my parents migrated into a more middle-class life, owning their own home was a goal that was always out of reach. Instead, we moved from apartment to apartment, opting for more room and more convenient locations as their tight budget allowed. Like so many people in the neighbourhoods I grew up in, my parents sometimes struggled to provide the kind of life they wanted for their children, and occasionally their financial concerns created friction between them. But I don't remember much of that. What I remember is the extraordinary amount of attention, love, and patience I received from these hard-working people.

When I think of it, the patience my family exercised with me might have been the most extraordinary thing. To say that I was a busy child is an understatement. From the moment I could get around on my own, I was getting around on my own. Bursting with energy, I wasn't easily distracted by books or television or playthings. In fact, the only toy I was ever really interested in was a ball. My parents quickly learned that the best way to entertain me and channel my energy was to throw me something round and bouncy. And then I would be happy for hours.

Once I was in elementary school, I expended all that physical energy on sports. On the weekends and in the summers, I would hang out at the local recreation centres, swimming or playing wall ball, volleyball, tetherball, or table tennis. In the schoolyard and at the rec centre, these games were the dominion of the boys, so they became my playmates and competitors. They sometimes resisted or teased me about preferring to play with them instead of the girls. But for a very long time, I was taller than any of them—and stronger. I could throw a ball farther and harder, jump higher, run faster. Eventually, they gave up smirking when I joined them for a game of wall ball or brought out my baseball glove.

I drew a lot of confidence from my strength. And my physical abilities convinced me that the boys were wrong—there weren't any sports or activities that girls couldn't do as well as they did. So whenever I heard a boy trying to belittle or exclude one of my female classmates, I'd challenge him. It was hard to argue with a girl who could belt a baseball right out of the park.

As you might imagine, that desire to be physically active posed a few problems in school—even nursery school. To four-year-old me, the purpose of naptime was a complete mystery. I would put my mat down like everyone else, then sprawl on top of it. As the rest of the little kids drifted off, I'd stretch out, wide awake, my legs and arms twitching and jiggling impatiently until we were allowed to get off the floor once more. I didn't do much better at elementary school. Although I got decent grades, most of my early report cards commented on the trouble I had sitting still and focusing on my schoolwork. When I was about ten, my mother, who was at that point working in a doctor's office, heard about a miracle drug that apparently helped children like me settle down. She and I visited my pediatrician and came away with a prescription for Ritalin.

The medication did indeed reduce my urge to keep my body in motion. After a few days taking the little pills, I was surprised at the stillness that had settled into my limbs. In the classroom, I realized that my attention didn't stray from the teacher or the blackboard the way it usually did. I could ignore the window with the schoolyard beyond, the asphalt and ball hoops that usually called to me throughout the lessons. When recess came, I went outside to play, but not with an explosion of pent-up energy and the feeling that I had just been released from captivity. These sensations were interesting, and my new behaviour seemed to delight my teacher. But I didn't really feel like myself.

And I guess I didn't seem like myself to my family either. After only a few months, my mother stopped giving me the pills.

My parents weren't worried that I wasn't going to be an elementary school academic star. And they didn't mind the extra energy it took to keep up with me. In fact, my father seemed to recognize a kindred spirit—someone who was as interested in sports as he was. My dad was gifted at many sports, but by the time I came along, his main activity was baseball. When I was about nine years old, he began taking me to his games. The players allowed me to warm up with them on the field, and once the game started, I was the bat girl. Afterwards, I would join the men at the bar for chicken wings. Dad's baseball games got me out of the house and let me run off energy, but they also introduced me to the joyful camaraderie of team sports.

Dad also often took me to work with him. He was the registered massage therapist at a fancy squash club in north Toronto. When he had shifts in the evenings or on weekends, I would join him. Sometimes I would watch him give massages, but I spent most of my time in the club's gym, using the exercise machines and learning to lift weights. I loved spending time with my father and being invited into his world this way.

No matter how exhausting it must have been to keep up with me, my mother always responded with gentleness and patience. But then she was kind and gentle with everyone. I think my mother's approach to people was heavily influenced by Salvo's sacrifice. For a time, she worked in a doctor's office in the Kensington Market area of Toronto. The practice included a lot of patients who were poor and struggling. My mother always gave them her own phone number so they could call if they needed a last-minute appointment or had questions. In the evenings, I could hear her warm and patient tone, always offering reassurance, as she promised to squeeze them in the next day. When I asked her why she invited the patients to call her at home, she would explain that it was important for people to know they had support. It mattered that they be given a sense of their own importance, especially if they had very little in their lives. She could do this in a small way, and so she did.

The only time I ever remember my mother voicing frustration with me was on Sunday mornings. Every Sunday, she would produce my church clothes—skirt, tights, fancy shoes. I couldn't bear any of them. They were uncomfortable and restrictive—and impossible to run in, had I been allowed to. Worse still was getting my hair done. Early in the morning, my mother would bring out a brush and a hair dryer. She would try to make me sit still as she worked her two implements of torture, struggling to straighten and style my curly hair. It would bring me to tears every time.

Eventually, when I was about ten, she just gave up—content, I suppose, to have one daughter who would look appropriate at church.

My sister, Diana, three years my senior, couldn't have been more different from me. She adored the dresses, fancy shoes, and hair ribbons that Sundays demanded. She played lovingly with the dolls and tea sets that I steadfastly ignored. Stranger still, as far as I was concerned, she wasn't interested in baseball or soccer or sports of any kind. Sometimes, I suspected that she was disappointed we didn't like to do the same things—but I refused to cooperate whenever she tried to cajole me into playing house or Barbies. She didn't complain or try to make me feel bad about it, though. Like my mother, she was patient and accepting.

My paternal grandparents also played a big role in my life. They gave up the diner just before I was born, and their home became the hub for our extended family. They spent a good portion of their new-found free time doting on me and my sister. I realized early on that they found me a handful—they simply didn't have the energy to keep up with me the way my parents and sister did—yet some of my warmest memories are of their affectionate companionship as they walked me to school each morning during the years we lived with them.

My parents, Diana, and I also spent lots of time with our maternal Italian relatives. Between the two families, there was always some dinner, party, or other gathering to attend—events that flowed with food, drink, and noisy conversation.

By the time I hit middle school, my athletic energies had been funnelled into team sports, in particular the girls' basketball team. The demands of competing lent a satisfying routine to my days. I would be up early to go to school. After school, I'd be at practices or games. I would rarely walk in the door before 7 p.m. I'd eat supper, have a bath, do my homework, and collapse into bed.

My father was, as always, encouraging of my devotion to sport and my team. He would often attend my games. After one of them, he struck up a conversation with a referee. "You've got a talented kid there," the official said. Then he suggested that my father enrol me in Albert Campbell Collegiate in Scarborough, a suburb east of Toronto. The school was a standard public high school, but it apparently had an exceptional girls' basketball program—the best in the country. The team's coach, Brian Pardo, was not only extremely dedicated but also well connected in the US basketball world. Since he took his players down to elite basketball camps and tournaments in the States on a regular basis, pretty much everyone ended up with scholarships to play US college ball. My father was sold.

At that time, we lived in a suburb north of Toronto, so the only way for me to attend Albert Campbell would be if we all moved to Scarborough. Perhaps because of all the relocations we'd already made, it seemed to be a fairly easy decision to make. Or maybe it was simply my family's innate generosity and selflessness that meant this upheaval hardly caused a ripple. Looking back on it, however, I now see just how extraordinary a decision this was. My sister was already in grade eleven. She would have to leave behind all her friends and finish her high school years at a school where she knew no one. My parents would be faced with even longer commutes on congested highways. And yet, Diana never grumbled or showed the least bit of resentment. My parents never said a word about their own inconvenience.

And so, in the summer of 1988, we moved to a rented house twenty kilometres from our former home. At the time, that area of Scarborough was a bit rough, but I didn't mind. Our new bungalow was roomy, and it even had a pool in the backyard. I was delighted.

As soon as I stepped foot on the court at my new school, I knew I had come to the right place. Brian Pardo was a gifted coach with a great eye for talent. When he'd moved to Albert Campbell, he had brought with him some of the best players from his previous school, and he had continued to attract talent.

Coach Pardo was never nasty or harsh, but you quickly learned to listen to his advice. It was clear that building a great team consumed him, and that he was putting in even more effort than he expected from his players. He spent untold hours at the school—not just at the practices and games but also supervising the gym so that we could go in at any time to practise on our own. He was the audio-visual support person at the school, so he taped all our games. We would spend hours in his office watching the films as he helped us analyze our play. Indeed, his office was a hub for us. We'd hang out there instead of the student lounge, chatting with each other and with him. I would often go there to work on my homework or type my essays.

Pardo's open-door policy extended even further. He'd invite the players to his house for barbecues and dinners with his young family. It brought us all close together—making us an even stronger team, certainly—but he also supported us as individuals. He talked with us about our futures, encouraged us to think about our post-secondary options, helped us fill out university applications, and sent videos of our play to schools in the US and Canada.

During my years at Albert Campbell, Pardo became like a second father to me, and the gym and his office like a second home. He was there when I needed advice or support. And he kept me focused. Whenever he sensed that I was at loose ends, or perhaps tempted by the kind of social life some kids at the school enjoyed, he'd get me doing something concerned with basketball or my educational future.

Under Pardo's friendly and nurturing guidance, we became a tight circle—on the court and off. In the summer months, my friends from the team would often come over to my house to swim and hang out by the pool. In our final years of high school, we'd sometimes go to parties or dancing at clubs. Partly because of my height, I always looked older than my years. By the end of high school, I had no problem getting into clubs, even though I wasn't yet nineteen.

When I was in grades ten and eleven, our team won back-to-back gold medals at the Ontario championships. (There were no national championships for high school basketball.) In grade twelve, we had to settle for a bronze. But by that time, the scholarship letters were rolling in for many of us. In the end, I received more than sixty offers. I chose the University of Arizona in part because of its great basketball program and wonderful coaches, and in part because my yiayia and pappou had begun to talk about spending the winter months in the state, and I hoped to have my family, always such a big part of my life, close by.

I really wasn't oversimplifying when I told the therapist my childhood was unequivocally "happy." I always had friends and was well liked at school. When I required expensive running shoes or money to travel to tournaments and camps with my team, they appeared. When I needed a ride to a game or practice, one of my parents took me. I didn't worry or feel guilty about what my parents sacrificed to make those things happen. If I didn't have time to help out around the house, little was said. My parents, my sister, my grandparents—nobody complained much or voiced displeasure with their situation. Or at least I never heard them do so. When my sister and I later reminisced about our childhoods, we'd sometimes remark that it was as if we had lived in two different homes. "Ace, you slept through everything," Diana would say.

I knew she was right. I went to bed so early that anything that happened in the evening was lost to me. One morning, for instance, I woke up to see potting soil all over our living room carpet. I shrugged it off and went to school. Later my sister told me the soil was evidence of a blow-up my parents had had the night before. A plant had gotten knocked over during the argument, and I had slept through the whole thing. But my parents' occasional disagreements never turned into lasting bitterness—tension didn't linger in the house, and my family always forgave and forgot.

Of course, there were sad times, when the illness or passing of a friend or family member moved us to say a few prayers to God and to Salvo. But if I cast my mind back, searching for moments in my childhood when I felt really sad or vulnerable or afraid of other people, I don't find much. There is only one time that I ever remember losing this certainty, of feeling nervous about my own safety.

I was eight or nine. It was a warm summer day, and I had gone to the park for a game of wall ball. The boys and I were playing an elimination version, and I kept hitting the ball so they couldn't reach it. One by one, they were forced to the sidelines. When the game had started, they were teasing me about not being able to keep up because I was a girl. But as each boy got knocked out, their taunts became nastier and nastier. When they moved past saying mean things about me and began making fun of my grandmother, I got scared. I thought they might start throwing their fists instead of insults. I dropped the ball and sprinted across the park. Three or four of the boys took after me as I raced down the sidewalk and around the corner. As I got close to our house, I could see my grandmother out front, watering the lawn. When she saw the boys on my heels, she waited until I was past her and then aimed the hose straight at them. I watched as the water splashed at their shins until they escaped its reach.

As the boys made their soggy retreat, I felt a wave of relief. I was safe. Protected by a tiny but strong and fearless woman with a garden hose. I think that long-ago afternoon stands out so clearly in my memory because it was such an anomaly. And even as I ran from the boys, part of me suspected that if I had stood my ground and challenged them, I would have scared them off. But I wasn't entirely sure of that, so I felt a frisson of fear. This was really my first memory of being afraid of someone, of being frightened that I would be physically hurt. And it would be the last memory like that for many, many, years—until I discovered how cruel and heartless some people can really be.

That fear-free, happy childhood meant that while I was proud of and inspired by Uncle Salvo's story, its lessons were a bit abstract to me. Uncle Salvo's example was something my grandmother found solace in and my mother and her siblings took strength from when times were tough. It wasn't until I was an adult, however, that I began to think of Salvo's story in a more profound way. That I began to pray to him when I needed faith and guidance. And then, that day in the fall of 2015, when the DA asked if she could use my assault to press charges against Bill Cosby, Salvo's story suddenly returned to me in a powerful way.

My uncle's supreme selflessness served as a beacon for me then. I knew that engaging once again with Cosby and his people, being drawn back into their toxic world, would be a personal sacrifice. *Nothing* like what Salvo had done, certainly. There was no equivalency here. And yet, his story put my decision into context. It served as a reminder that there were things more important than my own comfort or security. That there were other women who I would be standing up for. Women who had not been given the opportunity to fight.

Until that night in Bill Cosby's house, I had led a blissfully sheltered life. I had been given everything. But that happiness hadn't really kept me in a bubble. I was always aware that outside my comfortable life—all around it, in fact—people struggled and suffered. And that they made sacrifices, large and small, to protect their loved ones—and perfect strangers, too. And that there were moments when a person might be called on to do something, perhaps even something extraordinary.

Life had never asked anything of me. Not really. And now it was. I couldn't turn my back on that.

CHAPTER 4

COMING OUT

After Dolores Troiani, my lawyer, called and asked whether I would cooperate with the Montgomery County DA's office if it decided to bring charges against Cosby, I phoned my mother. We talked for a while about taking part in a criminal case. Fortunately, the civil settlement meant that I had a financial cushion that would allow me to take time off work and cover the expenses my family and I would incur if we participated in a trial far from home. It was the psychological and emotional costs we had to consider. We thought we understood the difficult road ahead. The civil suit had, after all, been gruelling. But we both agreed that we had to do this thing, no matter how painful.

I called Dolores to let her know. She sounded cautious but optimistic. She said she would keep me apprised of any developments. I didn't speak to Bebe Kivitz, the other lawyer from my civil case, right away. She and Dolores were no longer law partners, but I'd told Dolores that I would very much like to work with both of them if we moved forward in a criminal trial. Several weeks later, I got a call from Bebe.

"Are you sure, Andrea?" she asked, almost as soon as we started talking. "Are you ready for this?"

I was startled. Bebe's voice vibrated with concern. It wasn't a tone I had ever heard from her before, and it sent shivers racing through me. Bebe knew the magnitude of what lay ahead. I had thought I understood, too, but her concern reminded me that I had never been through a criminal trial before. She had. And yet she sounded worried. That terrified me.

What am I doing? I thought. What have I got myself into?

I took a deep breath. Going forward with the case was the right thing to do, I reminded myself. I couldn't think beyond this. The only way I could fight the panic in that moment was to reassure Bebe.

"I have to do this," I told her. "I'll be all right."

When I had talked things over with my mother, I had framed the question for myself in the most simple of terms: I was going to tell the truth. And telling the truth was something I'd always done.

Perhaps because we had Salvo in our family—the standard-bearer of doing the right thing—we all put great stock in telling the truth. When I was young, my nonna illustrated one of the reasons we needed to tell the truth with a little story. "It's like the bird that sits on a branch in the winter," she explained. "He may poop into the snow below, and no one will know what he has done right away. But eventually the snow will melt, and the evidence will be all over the ground. You can try to keep things a secret, but sooner or later the truth always comes out." As a child, whenever I did something I shouldn't have—broke a dish or lost a new sweater—I thought of that little bird. And I always fessed up.

My mother's gentle soul demanded only honesty and a bit of genuine remorse when I goofed. My father sometimes grumbled a bit more, but he too was easy on me. So I learned very early that telling the truth was relatively pain-free. And perhaps because of that—or just because of my innate temperament—lying was tough.

Even though the Cosby-related truth-telling was much graver than anything I'd done in my younger days, there was something about it that recalled an experience that had introduced me to the perils of being completely honest.

Bebe's call reminded me of it.

The initial attempt to press criminal charges, back in 2005, and the subsequent civil suit with Bebe and Dolores had taught me that I wasn't going to be in this alone. I was going to do this with my family by my side. And the pain and trauma I would face, well, they would experience it too. In fact, they might well suffer in ways that I wouldn't. In ways that I couldn't even imagine. It reminded me of the first time I had caused my family pain by telling my truth.

The summer I was ten, I spent several weeks at a sports camp in Northern Ontario. One night, while I was lying in my bunk, an enormous horsefly landed on my forehead and took a bite out of it. The next morning, one of the counsellors noticed my swollen red face and asked me what had happened. When I explained, she told me to come with her to the first-aid office. "I'll put something on that so it doesn't get any worse," she said.

When we got to the medical hut, she dug around in one of the first-aid kits for some antibiotic cream. She was about sixteen years old, slender and sporty. I tried not to stare at her, but my gaze kept drifting back to her soft brown hair and her brilliant green eyes. I felt a sort of nervous excitement. By the time she'd finished dabbing cream on my forehead, I had forgotten about my throbbing head and was feeling strangely rattled and self-conscious.

For the rest of my time at camp, every time I saw the counsellor or was near her, I felt a happy trembling in my chest. At night in my bunk, while other girls talked about the events of the day, I thought about her. I knew this made me different. This wasn't the way the others felt. When my friends had crushes, they had crushes on boys.

I had always enjoyed the company of boys. But once I was in middle school, a year or two after my experience at camp, I spent a lot less time playing with them. My park-based wall ball games and my recess baseball games had been crowded out by hours spent playing on the girls' basketball team. Yet while I was spending less time with boys, the rest of the girls I knew were trying to spend *more* time with them. They talked a lot about the boys they liked. And there were plenty of flirtatious exchanges between the girls and the boys in the hallways and the schoolyard.

I decided that I should see what the fuss was about, make an effort to join the romantic world of my classmates. It wasn't hard. I knew there was a boy who had a big crush on me. In short order, we were going out. I liked the boy—he was perfectly likeable. But I didn't get that buzzing feeling I'd had about my camp counsellor. My heart didn't race when I saw him or thought about him. I wasn't interested in becoming physical with him. Kissing was okay, but I wasn't tempted to go any further.

I realized, however, that there were a few girls who made me feel light-headed and giddy when they moved into my orbit.

It was becoming pretty clear to me what was going on. I was gay.

I don't know exactly when I first understood the concept of homosexuality, but I do know when I realized that many people view it as a very negative thing.

In mid-June 1985, when I was twelve years old, news broke of a terrible crime that had taken place in High Park, in west Toronto. A high school librarian named Kenneth Zeller was beaten to death by a group of five teenage boys. After an evening out with friends, the boys had gone into the park looking for a gay man to attack. They headed to an area known to be a meeting place for this community. They discovered Zeller on a walking path and chased him all the way to his car. He managed to get into his vehicle but didn't have time to lock the door before the boys descended upon him. A few days later, all five were arrested. The case and the subsequent trial were discussed on the news and in the schoolyard for months.

I don't remember if anyone from my Catholic middle school ever talked with us openly about homosexuality or about the murder, but all of us understood at some level that while Kenneth Zeller did not deserve to be attacked, homosexuality was a grievous sin—at least according to the Church and most people we knew.

Despite that, the media coverage of the case, while not exactly sympathetic, did make mention of the boys' homophobia. So the horrific Zeller murder brought me two insights: First, there were people like me out there—maybe many people like me. And second, the rest of the world viewed us with tolerance at best and downright hatred at worst.

My parents, my grandparents, my aunts and my uncles were either devout Greek Orthodox Christians or Roman Catholics. I was pretty sure I knew where they all stood on the issue, although it wasn't something that was ever discussed openly with us children. If they knew I was gay, none of my family members would respond with hatred—I was certain of that. But they wouldn't approve either. I decided to keep my feelings to myself.

Looking back on it, I'm a bit amazed by how little the anti-homosexual beliefs that pervaded my education, religion, and home life affected how I felt about myself. I know so many gay people who struggled to accept their sexual orientation. When they first recognized what their feelings meant, they desperately wished them away. They were sometimes beset with self-loathing and consumed by a desire to be "normal." They sometimes felt lesser than their straight family members and friends; they sometimes spent significant portions of their adult lives in denial or hiding. Some tried to change themselves. But I entertained none of that.

I didn't for a minute feel there was anything wrong with me. And I never seriously struggled to change myself. Why would I? This was just the way I was. It felt natural and essential to my being. And since God had made me, he had made me this way. The Almighty didn't make mistakes. This just couldn't be wrong.

By the time I got to high school, I knew I wanted to begin dating. But starting a relationship with one of my classmates or a teammate didn't seem possible. I spent a huge amount of time being physically close to other girls—on the basketball court, in locker rooms, sometimes even in hotel rooms when we travelled for tournaments. I understood that if some girls were uncomfortable with my sexual orientation, all these situations would become awkward, even for those who weren't bothered by the fact that I was "different." I did, however, talk this over with Coach Pardo. He was, as always, remarkably supportive. "What do you care?" he said, with warmth and affection in his voice. "Just be yourself." Still, I decided that keeping that part of me hidden from my teammates and classmates was the best way to go.

Nevertheless, sometime in tenth grade, I struck up a friendship with an older girl, a friend of my sister's. I knew immediately that she understood me, and that her interest in me was not purely platonic. Because the young woman lived in our old neighbourhood, we began to write letters to each other. Gradually, in those letters, we started to explore how we really felt. After a few exchanges, they turned into full-blown love letters. And we began to meet whenever we could.

Now that I was involved with another girl, I didn't feel guilty about acting on my feelings. My romance with my sister's friend was no different in my mind than if I'd taken up with some boy from my tenth-grade class. I had nothing to apologize for. That said, I was intensely private. I hadn't said anything to anyone about this new relationship (but I don't suppose I would have told my parents or sister if I were corresponding with a boy either). Someday I would have to tell my family that I was gay, but I wasn't in any rush to do that.

And then, one evening after I had come home from a practice, my mother approached me with a letter in her hand. It was one of the notes my girlfriend had sent me.

"What is this, Andrea?" she said in a shaky voice. "What does it mean? Why is this girl saying these things to you?"

Like my grandmother, I believed it was important to tell the truth, but this was a moment that made me realize that perhaps it wasn't quite as straightforward and easy as I'd thought. I couldn't think of any way to avoid telling my mother that I was gay, and yet I was scared to do it.

I knew my mother had very clear expectations about the ways girls and women should operate in the world. From the very start, I had defied those expectations. She had accepted that her younger daughter was a "tomboy," but I knew she wouldn't have such an easy time dealing with my homosexuality. In fact, I was quite certain she would be devastated.

As my mother waved the letter around in the air and tried to get me to talk, I collapsed on a kitchen chair. Fear kept me silent. I never seriously thought that she would disown or reject me. But I wondered if her disappointment would put distance between us, at least for a time. Mostly I was worried about how much pain I was going to cause her. How much heartache I might cause my father and my grandparents.

Eventually, in halting words, I explained that I liked the girl. In a romantic way. I was attracted to girls, not boys. I was gay.

My mother's face crumpled. She didn't say anything for a minute. Then she shook her head. "But, Andrea," she pleaded, "this is against our faith. Against our Church."

"Well, I guess I don't belong in the Church, then," I said.

The look of pain on her face deepened.

For the next few months, tension floated between us. I could see that my sexuality was a great concern to her. She clearly thought it was some kind of defect, and she worried out loud that she might have done something to cause it. She even wondered if it was her fault because she had allowed me to spend all my time playing sports with boys. She fretted about my soul, and yet, she also worried about how she might have made me feel all these years. Had she tortured me every Sunday and holiday, trying to make me wear those dresses?

I could shrug off her concerns about my standing in the eyes of God. I could reassure her that she hadn't contributed in any way to my orientation. But I couldn't get rid of the guilt and sadness I felt at causing her so much pain. I could see that the idea of a gay daughter was almost beyond her understanding. She knew no gay people. She had no vocabulary to discuss it. And she certainly didn't have anyone in her world who could reassure her or give her guidance.

I know she told my father that I had said I was gay, but I don't know what his reaction was. He never said a thing to me. In the end, it seemed as if they both decided that we were all going to carry on as if the love letters had never existed. I got the feeling that my parents were hoping this was just a phase that might disappear after a time.

But of course, it wasn't.

Near the end of high school, I started dating another girl. My mother's distress at this news was so intense that I decided to escape the house—for a few nights, I slept on a cot in Coach Pardo's family room. When I returned home, everyone had settled down, and we once again fell into silence about my sexuality. It would take my mother many more years to fully accept this part of who I am. And I no doubt slowed the process considerably when I started a brief relationship with a man I met just after I returned to Toronto following my European pro basketball years. We were introduced by friends and quickly hit it off. Our shared interests and enjoyment of each other's company drew us closer together, until our friendship grew into romance. But once we got serious, I realized two things: one, I didn't want the kind of family life he so clearly hoped for, and two, I simply didn't have the same sexual attraction to him that I had felt for the female lovers I'd had. In other words, my very deep affection for him hadn't translated into physical desire the way I thought it might. When my mother heard that we had broken up, her raw disappointment made it clear that she was still struggling to accept my sexual orientation.

Coming out was a process for me and my family, as it is for so many others. And it was the first time I realized that the truths I carried could hurt those who loved me. I saw this again—vividly, strikingly—the day I called my mother on the phone to tell her what Cosby had done to me. While my family's love and support had helped me deal with my pain through the attempted criminal case and civil trial, my truth had caused them intense pain of their own.

And now, ten years later, it was happening all over again.

It wasn't just that my family members would once again be thrown into the spotlight. It wasn't just that they would be worried about me, and that because of their love and empathy, they would experience the pain of the trial and the media attention along with me. It was also that my mother would be intimately involved in the legal proceedings. She would almost certainly be called to the witness stand too.

When I'd first told my mother of my assault, back in January 2005, she was horrified. Like me, she had a hard time comprehending how Cosby could have done such a thing. When you're grappling to make sense of the unimaginable, sometimes your focus lands on the questions you think are most likely to be answered. In the days after my assault, the question that dogged me was about those three blue pills. What had Cosby given me? That mystery drove me to the Chinese restaurant, and then to that awful conversation with Cosby back at his house, when he sidestepped my questions about the drugs. He'd even suggested that I'd enjoyed the encounter, saying, "I thought you had an orgasm." He clearly wasn't going to give me any answers.

A year later, my mother became absorbed by that same question. Before she even knew I'd been raped, she noticed a personality change in me. I wasn't socializing with friends, or even family. I didn't want to go to my sister's place or play with my nieces. I had lost my appetite and wasn't eating. At night, she and my father would often hear me cry out in my sleep. She knew I was having nightmares all the time. Once I'd disclosed what happened and told her I had been given some sort of medication, she began to wonder if the drugs had caused part of my physical and emotional transformation. And she couldn't forget the potential danger Cosby had put me in by knocking me out. How could he have known that I wouldn't have an allergic reaction? How could he have known that he hadn't given me too much? How could he have known that I would wake up at all? All her medical experience intensified that need to know.

She said she was going to call Cosby and find out what he'd given me. I begged her not to. I was afraid of what he might do to us if he thought we were stirring up trouble for him. I had never been very fazed by his extreme wealth and power when I first knew him at Temple, but now that

I realized what a dangerous man he was, I saw how he might be able to use his influence to punish us in some way.

My mother was insistent, though. "If you don't give me his phone number, Andrea," she said, "I'll just get on the plane and go there." I gave her the number for Cosby's answering service in New York. She left a message.

About a day later, Cosby called her back.

The first thing my mother asked him was what he had given me and what he had done to me. He insisted I get on the phone too. I got on an extension line, then explained to my mother how he gave me the pills and what he had done sexually, including the digital penetration and the masturbation. This was all new to her—I hadn't told her the specifics before. Then Cosby jumped in, claiming it was all consensual.

"Mom, she even had an orgasm," he said. (Cosby always called my mother "Momma" or "Mom," although she was younger than him. She had met him backstage at his Toronto concert in 2003, but their relationship was not familiar, never mind familial.) And he tried to offer her a little reassurance: "Don't worry, Mom. There was no penile penetration."

I couldn't listen to another word. I hung up the phone. In shock, my mother said nothing about his claims. Instead, she returned to the question of my drugged state and asked for the name of the medication I had been given. Cosby told her that he would go upstairs and check his medicine cabinet to find the name of the pills. When he got back on the phone, he said his eyesight was bad and he couldn't read the bottle. He said he would mail her the name of the drug.

The conversation continued.

My mother wanted to know why he hadn't called 911 when I passed out. What if I'd never woken up? she pressed. Didn't that possibility occur to him? He didn't answer her questions.

They talked for more than two hours, but by the time my mother got off the phone, she still didn't have her answers. Cosby's last words to her were that he'd call back in a while to find out how I was doing.

Of course, no note about the drug arrived in the mail, and by the time Cosby called back, three or four days later, my mother had a new plan.

On the day I told her of the assault, my mother had talked to my brother-in-law, Stuart, and explained that she was trying to reach Cosby on the phone. Stuart suggested that she tape any conversations they had (which is legal in Canada). But Cosby had returned her call before my mother could get her hands on a tape recorder.

When he phoned the second time, however, Mom had picked up a recording device at Radio Shack. She switched it on as soon as she heard his voice. Cosby seemed a bit suspicious—he said he heard clicking on the line—and he wouldn't talk about what he'd done to me or what types of pills he had given me, even though my mother asked again about the name of the drug. Instead, he started talking about paying for my massage therapy schooling—if I kept up a 3.0 grade point average. As if he were some kindly benefactor, trying to guide a young person's future. The offer came out of left field. It was certainly nothing we had asked for or wanted. (A few days after that, a man from the William Morris Agency, Cosby's talent agency, called and offered to fly us to Florida to meet with Cosby so we could talk further about school. He also said that Cosby would pay for any therapy I needed.)

My mother was angry. She kept pushing for more information. Eventually, Cosby said, "Mom, I'm a very sick man." My mother told him that he certainly was sick. His final words, as he got off the phone, were that it had taken me, Andrea, to "stop" him. My mother didn't know what to make of that.

Those phone conversations meant that my mother was almost certainly going to be involved with the trial—we knew that. She hadn't had to testify in the civil case (although she had made a statement to the Cheltenham Township police in Montgomery County), but now she would have to take the stand to describe her conversations with my assaulter. And she might not be the only one called to testify. My mother and I had told my father, sister, and brother-in-law what Cosby did. Stuart had given me advice about going to the police, recording phone calls with Cosby, and contacting a US lawyer. There was a chance he might be called to testify too.

In so many ways, I was lucky to have my mother in this fight with me. So many victims of sexual assault can't count on their families to back them—or even believe them. But my family's involvement worried me too. Going to trial was not just about standing up for myself, or for other victims. Its effects would reach out and sting all those who loved me. Whatever was in store for me, whatever Bebe was afraid of, was in store for them as well—especially my mother.

When I came out to my mother all those years ago, I thought it was probably the most difficult truth I would ever have to share. And I had seen how honesty can sometimes, unavoidably, cause pain for those you love. But this new moment of truth was going to be more traumatic than anything my family and I had suffered so far. Yet I knew in the end that none of that really mattered. The truth mattered. Telling the truth to address a wrong. There was no question, no debate. We were going to move forward. I found the inner strength to do that. I just prayed my family would too.

CHAPTER 5

MIND, BODY, SPIRIT

In the summer of 2015, the Montgomery County DA Risa Vetri Ferman was still considering whether to go ahead with a criminal case against Bill Cosby. Kristen Feden, an assistant DA, and three Cheltenham Township police officers—Sergeant Richard Schaffer, who had worked the original case; Detective Jim Reape; and Detective Mike Shade—all came to Toronto to interview me and my family. They needed to go over the details of my original statements and to assess whether I would be able to endure a criminal trial.

I remembered Richard well—he was patient and supportive when I had worked with him a decade earlier. And I liked Kristen immediately. She struck me as extremely smart and intuitive, with an intensity and passion that was contagious. I could see I was in good hands.

Nevertheless, it was a stressful few days. My parents moved into my tiny Toronto condo for the weekend, while I tried to sleep on my couch. Between the three of us and our three dogs, we didn't have an inch to move, which only made the tension arising from the interviews worse.

As we sat in my cramped living room, Kristen acknowledged that the process would open old wounds, but she encouraged me to relax, be myself, and share as many details as I could remember. Over the course of the two days, we talked for at least ten or twelve hours, and by the time we said our goodbyes, I was completely drained.

Once my parents headed home, I sat in my now-quiet condo and had a good cry. As I said earlier, I've never shed tears easily, but the weekend had made it clear that Kristen was right—old wounds were festering. And the flood of pain reminded me of how much Cosby had broken my spirit, and how profoundly he had changed who I was. I had done much healing and had devoted myself to looking forward, but now I was going to have to turn around and look back. I was going to have to relive my past. The only way to be a credible witness was to be in touch with that pain. I had to make myself raw again and then find the emotional and mental toughness to share it and not fall apart.

When Dolores had asked me if I wanted to go ahead with a possible criminal case, I thought I could muster that strength. But a few months later, in early December 2015, something happened that cast that belief in doubt.

In truth, it wasn't just my own pain I had been struggling with. Since the appearance of the Buress video, the flood of Cosby victims telling their stories hadn't slowed. In fact, by September 2015 more than fifty women had gone on record about being sexually assaulted by Cosby, and *New York* magazine had published a stunning issue featuring thirty-five of the other accusers. Kristen had advised me to turn off the news to protect my own psychological well-being. But even if I snapped off CNN every time another panel discussion of Cosby's case filled the screen, the stories were everywhere. Besides, I couldn't turn my back on the other women. Their accounts of suicide attempts, divorces, lost careers, mental health struggles, shame, secrets, and heartache deepened my revulsion for Cosby. I had worked so hard to forgive him for what he had done to me, but now I struggled with renewed bitterness with every additional revelation. I did my best not to take on these women's anguish and to remind myself that this was Cosby's burden, not mine. But I wasn't always successful in that.

Part of what made it so difficult was that the existence of all those other victims rewrote my own history in a way. When my criminal case had failed, I was worried about future victims. But I had no idea then of how many lives had *already* been scarred by Cosby before I even met him. I felt absolutely no resentment towards the women who had been victimized before my own assault and had stayed silent. I understood the many reasons why they had. But now, I could see that my experience was just one small link in a vast chain of predation. And I couldn't help thinking that the failure to prosecute Cosby in 2005 had been a moment lost—not just for me but for all those victims. My pain and disappointment back then must have been shared by so many. It had all been beyond my control, and yet it weighed on me now.

I was also continuing to struggle with the sudden loss of the relative anonymity I'd enjoyed since the civil settlement. I wasn't talking to the press—nor were my lawyers—but the media frenzy, ignited in fall 2014 and then fuelled by the release of Cosby's deposition the following summer, had not abated. Cosby's lawyers had gone to a judge and asked for an inquiry into the release of the damning deposition, in which he admitted drugging and having sex with me. They were accusing Dolores—and by extension, me—of somehow facilitating the leak. The judge rejected the petition, but that, along with articles like the one in *New York* magazine, kept my name in the news and my picture popping up on websites.

Over the course of the summer, there were frequent reminders that my privacy and my private life were over. One afternoon, I walked into my corner store for a quart of milk, and the man at the cash register looked up at me.

"I know you," he said.

Of course he did. The shop was steps away from my condo. I stopped in all the time. But I could tell this wasn't what he meant.

"I saw you on the news. I know what happened to you."

I felt sick. I was no longer that tall, pleasant woman who occasionally stopped by for a few groceries. Now, to this man, I was simply a rape victim and Cosby's accuser.

I also noticed several no-shows at the massage clinic, and by the fall of 2015, it was clear these weren't random missed appointments. I was losing clients—people who, for whatever reason, didn't want to associate with me any longer. The Cosby firestorm had clearly changed the way some saw me.

Of course, people who didn't know me even a little bit suddenly had strong opinions about who I was and why I had accused Cosby. Each time I went onto my Facebook or Twitter account, there they'd be. The private messages or public comments attacking me as a racist gold digger or jilted lover. The suggestions that I had been the predator because I went to the house of a married man. The sneering questions about why I would willingly take pills from someone. There were even death threats. As fast as I could block the trolls, they popped back up with new names and new messages.

On top of that, I was being undermined in another unexpected way. Bruce Castor, the DA who had declined to prosecute my case back in 2005, had stepped away from the district attorney's office for a number of years. His assistant DA, Risa Vetri Ferman, had taken over after his departure, and she was the one who'd reopened the investigation in 2015. When the story got out that Ferman was looking into this old case, Castor was quoted in the *Philadelphia Inquirer* as saying that I hadn't given the police sufficient evidence and that was why he had refused to prosecute in 2005. He then said on Facebook and Twitter that my statement to police and the ones I made in my civil case were inconsistent.

There was some truth in this.

I *had* made errors in my initial statements to the police. When I first met with the Durham Regional Police in Canada, I was caught up in a crazy brew of emotions. I was scared to share what had happened to me with complete strangers. Scared that they wouldn't believe me or would respond with dismissive disgust. I felt humiliated talking about my body and relaying the graphic details of what Cosby had done to it. I felt sick trying to describe that horrible evening—I found myself overwhelmed by flashbacks. And as I answered questions, I was pierced by moments of terror at the thought of what Cosby and his people might do if they found out I was talking to the police. At the same time, I also felt relief, as if

I were spewing forth a toxic mess that I'd been trying to keep inside. At several points, I had to fight the strange urge to smile. These emotions had me operating in a tornado of confusion and battling to reach through it to describe events.

There were, however, details that were still crystal clear to me. Eating dinner. Getting up to go to the washroom while Mr. Cosby disappeared upstairs. The three blue pills in his hand when he returned. The way he encouraged me to swallow them: "These are your friends." The physical feelings that overcame me shortly after. And the attack on the couch. Then waking. Being offered that blueberry muffin and tea.

Yet even at the time of the actual assault, many other things were a blur. I don't really remember the drive home. I don't remember much about the days that followed, except that I went to work and was concerned about what pills I had taken. What's more, by the time I contacted the police, I had spent more than a year trying to forget everything that had happened. In those months, I tried to think about my time in Philly as little as possible. I wanted to leave it all behind—the good and the bad.

So in 2005, when the Durham police officers and later the Montgomery County officers started to ask me questions about my history with Mr. Cosby, it was as if I were trying to piece together events that had happened decades, not simply months, before. When the Durham officers asked if I had ever been *alone* with Cosby before the night of the assault, I said no. To be honest, I don't know now if I answered that way because I was thinking that I had never been alone with him like *that*, or if I had just temporarily blanked out on all the previous visits with him. When they asked how long I had known Cosby, it felt like advanced calculus. I came up with six months, instead of the actual eighteen.

Even the date of the assault was beyond my grasp. When I talked with the Durham police, I'd conflated two events—the night of the attack and the night, weeks later, when I'd joined the group dinner at the Chinese restaurant and later drove to his house to confront him. By the time I went down to Pennsylvania to meet with the Cheltenham Township police, I realized that I had compressed those two nights. I had pieced together a more accurate chronology by then and was able to give the police a less garbled account of events.

This confusion, which I would later learn is extremely common among victims of sexual assault, was the "inconsistency" that Castor was now referring to—out of context, and in a way that I could not address.

Unfortunately, that *Philadelphia Inquirer* article and the Facebook and Twitter posts that Castor made were not the end of the matter. A statewide election, which included a race for district attorney of Montgomery County, was scheduled for November 4, 2015. Risa Vetri Ferman had decided not to run. Instead, her assistant, Kevin Steele, had put his name on the ballot. And so too had Bruce Castor.

Now that so many other women were speaking of their bad experiences at the hands of Bill Cosby, Castor must have realized that his failure to lay charges in 2005 and the current DA's reopening of the case might play against him and his bid to reclaim his former job. Whatever his thinking was, he resumed talking about the case in the early fall, when he claimed in a social media post that the accusations I'd made in the civil case were much more serious than anything I had reported to the Cheltenham Township police, which just wasn't true. "Troublesome for the good guys," he wrote, meaning the DA's office. "Not good." He also opined to a Pennsylvania newspaper that reopening the investigation before the election was a scheme to garner favourable press for the current DA team—without any of them having to worry about the actual viability of the prosecution.

Castor's various comments made my heart sink. If he won the election, he would almost certainly drop the case. Even if it somehow miraculously proceeded under his stewardship, I knew I wouldn't be interested in participating in a criminal trial. I couldn't possibly trust the process after Castor had undermined my credibility. And even if he lost and charges were laid, he was describing the case as impossible to prosecute and claiming that it had been opened only as a PR ploy for Steele's election bid. In other words, he was once again saying that my testimony could not be relied on.

Castor's dismissal of my account of the assault was wounding to me, but Dolores was alarmed by the more far-reaching implications of his pronouncements. He was playing politics with the case—and he could well be prejudicing everyone who might be involved, including potential jurors. She advised me that the best way to stop Castor's attacks was to sue him for defamation. At the end of October, a week before the election, we did just that.

When the papers were served, Castor lashed out at me and my lawyers. Speaking again to the *Philadelphia Enquirer*, he claimed that just like the investigation, this suit was a campaign stunt for Kevin Steele. He called our actions despicable and said, "I'm a lawyer. I'm not afraid of court. I think the people who filed the suit ought to be afraid."

In the end, Castor lost the election, and then he tried to countersue me, Dolores, and Bebe, saying that our suit had contributed to his defeat. His case was dismissed, but ours continued. I understood the importance of proceeding with it. It wasn't just about trying to make sure that a criminal case wouldn't be decided in the papers; it was also important to fight the smear tactics, to push back against the relentless campaign to discredit those of us who were sharing our stories. Many of the women who'd come forward had come under attack from Cosby and his team. A number of them—some represented by Gloria Allred and her daughter, Lisa Bloom— were now suing him for defamation. For so many of these women, the statute of limitations had taken away their right to a day in court. But they could still stand up for their truth.

Defamation suits were an important tool for us, one of the few ways we could protect our truths and our reputations. I knew this. In fact, in 2005, Dolores and Bebe had launched a defamation suit on my behalf against Cosby's lawyer, Marty Singer, and the *National Enquirer* over that interview in which Cosby had talked about being exploited by his accusers. Singer had arranged the interview, which appeared to have been granted in exchange for the *Enquirer*'s agreement to shelve a piece they had done with Beth Ferrier. In it, she described her assault by Cosby. (Beth even submitted to a lie-detector test to support her claims. She finally got her story published several months later, when she told it to Nicole Weisensee Egan at the *Philadelphia Daily News*.) We settled that defamation suit at the same time as the civil suit. Still, the legal battle with Castor weighed heavily on me, adding to the stress that the Hannibal Buress video and the possibility of a criminal case had already brought to my life.

It was early December 2015, and I was driving down a busy Toronto street, heading to meet a client for a massage appointment. I had spent the morning reading a hundred pages of documents related to our suit against Castor. It was tough working through the legalese, and tougher still to see all the material Castor's legal team had collected about me. My medical records. Tax returns. A psychological assessment I had been forced to endure. His lawyers had even contacted the manager of the massage clinic to get my employment records. What's more, Castor had been using motions related to the suit to release my initial police statements to the courts. The process made me feel vulnerable, stripped bare—all those details of my private life printed out, copied, and circulated for so many to pore over. That vulnerability stoked feelings that were becoming close to paranoia.

As I read through the documents that morning, I found myself glancing up to the streetlamp outside my living room window. For a while, I had been wondering if there might be a camera hidden there, peering into my apartment and feeding video of me to those who were hoping to find some dirt. By the time I'd reviewed all the documents, hours had slipped by, and I realized that I was in danger of being late for my first massage appointment of the day. I rushed out of the condo, adrenaline pumping, barely checking for photographers as I tore out of the parking garage.

And now, ahead of me on the road, the traffic had slowed to a crawl. I inched along, growing more and more frustrated to be in yet another situation I couldn't control. Why hadn't I left earlier? Why hadn't I been paying more attention to the time? What would my patient think, sitting there, no doubt in pain and discomfort, wondering where I was? I felt an urge to press my foot hard against the gas pedal, to blast forward and push the car in front of me out of the way. The sound of metal scraping metal filled my imagination, and then my heart started hammering in my chest and my throat tightened. My hands clenched the steering wheel as

I concentrated on keeping my foot off the gas pedal. Sweat bloomed on my forehead, along my scalp, across my chest. I was terrified. Terrified by my desire to step on the gas. Terrified by some inexplicable doom that seemed to be descending on me. Just terrified, without reason.

By the time I got to work, I was shaken, but luckily I was able to spend a few minutes calming down before I had to see my patient. In the coming days, though, I didn't feel like myself. I was experiencing tightness and pain in my chest, a heaviness, feelings of dread—all classic signs of heart trouble in women. I went to my doctor and then the hospital to get some tests done.

The diagnosis was that my heart was fine. My chest pains were the result of anxiety; the incident in the car was clearly a panic attack. I was both relieved and surprised. I had, in the aftermath of my assault, suffered from stress, anxiety, and depression. I had never, however, had an anxiety attack. I wondered if I would have more unpleasant firsts in the months to come. The Castor suit was far from over. And if Cosby ended up being charged, the pressure in my life would increase exponentially. I've got to do something, I told myself, if I'm going to get through this in one piece.

Then I reminded myself: *Mind, body, spirit.*

The anxiety attack had reminded me how interconnected our minds and bodies are. But I also knew there was another dimension to life that was just as important to well-being, and without it I simply couldn't be as strong as I needed to be. And that was my spiritual self.

When I was sixteen and first told my mother about my sexual orientation, I had also admitted to her that I no longer felt at home in the Orthodox Church. I simply couldn't find peace in a place that wouldn't accept who I was. I hadn't lost my faith in God or in Jesus. I had simply lost my old ways of connecting with it.

By the time I left for the University of Arizona, I hadn't gone to church for more than a year. I hadn't thought I missed it until I noticed how central religious faith was for many of my teammates and classmates. A number of women on the basketball team were members of a Christian athletic alliance on campus. Before each game or practice, they would gather in a circle, hold hands, and say a prayer. Sometimes members of the opposing team would join the prayer circle. These same teammates also often talked about how their faith shaped their approach to competition—they believed in being good sports and competing in a way that was positive and generous. They did not embrace winning at all costs. All of this spoke to me; it was how my mother and father had taught me to approach sports—and life itself.

The examples set by my Christian teammates had me questioning my own spirituality. Where did I stand? What did I believe in? I had no answers, and that truth left me feeling empty.

There was a Catholic church on campus, and I decided to attend services with a few friends. After a couple of Sundays, however, I abandoned the effort. I couldn't ignore the fact that the Church didn't want me as I was, that the Catholic Church thought being gay was an abomination. There seemed no point in searching out another Christian denomination either. As far as I knew, they all shared similar views on homosexuality. As much as I would have liked to worship with other students and be part of a faith community, it didn't seem that I would find the answers I was looking for that way.

And then, the summer between my second and third year, I met someone who led me into a life-changing spiritual awakening.

It was mid-June and I was at the Toronto Pride parade with some friends. We had stopped for a drink on a restaurant patio when my friend Voula recognized someone she knew. The woman's name was Karen. I was instantly struck by her radiant smile, and when she took off her sunglasses, our eyes locked. That was it.

In just a matter of days, our lives had become entwined. It was my first really serious relationship. I was twenty-one; Karen was thirty-five, with two small children. A deeply nurturing, loving person, she immediately took me under her wing. She was a wonderful lover, but she also taught me so many other things. Food had always been a huge part of my family life, for example, but I had never thought too much about what I was consuming. Karen taught me about good nutrition and about how to cook new and healthy foods. We did yoga together, and she showed me how to meditate. She also talked with me about holistic medicine and vibrational and energy healing. And she introduced me to the remarkable natural world of the Ontario North.

I had always been a city person. For a few summers I had attended sports camps in cottage country, but most of our family holidays were to beaches—Florida in the winter months, Wasaga Beach on Lake Huron when summer arrived. Karen was, by contrast, a true nature lover, and she spent as much time outside as possible. We rollerbladed, swam, and skied. And throughout the two summers we were together, we would head up north with her kids as often as possible, to camp or stay at some borrowed cottage. During the school year, she occasionally came down to Arizona so we could spend time together and explore the gorgeous southwest landscapes as well.

The scenery and fresh air were great, but the spiritual aspect of our times outdoors was perhaps the most revelatory for me. Karen believed that "spirit" was not something that resided only in humanity. Every part of the living world was imbued with it—and she believed that recognizing that truth and connecting with that greater spiritual universe was essential to inner growth.

We had been talking about this during one of our summer hikes through the northern boreal forest when Karen suggested we try to connect with the spirit of the earth. We had come across some huge pine trees, and Karen wrapped her arms around the trunk of one. I did the same.

I'm not sure how long we stood there, but it felt like forever and yet no time at all. My body rippled with sensations—the rough bark pressed into my cheek and forearms; the sharp, resiny smell of sap filling my nostrils. I was aware that the uneven ground beneath my feet was actually the contour of roots running deep into the cool, rich soil. The tree was so huge, so alive, so connected to all around it.

As I was thinking this, Karen suggested we lie down on the ground, beneath the tree. Looking up through the branches at the blue sky, I felt relaxation and peace wash over me. I thought that for the first time, I really understood the meaning of "Mother Earth." I did indeed feel as if I was in the embrace of a vast living being, and for the first time in many years, I felt that my spirit was being fed.

While Karen was showing me how to grow spiritually through a connection with nature, she was also making me aware of the power of feminine energy. One summer weekend, we packed a few bags and headed to a retreat in the Hockley Valley, north of Toronto. The two-day workshop we had enrolled in was designed to help us get in touch with our emotions and embrace our sexual energy.

That intense and challenging weekend made me realize that while I had always accepted my sexual orientation, I hadn't fully embraced my sexuality itself. It was just something I'd never been comfortable with. The discussions and meditative exercises helped me find the power in my sexual self and learn to celebrate that essential part of my being. And with that revelation and release, I had the grounding I needed to be open to a deeper spiritual journey.

I had always been an intensely physical person, and until my university days, I'd seen my religion—indeed my mind and spirit—as something very separate from that body. Karen and the things I learned during the retreat showed me that this wasn't true. Now I was finding out how other spiritual practices also embraced the connection between mind, body, and spirit in profound ways. I was learning that I was much more than a duality of body and mind, that I could have a rich interior life, and that my soul could interact with the world around me, as long as I transcended my own ego.

During my time with Karen, a number of books gave me insight into my internal life as well, including *The Artist's Way* by Julia Cameron and *The Alchemist* by Paulo Coelho. I was fascinated by many of the new age ideas and approaches, but I still felt that I hadn't landed on spiritual beliefs that could fully sustain me.

Eventually, after almost two years of a long-distance relationship, Karen and I broke up. While the age difference had never mattered to either of us, we were simply at different stages in our lives. I wanted to play pro basketball—either in the WNBA or elsewhere. I might have many relocations in the years ahead of me. And I wasn't ready to settle down.

Even though our relationship had ended, Karen's spiritual guidance continued to influence my life. In time, my spiritual seeking led me to the Kabbalah, a form of Jewish mysticism, and to Zen Buddhism. While I found many of the ideas in the Kabbalah absorbing, there was something in the style of devotion and its emphasis on following a leader or teacher that didn't suit me. I was still seeking, and I wanted to be open to other ideas, to continue to explore the possibilities. And I wanted to learn how to guide my own spirituality. Zen Buddhism's use of meditation to achieve enlightenment and its emphasis on intuition, however, appealed to me.

I then became fascinated by how quantum mechanics might reflect some of the principles of ancient Eastern mysticism. That in turn led to an interest in quantum medicine, or how the quantum theory of physics could explain the connections between human consciousness, energy, and healing. (Adam's DreamHealer books introduced me to some of this theory.) I found bliss in deep breathing, slowing my heart rate, and transcending consciousness using the healing techniques I was learning. Studying all these schools of spiritual thought brought me a greater understanding of what gave me joy and peace—and brought real positivity into my life.

And yet, throughout this journey, I never left Christianity behind. I knew that my connection to it was still deep, and that my family history made its great wisdom and meaning impossible to ignore. That awareness really took hold during my time in Italy.

Playing professional basketball in Sicily in 1999 and 2000, after college, was an intensely lonely time for me. Because I had learned a little Italian from my mother and grandmother, I was able to pick up the language quickly, but I understood more than I could say, and I found it hard to make friends readily with the other women on the team. My mother came to stay with me for a month, which helped, but the real lifeline was my

Italian family in Sicily and Naples. They invited me to visit on a number of occasions, and it was a great solace to join them for warm, chatty seven-course dinners in their comfortable homes. In mid-September, during my second year in Italy, my great-uncle Sandro mentioned that a national day of celebration for his brother Salvo was coming up on September 23. Did I want to join him, his wife, and their daughter for the occasion? I said yes and immediately bought a train ticket to Naples.

The sky was heavy and grey when we left Uncle Sandro's house to start our day of remembrance. We went first to the Church of Santa Chiara, where Salvo's remains rest in one of the chapels. The basilica is set amidst an enormous and imposing religious complex that also includes a monastery, a museum, a second church, and many tombs. More than six hundred years old, the basilica itself, like so many churches in Italy, is a magnificent structure, with soaring ceilings and a long arch-lined nave. Despite its huge capacity, the church was packed when we arrived that Sunday morning and headed to the pews reserved for Salvo's family.

The mass, dedicated to Salvo's memory, was beautifully sad and moving, the emotion in the pews as intense and immediate as if Salvo had died only days before. My grandmother's sorrow at his loss had always been apparent, but I was struck by how much he meant to so many people who had never met or known him.

After the service, I prayed for a while before Salvo's tomb, and then we joined others for a short procession to the Piazza Salvo D'Acquisto, a public square that has a modern sculpture dedicated to Salvo. About fifteen feet tall, it has a dark steel background with angular human figures cut from the metal. In front of this pattern of people stands a simple geometric representation of a man spread-eagled in a stance of protection. I was again overcome with the solemnity of the occasion, people's obvious reverence for the young hero, and the sense of mourning for his loss.

There are many, many monuments and plaques dedicated to Salvo between Naples and Rome, including a bronze statue on the Via Aurelia near Palidoro and an imposing monument of four huge rough-hewn blocks of marble outside the Torre di Palidoro, on the very spot where he died. But instead of touring these sites, my great-uncle drove to the town of Cisterna di Latina. The square outside the train station there features a wonderful bronze statue of Salvo standing tall and gazing into the distance, his Carabinieri jacket slightly undone, his cap between his feet.

As I stood under the dull low sky, a fine mist filling the air, I found myself trembling with emotion. When I was a child, I had always thought of Salvo's story as a kind of fairy tale. There was a lesson in it, but it felt more allegory than personal history. But this day of observance, spent with people who'd known him and those he'd saved, made his sacrifice immediate and astonishingly real to me. Salvo was younger than I was when he'd made his decision to exchange his life for those of the twenty-two villagers. He had decided to put his young soul into God's hands in order to preserve the lives of others. His action was unimaginably brave. For the first time, I understood the true heroism of it—and the profound act of faith that it was. I was blown away.

By the time I was on the train back to Sicily, I knew one thing: my spiritual seeking would continue, but I would never be able to embrace a faith that did not have room for God, Jesus, or Uncle Salvo.

It would take another decade before I discovered that inclusive faith. It was a quiet winter afternoon in 2011, six years after my civil case against Cosby. I was no longer in therapy and had put my life back together in many ways, but I was still working to understand the world and to keep myself spiritually, emotionally balanced and well. I was at my aunt Paola's house, visiting with my grandmother. Nonna and I were sitting on the living room couch, watching TV, when Paola came into the room with a book in her hand. She held it out to me. "Here, Andrea," she said, "I think you might find this interesting." It was *Man's Eternal Quest* by Paramahansa Yogananda, a collection of essays about finding God in daily life.

Paramahansa Yogananda was a yogi and guru who came to the United States from India in 1920. He was also a believer in Jesus Christ.

His teachings blended ancient Eastern religions and Christianity, and he introduced the spiritual practice of Kriya yoga to North America, earning him the moniker The Father of Yoga in the West.

Man's Eternal Quest spoke to me in powerful and profound ways. It led me to Yogananda's next book, *Autobiography of a Yogi*, and to the spiritual organization he founded in 1920, the Self-Realization Fellowship (SRF). I enrolled in correspondence courses and began to attend an SRF temple in Toronto.

A number of Yogananda's ideas resonated with me right from the start. He spoke of different consciousnesses that worked together—including a Christ consciousness and a Cosmic consciousness. His discussion of Christ allowed me to understand how my Christian faith could fit in with other spiritual beliefs and practices. Indeed, Yogananda's concept of the moral dimension of life struck me deeply. He described life as a "joyous battle of duty" that at the same time was only "a passing dream," a thought that seemed aligned with Salvo's great legacy. And when I read Yogananda's words on the importance of a minimalist approach to life, his rejection of accumulation and consumption, I couldn't help remembering my nonna's simple bedroom. I understood the spiritual freedom that I might gain by leading a materially spare life.

His teachings also focused on the body as a reflection of the spirit and explained how divine energy sustains the body. Mind, body, and spirit, he taught, were inextricably intertwined. Exercise, relaxation, a good diet, and an "undaunted" frame of mind strengthened the soul, just as the soul strengthened the mind and body. And it was necessary to strike a balance: "To be too calm is to be lazy; to be too active is to become an automaton."

While Karen had introduced me to yoga and meditation, Yogananda's teachings allowed me to engage in these practices in a deeper, more sacred way. Many of the meditation techniques that Yogananda taught were designed to help a person recharge the physical self by connecting to cosmic energy. Meditation, he explained, was to free your soul from the constraints of your body and your daily concerns. When I was younger, I had never thought of my body as something that could impede me, but my assault had changed that. I knew that I could benefit from escaping its pain and limitations. Just as Yogananda claimed, the deeper and longer I was able to meditate, the more rejuvenated and restored I felt. Meditation became an indispensable part of my day, and the way I rebuilt my positivity and balance whenever I felt off-kilter.

And perhaps most important, Yogananda wrote movingly about the power of forgiveness. Christ's prayer for forgiveness for the Roman soldiers who were about to crucify him ("Forgive them, Father, for they know not what they do") was one of his most glorious acts, Yogananda said. And he explained how forgiveness was a way to maintain your own connection with the divine. "Why forgive one who wrongs you?" Yogananda wrote. "Because if you angrily strike back you misrepresent your own divine soul nature—you are no better than your offender." Forgiveness, Yogananda explained, was a way to escape the burden of bitterness and anger, to escape the cycle of suffering unleashed by a thirst for retribution.

For years, I had known that putting the past behind me meant forgiving Cosby in some way. Yogananda's writings inspired me to commit fully to forgiveness and work continually to maintain that state of mind.

The teachings of Yogananda and the lessons I studied through the Self-Realization Fellowship had been a big part of the contented life I had managed to establish for myself before the Cosby case hit the news again in 2014. Indeed, after I experienced that panic attack while driving, I had gathered myself by doing a short meditation in my office before seeing my patient. But the fact that anxiety had so overtaken me both on that commute and in the days that followed made me realize that I wasn't as strong as I needed to be. I clearly had to work harder to ground myself, to relinquish anger and bitterness, to find peace, and to bring balance back to my life. I needed to work more consciously to live in a state of forgiveness, as I'd been able to do just a year or so earlier. To achieve any of this, I was going to have to take my athletic discipline and apply it to strengthening my soul even further. If I was going to be able to do this, if I was going to be the best witness I could, if I was going to stand up for what I believed in and for all the women who couldn't, I needed to be strong in mind, body, and spirit.

In the coming months, I would have to dig deeper than I ever had before. I just hoped and prayed I had it in me.

CHAPTER 6

SOLIDARITY

Not long after my panic attack, the Christmas season was upon me. It was a busy time, with gatherings and parties with both sides of my extended family. Looming over all these good times, however, was what I knew awaited me in the new year. I'd had a call just after Christmas from Kristen Feden, the assistant DA. Big news was days away.

On December 30, 2015, my phone started to beep. I knew immediately what the texts, emails, and Facebook messages were about. More than ten years after I'd reported my assault, the district attorney's office of Montgomery County, on behalf of the Commonwealth of Pennsylvania, had issued an arrest warrant for Bill Cosby. He was charged with three counts of aggravated indecent assault: one count for penetrating my genitals with "part of his body," one for assaulting me while I was unconscious, and one for assaulting me after he'd administered drugs or an intoxicant to render me defenceless.

I turned on the TV. There he was, wearing a soft toggle-front cardigan. He was carrying a cane (Cosby had a condition that was making him blind) and was supported by people on either side as he walked carefully into the Montgomery County District Court in Norristown, Pennsylvania. America's Dad had morphed into America's Ailing Grandpa.

I wasn't surprised, of course, but I was nevertheless shocked that it was really happening. And then, as I watched, I was overcome with relief. I wasn't seeing a fragile old man; I was seeing a predator in a comfy sweater. Finally, I thought. Now he can't hurt anyone else. Later, Cosby would be released on $1 million bail, but even this news wouldn't dampen my feelings. Now he would be under some kind of surveillance. Now the world would be a little bit safer.

I turned to my phone. I would respond first to my parents and sister. Next, I would send a note of congratulations to the district attorney's office. And then it would be time to connect with my teammates.

Throughout my life, there was never a moment when I didn't have friends. But I've never had a particularly large group of friends. When I was small, we moved around a lot, which made sustaining relationships hard. And of course, my athletic interests meant I played mostly with boys, but I didn't hang out with them after our games. Then in my teen and college years, my basketball schedule restricted my socializing. Having a fairly small social group was something I was used to, a habit I carried with me in my early working years. And after my assault, trust issues kept me from widening my circle much beyond a few close friends and my family.

But ever since I was twelve, I'd always had teammates. I'd been closer to some than others, but the group dynamics, the camaraderie, the mutual respect and support had provided me with so much comfort over the years. And I had always drawn great security and confidence from being on a team. That's why, when Dolores told me that she and Bebe were no longer practising law together, I insisted that if I was going to work with the DA on a possible criminal case against Cosby, I wanted Bebe to represent me as well. I then sent them both an email, explaining why this was so important to me.

The three of us had been a team—a *great* team—and Dolores and Bebe complemented each other in a powerful way. If I had only one word to describe Dolores, it would be "tough." Dolores wouldn't be in the courtroom questioning witnesses this time—that was the district attorney's role.

But I knew her steeliness would be invaluable in dealing with the press. During the civil case, she took the reins when it came to reporters. When she said "No comment," it was immediately clear that all talk was over. Even when she answered questions, she could be stunningly abrupt. Many times, her response was a single word. With Dolores representing me, I knew we'd have complete control over the messaging that came from our side.

Where Dolores was tough, Bebe was strategic. Lively and energetic, she had a soft touch when working with traumatized people and a sharp legal mind. She was a master of the technical details, the minutiae of legal motions and procedures. The two of them were really a one-two punch when it came to the law.

But frankly, I was after more than just the amazing combination of skills when I asked them to reunite for my case. My insistence was also rooted in a visceral need to feel part of a strong front, to put the team back together. It broke my heart that tension seemed to have developed between them, and that their business separation had meant a social separation as well. At that point in my life, I just wanted to see people coming together and supporting each other. And despite the fact that it really wasn't my business, I desperately wanted them to work together again so they could figure things out. That they did so gave my spirits a lift during the difficult months leading up to the trial.

Yet Dolores and Bebe weren't my only teammates, my only team.

When the Cosby case re-entered the news in 2014, I began to think of those women who had provided me with support in my civil suit—the twelve Jane Does. I wondered how they felt reading the articles that popped up after the Buress video, how it affected them to see their stories recirculated, and how they felt about the new Cosby victims appearing almost daily.

After the civil case, Dolores and Bebe had thanked the Jane Does on my behalf, but they advised me against contacting any of them myself. Since I was constrained by the non-disclosure agreement, any interaction with the twelve witnesses or other women who had contacted my lawyers around that time was fraught with risk. But it was tough and isolating to keep my distance from these women—the only women I knew who had also been sexually assaulted, and who might well have the same emotional struggles I had. I had prayed about it, but eventually I had to move on. Now that our pasts were being rehashed in public, however, I was beginning to think that we needed each other. And perhaps now I could be there for them.

I tried to find some of the women on Facebook. The first two I reached out to were Barbara Bowman and Donna Motsinger. Both had appeared as Jane Doe witnesses in my civil case, but Barbara had spoken publicly about her assault while that suit was still unfolding. I didn't know Donna's story until late November 2014, when she decided to go public in the wake of the Buress video, saying she felt guilty for not sharing her story earlier. Now she wanted to support those women who had already come forward.

Her story was sadly familiar, even though it preceded mine by more than three decades. Donna alleged that in 1971 she was waitressing at a restaurant in Sausalito, California, when Cosby came in. He chatted with her and invited her to accompany him to his live show that night. During the limousine ride over, Cosby offered her a drink. After taking a few sips, she immediately began to feel odd, and then she remembered nothing until she woke up the next morning in her own bed. She was certain that she'd been sexually assaulted.

After approaching a few of my Jane Doe witnesses individually, I discovered another way to connect with Cosby survivors. In January 2015, a Facebook group called "We Support the Survivors of Bill Cosby" (@WeStandInTruth) had been created by a man from Saskatoon. It had quickly ballooned in size with members from all over the world. I was buoyed to see a public forum of supporters like this. Despite some serious blowback after the Buress video (his TV shows had been taken off the air, some concert dates had been cancelled, universities and colleges had rescinded honorary degrees), Cosby had continued his "Far from Finished" comedy tour that winter. In January, he had performed in three cities in my corner of Ontario: Kitchener, London, and Hamilton. There were small protests at the Kitchener and London shows, but when it was reported that at the latter Cosby had made a spontaneous joke about how dangerous it was for women to drink around him, protestors turned out in force outside the Hamilton theatre, chanting, "We believe the women!" Despite my disappointment that those shows had sold out, I was encouraged by the growing protests—and happier still that someone had created a permanent virtual hub for supporters to express themselves. "We Support the Survivors of Bill Cosby" also quickly became a meeting place for survivors.

Through the group, I connected with a number of other Cosby victims. Although we sometimes knew each other's stories, I made sure not to talk about the details of our experiences when we chatted. During my civil case, I'd learned that defence lawyers could subpoena my messages and texts. If they looked through my correspondence with other Cosby victims, they would no doubt be hunting for any suggestion that we were "colluding" to manufacture or bolster our own accounts. They might twist even the most innocent exchanges to try to make this argument. I didn't want to jeopardize any future legal cases, so I kept my interactions brief. My purpose was simply to let other survivors know I was there, I was listening, I felt their pain. And for me, the group offered a sense of being part of a larger community of people who understood each other at a profound level and drew strength from that bond.

Getting to know the other Cosby survivors was a great comfort in many ways, but it also brought me new points of pain. Their stories cut into me. So too did the secrets I carried. In the early days of 2015, before the deposition was released, I knew things these women did not. Most had the same questions I'd once had: What did he give me? Why was I unable to resist? Why did I pass out? But I knew from the civil trial that the answer was likely Quaaludes. Cosby had admitted to getting seven prescriptions from a Dr. Amar in Los Angeles. He explained that when he'd initially requested Quaaludes, the doctor asked if he "had a bad back or anything." Cosby said yes. But he never took the pills himself. Instead, he kept them to give to women before sex. Because of my NDA, however, I couldn't share this information.

Even so, over the months, a number of women became my good friends, including Heidi Thomas, Patricia Steuer, Barbara Bowman, Donna Motsinger, and Lili Bernard. In the late spring of 2015, I decided that I wanted to mark these new relationships in a lasting way. I didn't have to think long about how to do it: within days, I was at the tattoo parlour.

I have always loved getting tattoos—and I started young. I was fifteen years old and on holiday with my family in Daytona Beach, Florida, when I got my first one. My mom and one of her friends had been daring each other to get inked for some time. Mom and I were out shopping when we passed by a tattoo shop. With her friend's challenge in mind, Mom decided to pop in and ask what was involved. The tattoo artist assured her that a very small tattoo would take only five minutes or so and could be placed where no one would see it. True to her spunky nature, my mother decided to get one on the spot. And once I was looking at the designs, I knew I wanted one too. My mother could hardly say no, so the tattoo artist agreed to etch a loonie-sized basketball tattoo on the right side of my chest. Inside he put "33," my number on the Albert Campbell team.

At the end of high school, I had my girlfriend's zodiac sign tattooed on my lower right abdomen. When I got to the University of Arizona, I discovered that tattoos were almost a rite of passage in women's college ball. This time, I had my inner wrists decorated with the Japanese characters for "earth," "angels," "spirits," and "destiny." When I was in Italy, I decided to memorialize the achievement of making a pro ball team by having a pair of wings etched on top of my shoulders—a fitting emblem, I thought, for my life as it was taking off. When I was living in Philly, I picked up a book on polarity therapy and saw the caduceus symbol—the staff and two snakes— on one of its pages. I had always felt a calling to be a healer like my father, and in that moment, I recognized the extraordinary power of that symbol. Since it was a reflection of how I wanted to spend my energy going forward, I decided to make it part of my physical self too. I had the caduceus inked onto my arm.

And then, for five years after my assault, I didn't return to a tattoo parlour. In about 2009, however, I decided to start the process of getting "sleeves," large tattoos made up of various designs on each arm. Despite what some might claim, getting inked is very painful. And yet tattoos can be addictive, and in my early days, I withstood the pain for the thrill of seeing small pieces of art blossom across my body. When I started the sleeves, however, I began to see the pain in a different way.

The bite of the needle now seemed to be a reflection of the pain in the world around me and the pain in my own soul. As the tattooist worked his way up my arms, I felt as if my stinging flesh was bearing testimony to everything I had gone through. When I looked at the final art, I saw a lifelong reminder of how I had endured that pain and survived. I found the many sleeve sessions—and the tattoos themselves—remarkably therapeutic.

And by early June 2015, I was thinking about tattoos again. Yogananda counsels that it is good to rise above the body, so I wasn't sure that he would think the skin was the best place to store memories or express yourself. And yet, I'd always found the tattooing process spiritually uplifting, and now I felt ready for a little more of that cathartic art.

To honour the new women in my life, I chose a drawing of a cluster of pink gladioli for my left shoulder. The gladiolus flower symbolizes strength of character, remembrance, faithfulness, and moral integrity; Lili Bernard had also told me that in Cuba, her birthplace, the pink versions of the flower were a symbol of peaceful protest.

In fact, it was Lili's use of the pink gladiolus in her own protest that inspired my choice of tattoo. On April 30, 2015, many months before my criminal case was restarted, Lili Bernard and her lawyer, Gloria Allred, went to the police in Atlantic City, New Jersey (the state has no statute of limitations for sexual assault), and told them her story. Lili had been an actress in the early nineties and was thrilled when she was cast as one of Dr. Huxtable's pregnant patients on *The Cosby Show*. He seemed enthusiastic about Lili's potential as an actor, encouraging her and calling her "one of my kids." In turn, Lili thought Cosby was wonderful—someone who truly cared about her future. Someone she could trust. And then, according to her, one day he drugged her and raped her. After the assault, she said Cosby told her, "As far as I'm concerned, Bernard, you're dead. Do you hear me? You're dead. You don't exist."

The abuse, both physical and emotional, so traumatized her that she became suicidal and wound up in the hospital. She recovered, and over the next two decades, Lili married and had six children. But the psychological wounds lingered, and by 2015, she had decided she finally wanted to see justice done.

A day after she and Gloria Allred met with the police, Lili travelled to Cobb County, Georgia, where Cosby was performing one of the last shows of his "Far from Finished" comedy tour. She stood outside the venue, holding an armful of pink gladioli, and told her story to the press.

When I decided to get a new tattoo, I remembered Lili's gladioli. The flowers would be a beautiful reminder of the many women who had become my friends and my teammates. I decided to give a nod to my heritage as well, adding the Italian words *amore, verita, coraggio*—"love," "truth," and "courage." The pain from being inked was again a release.

It took three sessions to finish the flowers, but by mid-July, the art was done and my skin had healed. I sent Lili—who had heard recently that the Atlantic City DA would not press charges against Cosby—a photo of the completed tattoo. Clearly we still had much to protest.

The supportive community I was building for myself grew even bigger when Barbara Bowman put me in touch with a woman named Angela Rose. Angela was kidnapped and sexually assaulted in 1996, when she was just seventeen. In 2001, she founded a Chicago-based non-profit organization called PAVE (Promoting Awareness/Victim Empowerment), which works to prevent sexual violence through social advocacy and education. PAVE also provides support for victims of sexual violence so that they can heal from their trauma. Throughout 2015, Angela and I exchanged emails and talked on the phone every few weeks. She not only offered me words of wisdom and support but also invited me to share what I'd learned over the years with other survivors.

So when the news broke on December 30, 2015, that the Montgomery County district attorney, Kevin Steele, had charged Cosby with my assault, my family celebrated with me, but so too did a great many women. Phone calls, text messages, and Facebook posts poured in. It was a tidal wave of support, but also a reminder that the legal proceedings were about much more than my individual case. I would be fighting for a whole community.

More moments of connection saw me through the new year. On January 31, 2016, a month after the charges against Cosby had been laid, I was on my way to a PAVE summit in Phoenix. Angela had asked me to talk about holistic healing for trauma. The event was a remarkable experience. For so many years, I had lived in the shadows. And yet here were people talking openly about trauma, and learning about active healing and recovery within a supportive, united community. Here were men and women committed to addressing the issue of sexual violence and working for societal change. I knew that whatever happened, I would stay connected to this organization.

After the summit, I got in my car and drove along the scenic Route 66 to Santa Fe, New Mexico. I was on my way to a small town outside of Taos to meet Donna Motsinger in person for the first time. When I first found out that Donna had the same birthday as my mother and was exactly ten years older than her, I saw it as a sign that we were meant to be close. What's more, she lived in one of my favourite parts of the world.

One thing that connected me to both Donna and Barbara Bowman was a love of the US Southwest (Barbara lives in Arizona). Since my university days, I had returned to the Tucson area many times. I always found the fragrant desert air in Arizona, the mesas, and the open skies to be healing. I also shared Lili's passion for California, where I had lived for several months after university, before moving to Italy. Since then, I had made a number of trips back to the West Coast, where the mountains, the ocean, and the salt spray always rejuvenated me and reminded me of the connections to the earth that Karen had taught me about. The new age culture that thrived in both places was also a draw for me. During the eighteen months I waited for the trial I travelled to both places multiple times, sometimes with my nieces and sometimes alone.

Sure enough, Donna and I hit it off. She reminded me of my mother in many ways. She has a bit of a hippie vibe—a relaxed and free spirit that made me feel at ease and understood. Donna's calm reassurance and obvious contentment gave me hope that I too could truly move past the trauma I'd been through and spend my future in a place of healing. We talked and talked throughout the two or three days we spent together. We had a lovely lunch in a restaurant her son managed in Taos. We visited art galleries, and we went on several beautiful hikes.

After the trip, I returned to Toronto feeling refreshed and energized. The Southwest had worked its magic on me once again, as did all of the wonderful connections I had made. But I could see that it would take some work on my part to keep that energy alive. While the PAVE summit and my time with Donna had renewed my commitment to go to trial, the road ahead looked long and challenging. Bebe and Dolores advised me that I wouldn't see the inside of a courtroom for at least another year, and maybe longer. I needed to stay committed. I couldn't lose sight of why we were doing what we were doing.

So shortly after I got back from New Mexico, I returned to my favourite tattoo artist and explained what I wanted. After a couple of sessions, the new tattoo was finished. The word "truth" was now emblazoned in flowing script across the top of my chest. Every morning when I looked in the mirror, I would be reminded of what was really important—and what I had been called to do.

The community I was becoming part of empowered me greatly. That—along with therapy and the meditation and study of the Self-Realization Fellowship—was helping me stay emotionally and psychologically grounded.

Yet when I look back on those many months, I can see that I wasn't entirely myself. And that my need for connection did not always manifest itself in ways I am proud of now.

One reason I'd ended my relationship with my girlfriend, Kristin, in the spring of 2015 was that I had developed trust issues. Another factor was that my life had become overshadowed by the Cosby firestorm. I found it harder and harder to be there for her—it was as if all my psychological and emotional energy was needed to fortify myself and to connect with people who were going or had gone through the same kind of struggle. Our parting was amicable. Kristin checked in on me frequently, and our romance gradually transformed into an enduring friendship. I was content with this. Or at least I thought I was.

Sometime in 2016, while I was on one of my trips to the US, I met a woman who had also been a victim of sexual assault many years earlier. She was in a long-term relationship, which was foundering, although she was still committed to making it work. We discovered that we had a lot in common, and I found great solace in being able to talk with her about our mutual traumas and challenges. We stayed in touch by email and text messages, and the next time I was in her city, we arranged to get together for a drink.

We met in the bar of the hotel where I was staying. Time flew by as we talked, and at some point in our conversation, the room around us seemed to dissolve. There were only the two of us, drawing closer and closer to each other. I was overcome by the surging need to make the space between us disappear altogether, to feel the heat of another body against mine. It was a desire I hadn't felt for a long time. And it was a warmth I'd thought I might no longer be capable of feeling.

We ended up in my hotel room, making love.

Once I returned home, we continued our chats and messages, and in the months leading up to the trial, I travelled to see her several more times. I have never taken physical intimacy lightly, never been very comfortable with casual hook-ups. I certainly had never before (or since) become involved with someone who was in a relationship. But the fact that she had a life partner must have played into the safety I felt with her. She understood me and what I had gone through—that provided the initial sense of trust. Added to that was my understanding that she was looking for nothing further from me. She certainly wasn't looking for a commitment of any sort, and neither was I. I didn't have that in me to give.

The last time we were together sexually was a few months before the trial began. We didn't talk about it being the last time, but I think we both knew it. I was about to enter the maelstrom of the court proceedings; she was going back to her partner and her life. We would continue to be friends—to be in touch through emails and texts—but that would be it.

I have to say, I do not feel good about our short-term fling. But I'm just too grateful for the much-needed intimacy that I can't find it in me to blame either of us for that misstep. Our affair gave me something I desperately needed: physical tenderness, desire, the feeling of being alive. Cosby had taken so much from me—and I was about to be dragged back into his blighted world by the upcoming trial—but he had not taken away my ability to be sexually alive with another person. I know how lucky I am in this. Many sexual assault survivors, including a number of Cosby's victims, can't say the same.

In the end, the liaison was about connection. And yet, if I'm really honest with myself, I recognize in the tryst my fundamentally altered state. Even while I was grounding myself spiritually and building a community of support, my emotions were raw and insistent.

And I hadn't yet been thrust into the crucible of a criminal trial. That, I knew, would be the real test.

CHAPTER 7

TRAINING CAMP

My trip to the PAVE summit and my wonderful visit with Donna couldn't have come at a more welcome time. I had needed the escape. On January 1, 2016, just a few days after the charges had been brought against Cosby, the *New York Post* ran an article about me titled "Cosby Accuser Used Settlement to Buy Ritzy Condo." The article quoted one of my neighbours, mentioned my building by name, and featured a photo of the facade with the street number clearly visible. It was upsetting to think that one of my neighbours was talking to the press about me. Worse still was the idea that while the media had always known how to find me, now the rest of the world did too.

On the same day the article appeared, one of Cosby's lawyers, Monique Pressley, did the rounds of the morning news shows. She told ABC's *Good Morning America* that the charges were "a game of political football" and that the DA was only "fulfilling a campaign promise."

Cosby's legal and public relations teams then continued their flurry of activity. On January 20, his lead defence lawyer, Brian McMonagle (Cosby had fired his longtime legal rep, Marty Singer), formally moved to have the case dismissed. That was followed on February 1 with a suit claiming that my lawyers, my mother, and I had breached the civil settlement by pursuing criminal charges, and that I had breached it by tweeting about those charges. (Cosby's lawyers in the civil suit had wanted a clause that restricted me from ever cooperating with a criminal investigation. Dolores and Bebe agreed only to a promise that I wouldn't initiate proceedings. There was nothing that said I couldn't cooperate with a criminal case if I was approached to do so. The suit would be withdrawn at the end of July.)

On February 2, the dismissal hearing was held. Bruce Castor testified that he felt his 2005 decision not to prosecute Cosby in my case effectively shielded the comedian from being prosecuted by the current district attorney as well. He also claimed that he had not put an immunity agreement in writing at the time only because Cosby thought it would look bad. And he asserted that he had pressured Cosby to make the deposition in the civil case, hoping that it would help me get some monetary compensation. Castor once again made an issue about my initial inconsistencies and the fact that I had stayed in touch with Cosby after my assault. He thought my behaviour was "inconsistent with the behaviour of a person who had been sexually assaulted." Meanwhile, the defence lawyers argued that too much time had gone by and evidence was no longer available to them. And then they claimed that Cosby was now too old and sick to be able to review what evidence was available.

The court rejected Cosby's petition to dismiss the case, but the motions continued, including one to suppress his civil deposition (which his lawyers claimed he'd made only because he was promised criminal immunity), and one to have DA Kevin Steele disqualified from the case because he had talked about it during his election bid against Castor. Both of those were rejected, but the judge did allow a motion to block excerpts from Cosby's 1991 memoir, *Childhood*, and the various interviews and stand-up routines he'd done over the years. As part of his early stand-up routine, Cosby had described how in his teen years he'd learned about a drug—the aphrodisiac Spanish fly—that you could slip into a girl's drink so she'd do anything you wanted. The prosecutors argued that this showed Cosby's early and sustained interest in drugging women for sex. But the judge wouldn't allow that line of argument into the courtroom.

My lawyers, Dolores and Bebe, as well as the DA Kevin Steele, kept me in the loop at all times. But whenever one of these motions popped into the news, I would hear from my mother or sister or other friends and relatives. People also reached out every time a story broke about Cosby's other accusers and the legal actions they were involved with. And there were plenty of those—including attempts to press charges in other districts, and defamation lawsuits launched by women whom Cosby's team had called liars. Cosby often tried to use the courts to silence those speaking out. Even before the charges were laid in my case, Cosby had filed suits against seven women for defamation. A week later, he filed another defamation lawsuit against model Beverly Johnson, who had accused him in the media and in her memoir of drugging her, although she did not believe he had raped her.

And then there were all the Cosby defenders who were busy proclaiming his innocence and decrying this so-called miscarriage of justice, including his family, his celebrity friends, and of course, his lawyers and public relations people.

And with every news item and announcement, my phone would start pinging and buzzing with calls and messages from my family. Despite all the things I was doing to ground myself, the constant communication was proving exhausting. Unlike the women I'd met through PAVE and the other survivors I knew, those closest to me simply didn't realize that their outrage and worried questions served only to remind me of my pain. What's more, their reactions to everything that was going on made me concerned for them. Just as I had feared when I agreed to cooperate in a criminal case, my family members were being drawn into the vortex. And they were suffering.

When we got together for Sunday dinners, I would notice this. Someone might mention the case, and then tension would crackle through the room. A little more alcohol than usual would be consumed. People would get testy with each other. There might be an argument. And I would leave the house, not only anxious about the legal manoeuvres but also sick with guilt about the stress my family was feeling.

I knew that if I was going to get to the trial in one piece, I needed to try to help them. And I needed to reduce the flood of negative stories and negative feelings around me. So I attempted to lay some ground rules. I suggested to my parents and other relatives that they try to limit their exposure to the Cosby news to avoid the negativity and hateful things that were being said about us and the other accusers. But they felt staying on top of all developments was a way they could be there for me, accompany me on this journey, and maybe even protect me. Their focus on the case was coming from a place of love—I knew that. Eventually I gave up telling them to stop following the news. "If you can't do that," I told them, "please don't tell me about what you've heard. Just assume that I already know." I explained that I just had to let it all go until there was something I could actually do. For the time being, I needed to let my lawyers, the DA, and God take care of it for me.

For the next few months, my mother, father, sister, and the rest of my family shared their upsets and outrages with each other, but they did their best to give me the space I needed.

My first concrete involvement with the legal proceedings finally took place in late spring. A pretrial preliminary hearing was supposed to have happened early in the year, but Cosby's legal team had managed to delay it to May 24, 2016. The prosecutors explained to me that the hearing was like a trial before the trial, but instead of determining whether Cosby was guilty, a judge would decide if there was enough evidence to move forward to an actual criminal trial. The plaintiff is not usually called to testify in these hearings. Instead, the DAs were planning to have portions of my 2005 testimony read to the judge. But she might still want to hear some of the details from me in person. I would have to travel to Montgomery County so that I'd be available if needed.

The day before the hearing, I flew to Philadelphia and checked into a hotel. Kevin Steele, Kristen Feden, and Sergeant Richard Schaffer came to see me there. I had heard so much about Kevin from Kristen—his hard work and leadership had played an important role in getting the case this far. But this was the first time I had met him in person. I was impressed by his sensitive and caring demeanour. I had a great group behind me.

The next morning, a detective picked me up in an unmarked car and drove me to a government office building across the street from the Montgomery County District Court in Norristown. I would wait there to hear if the judge wanted me to appear before her. As we got close to the courthouse, my pulse quickened. A line of huge news vans stretched around the courthouse block. Our car turned away towards a parking lot behind the neighbouring building.

I was led quickly out of the car and to one of the upper floors, where I was taken to a large room with a conference table and a number of couches. As soon as I entered the room, I headed over to the windows. No one other than the people in the DA's office and the detectives knew I was there, but the press had speculated that both Cosby and I might be in the courtroom—facing off, as it were. I suspected that the prospect of seeing us together had fuelled excitement.

The sidewalk in front of the courthouse was hemmed in by all the news vans, satellite dishes perched on their roofs. All the major networks seemed to be there—CNN, ABC, NBC, CBS, Fox—as well as a number of entertainment news shows. Big microphones and video cameras were being set up near the courthouse steps. Photographers and reporters were jockeying for position. Women's rights and anti-abuse protestors were holding signs and banging drums. Another group of people stood separately—possibly Cosby fans, waiting to greet him as he walked in. Apparently, it was just as crowded inside the courthouse. I would later hear that so many reporters and spectators had shown up that at least fifty of them had to sit in an overflow area outside the courtroom itself.

As I watched the crowd, I was struck by the enormity of what was going on. Suddenly the possibility of a trial felt very real.

And then, there seemed to be a flurry of activity at the front of the building. I was too high up to tell exactly what was going on, but later I would see the video of Cosby's arrival. A large group of people, including police officers, made their way around the side of the building. In their midst was Cosby. He wasn't using a cane, but he was leaning on the arm of his spokesperson, Andrew Wyatt. They slowly walked up the ramp that led to the entrance. Reporters called out and cameras flashed. Cosby waved. He and his entourage disappeared into the building. Once the commotion settled down, I realized that there was nothing to do but wait.

Three and a half hours passed. I wasn't called, but near the end of that time, someone took me downstairs to the room where grand juries meet. It was filled with audio-visual equipment and rows of empty seats. When Kevin and Kristen walked in, they looked relieved. "Good news!" one of them announced. The judge had ruled that our case could go forward.

Before they gave me more details, they introduced me to the other assistant DA who had been working hard to put the case together. Stewart Ryan was perhaps more matter-of-fact than Kristen, but his compassion was evident as soon as he began to speak. I would also come to appreciate his remarkable intelligence and formidable legal instincts. I was struck once again by how lucky I was to be on such a wonderful team.

Kristen, Kevin, and Stewart then walked me through what had happened in the courtroom. As they had warned me, large portions of my 2005 statements to police were read during the hearing. The Cosby camp had been quoting bits and pieces since the charges were laid, but this was the first time that many details of my story had been made public, including exactly what I remembered him doing to me on that couch.

Cosby's 2005 police interview was also read aloud. In it, he claimed that we had had a number of intimate encounters, including "petting," and that he had given me the over-the-counter allergy medication Benadryl because I complained of having trouble sleeping. (At the police interview, apparently, he had brought with him one and a half tabs of the drug to show the police, although the pills were pink and not blue.) In his statement, he also claimed that I didn't object when he put his hand down my pants. Now this information was certain to be splashed all over the news.

Although District Judge Elizabeth McHugh ruled that we did have enough evidence to proceed to trial, a date wouldn't be set for a while. Cosby waived his right to attend a subsequent hearing in July, when the charges would formally be read. He would leave it up to his lawyers to deliver his not guilty plea to the court.

When Kevin and the others had finished updating me, one of the detectives in the group, Jim Reape, told me that someone wanted to meet me. Gloria Allred had appeared at the hearing on behalf of her Cosby clients, who by this point numbered about a dozen. After the hearing, she had spoken to reporters on the courthouse steps, telling them that she felt the judge had made the right decision.

When Gloria walked into the grand jury room, we shook hands. "Andrea, you're very courageous. You're standing up for all the other women as well," she said. "Thank you." Then we stood together as Detective Reape took a photograph for me.

I knew the pretrial hearing was a taste of what was to come. Media scrums. Faceoffs between Cosby supporters and protestors. Cosby's lies. And the graphic details of my violation discussed on the news.

But all I could do was wait. It was not an easy time. The story stayed in the news for weeks thanks to both his not guilty plea in July and his various attempts to control the narrative. In September, his legal team made its first accusation of racial bias.

Another hearing was held on Tuesday, September 6, at the same Montgomery County courthouse. The judge heard requests from Cosby's lawyers that portions of his 2005 police statements and deposition be kept out of the trial. After the hearing, on the courthouse steps, Cosby's lead lawyer, Brian McMonagle (who I later found out was a friend of Bruce Castor's), declared that Cosby's civil rights were being trampled. He claimed that Gloria Allred, who was representing a number of the women who were offering to testify, "calls herself a civil rights attorney, but her campaign against Mr. Cosby builds on racial bias and prejudice that can pollute the court of public opinion." He also said, "Mr. Cosby is no stranger to discrimination and racial hatred. When the media repeats her accusations—with no evidence, no trial, and no jury—we are moved backwards as a country and away from the America that our civil rights leaders sacrificed so much for." Another Cosby lawyer, Angela Agrusa, told the crowd of reporters that the airing of accusations by other women was "a version of the 'shoot now, ask questions later' approach to judicial justice that you're seeing in the streets."

The idea that my accusation and the charges stemming from it might in some way be the result of racism had not been raised in earlier motions to dismiss the case. Perhaps for that reason, Los Angeles criminal defence lawyer Mark Geragos was later quoted in an Associated Press article suggesting that this might be the Cosby team's way of trying to influence the jury pool. Whatever the case, it was a distressing new aspect to Cosby's public protestations of innocence.

But there were other things that made 2016 an especially challenging year.

A US presidential election was, of course, slated for November. Generally I don't follow politics too closely, but Donald Trump's candidacy and campaign were impossible to ignore. In May 2016, the *New York Times* published an article quoting a number of women who claimed to have been sexually harassed by Trump. The paper also reminded readers of the three public accusations of sexual assault that had been made about him over the years, including a charge of rape from his first wife, Ivana (which she later withdrew). That a man who'd been accused of harassing and attacking women was the Republican choice for president deeply upset many, of course. The Cosby survivors and a lot of others vented their anguish in the Facebook group. But we had no idea how much more disturbing Trump's candidacy would become. On October 7, 2016, the *Washington Post* published a recording of a 2005 conversation between *Access Hollywood* host Billy Bush and Donald Trump. In it, Trump bragged that his fame allowed him to "do anything" he wanted to women. He could, he said, "just start kissing them . . . I don't even wait." He could even, he continued, "grab 'em by the pussy."

To all the sexual assault victims I was in touch with, this was an intensely upsetting statement. And once the tape was out, many more women—twenty-two in all—came forward to say that they had also been sexually assaulted by Trump. Each story delivered another shock.

When Trump won the election on November 8, 2016, I broke down in tears. To know that a man who'd bragged about his ability to assault women and get away with it was going to take up residence in the White House was beyond my understanding. So when I heard about the Women's March, organized to protest this outrage, I knew I had to go to Washington and be a part of it.

A number of women who were members of the Cosby Facebook group announced that they would be attending as well. Jennifer Litton Todd, a women's advocate, was organizing some of the Cosby survivors to march together. I said I would like to meet up with them at some point, but as odd as it may sound, I thought I needed to attend the march itself on my own.

My decision to walk alone was an intuitive one. I just knew that if I really wanted to absorb everything around me, I couldn't be distracted by conversations and socializing. I needed to have some sort of solitude among the masses, some quiet space amid the noise. And I wanted as much anonymity as possible. If I were in a group, with a sign, people might notice me, recognize me. I didn't want anyone snapping photos that could end up in the papers.

Around 10 a.m. on the morning of January 21, 2017, I stepped off a plane at Dulles International Airport, then picked up my rental car and drove to Jennifer Litton Todd's Virginia home. I knew that Jennifer would already have left for the march, but her husband had offered to drive me to the nearby commuter train.

When I stepped onto the train, it was packed. Many of the men, women, and children were carrying signs. A canopy of pink hats stretched along the entire car. I really had no idea where I was going, so I simply jumped off the train when everyone else did and followed them up the street. Within a couple of minutes, I was walking down a huge avenue completely engulfed by a sea of strangers—strangers who nevertheless shared a passion and energy that rippled through the air. A steady chorus of chants and cheers rose from the crowd as we walked. I stayed silent. I let the voices move through me, empowering me. I too would raise my voice, but not this day.

We marched past the Lincoln Memorial and its Reflecting Pool—those potent symbols of democracy. As we passed the White House, I was taken aback by the size of the police presence. The spirit of the protestors was peaceful but powerful; yet I could understand why the new president might be afraid. The people around me were demanding real change to a status quo that had served him so well.

Indeed, marching along with the crowd, I couldn't help thinking about how the last two years had opened my eyes to the enormity of the problem of sexual harassment and sexual violence. The stories that hit the papers, the accounts people posted on Facebook, the histories women shared at the PAVE summits—all suggested that my pre-Cosby experience was not the norm. Before I met him, I had never been sexually harassed. I had not endured crude remarks or sexual innuendoes from classmates or co-workers. I had never been coerced into sex. I'd had no terrifying moments at parties. No handsy bosses. No creepy teachers or coaches. I had never really been afraid for my personal safety.

What's more, I hadn't truly appreciated the crushing weight of patriarchy. Sure, my mother had wanted me to wear dresses and, later, date men. And boys had sometimes ridiculed me and other girls about our athletic skills or other abilities. But those were really the only times I remember feeling that I was not behaving as a girl or a woman "should." And they had been very easily shrugged off. Now, however, I was really taking in all the subtle ways girls and women were demeaned and demoralized. All the ways their authority was questioned or reduced. All the ways their ambition, competitiveness, and drive were stymied. I now recognized that a good many women faced this kind of vulnerability all the time. And the fact that a man like Donald Trump had just been elected to the most powerful office in the United States made that reality more evident than ever.

By mid-afternoon, after several hours on my feet, I'd decided it was time for a rest and something to eat. When the crowd moved past the Capitol Lounge, I ducked out of the march and found myself a spot at the bar, where I could watch the procession on television, see the signs passing outside the open windows, and chat to those on the stools next to me. After I'd finished my lunch, I went back outside and stood on the sidewalk as the last marchers passed down the street. There I struck up a conversation with two sisters who were also watching the last moments of the historic walk. They invited me to join them for a drink at another bar a short distance away. Marching alone had been an amazing experience, but now I was more than ready for company. I joined them for an hour or so, and by the end, we had exchanged email addresses. (A little more than two years later, after the second trial, I would get an email from one of them saying, "Congratulations! Now we know who you are. Wish we'd known back then!") And then I headed to the train and back to Jennifer's house to join the group that she had gathered together for the march.

That evening was an extraordinary one for me. A number of the women in the group were advocates working to promote women's rights and sexual assault prevention. Two of the women were also Cosby victims. One was Janice Baker-Kinney. On April 23, 2015, she, Marcella Tate, and Autumn Burns (all represented by Gloria Allred) had come forward with their accounts of abuse at the hands of Bill Cosby.

In 1982, Janice, then a twenty-four-year-old bartender at Harrah's Hotel and Casino in Reno, Nevada, was invited by a friend to a party that Cosby was hosting. When she and her friend got to the house where he was staying while performing at the casino, they discovered that they were the only guests. They decided to stay for some pizza and beer. Cosby offered Janice some Quaaludes. She was willing to take one—she had taken them before to relax—but Cosby insisted she take another, saying she'd be okay with two. She swallowed the second pill and then began to play a game of backgammon with her host. But before long, Janice passed out on the couch. She awoke briefly to hear her friend leaving. The next time she regained consciousness, she was in a bed, completely naked, and Cosby was touching her genitals.

For thirty years she had tried to bury the experience, feeling that she was at fault for taking the pills. But the steady onslaught of stories about

Cosby's sexual violence finally helped her realize that she too was a victim and needed to speak out.

I knew Janice's story and she knew mine, but we didn't talk about Cosby or our assaults that evening. Instead, we all relaxed, nibbled on snacks, and talked about the sights and sounds of our exciting day.

On the flight back to Toronto late, late that night, I marvelled at the show of solidarity I had just been part of. And I thought how important it was to have met Janice, to now be able to put a face to the name. That made me realize something else: Cosby's prolific history of assault hurt *so* many women. And yet that meant there were so many of us who could come together to help one another. So many of us who felt a visceral bond. It was a bond that started in pain, but it was also a bond that could mend. And its healing power was so much stronger than any blow Cosby had dealt us.

By the time the snow had melted in Toronto and the trees were ready to green, I felt as if I'd done as much as I could to prepare emotionally and spiritually for the trial. I was keeping in touch with my community, regularly doing three-hour meditations, and practising bio-feedback (a technique I had learned in my return to therapy) whenever I felt a little overwhelmed. I thought I was ready. But I was wrong.

Kristen and Stewart, the prosecutors in my upcoming case, came to Toronto over a weekend in mid-April—my birthday weekend. They had told me that they wanted to stage a mock trial to get me ready for the kind of questioning I would be subjected to by Cosby's defence attorneys. Since sitting on my sofa in my apartment would hardly feel like being in a courtroom, I booked one of the common rooms in my condo building. When Kristen and Stewart arrived, we sat down at the big boardroom table.

We spent a couple of hours going through documents that would be used at trial. These included my phone records from my time at Temple. But I already knew they would come into play. Cosby's lawyers, Brian McMonagle and Angela Agrusa, had been all over the airwaves in the previous month, talking about how many phone calls I'd had with Cosby after what they called the "alleged" assault. They claimed I'd spoken to him at least fifty times. The implication was clear: we were in constant touch because we had a close relationship—a relationship that hadn't changed after I had dinner at his house on that evening in January.

Of course, in the months after I'd been attacked, I still worked at Temple, and I still had to do my job. When Cosby phoned, I had no choice but to speak with him. When he left a message, I had to call him back. Many times, I simply left a voicemail with his answering service. But even when we did speak, our conversations were never personal—I tried to give him the information he was looking for and get off the phone as quickly as I could.

During their various interviews, McMonagle and Agrusa also shared details that had been part of the civil case. They were, therefore, breaching the non-disclosure agreement Cosby and I had both signed. These things seemed to be part of a concerted effort to sway potential jurors. I suspected that they were also trying to intimidate and unnerve me. And they certainly were. Every time I caught sight of one of them on television, I'd feel my heart race and I'd have to do a few breathing exercises to calm down.

But after a while, I started to draw comfort from their media campaign. I couldn't help thinking they were being fools. They were showing their hand. And that would backfire when we got to court and they weren't able to catch me by surprise on the stand.

In my condo meeting room that day, when we had reviewed all the evidence, Kristen told me that Stewart was going to play the role of one of Cosby's trial attorneys. "When he starts asking questions, just try to relax and be yourself," she told me. "And just as important, don't overthink things. Just answer the question."

Stewart then positioned himself directly across from me. As soon as he did, I noticed that his whole demeanour changed. His genial expression turned hard; his voice had an iron edge to it. The questions came hard and fast. There was no waiting for me to think through my answers or refine any points. He leapt on me at any pause or moment of hesitation. After forty-five minutes of being grilled, I was rattled and exhausted. Maybe I wasn't as ready as I'd thought I was.

Once Stewart and Kristen left, I went online and looked up descriptions of witness questioning in other sexual assault trials. There weren't many available trial transcripts, but what I found confirmed my suspicions: Stewart's interrogation hadn't been the least bit extreme or unusual. I clearly had more work to do. It didn't matter if I knew what the defence lawyers' approach was going to be. It didn't matter that they had showed their hand during all those TV interviews and in their public statements. Even if I wasn't surprised by their questions, I could still be knocked off my game by their blistering offence. Everything I had been doing in the previous year—the community building, the spirituality—had kept me going. But I now realized there was one more thing I had to do to get ready for this contest.

I had to *practise.*

I thought back to all those practices I'd had on basketball courts over the years, first with Brian Pardo in high school and then with my wonderful coach Joan Bonvicini in Tucson. When I was a child, I'd often struggled to focus. But basketball had taught me how to turn my attention to something for extended periods of time. It taught me to be in the moment at every second. To pay attention to what I was doing. It taught me about the importance of repetition in mastering a skill and being able to produce it when the pressure was on.

That was what you did in practice—you made the same passes or the same lay-ups over and over again, until every sinew in your body remembered exactly what to do once you started to move. I thought of Coach Pardo making us do shot after shot. And then, when we were near exhaustion, telling us to do a few more—but this time with our eyes closed.

This was the kind of thing I needed to do with the accounts of what had happened to me. Cosby's lawyers would try to trip me up, get me to stumble over my answers or details. As Stewart had done in the mock trial, they'd hammer away with questions I couldn't answer or at things I didn't remember. I needed to say, firmly and confidently, "I don't know," when that was the truth. When his lawyers went after my inconsistencies, I needed to respond with consistency: "I was mistaken when I spoke to the Durham police."

From both the mock trial and my online research, I learned that perhaps the most important tool in being an effective witness is the ability to listen. You have to pay close attention to what the lawyer has asked—and answer *only* that question. I couldn't allow myself to get off track, to try to offer context or additional details that the defence attorneys might be able to twist to their advantage. I needed to listen carefully to their words but not to the emotion in their voices—I had to ignore hints of derision, disbelief, annoyance, intimidation. And I had to try to keep emotion out of my own voice. I couldn't react when they spun their false narrative. It would be like doing a lay-up with my eyes closed—everything done with the utmost focus but without self-consciousness or analysis. The truth—telling the truth—as rote and automatic as possible.

To do that, I had to build my mental toughness.

I prayed to Salvo for that mental strength. Again and again, I went over the questions that Stewart had asked me. I employed the visualization techniques I had used in college when preparing for a game. But instead of "seeing" my arm rise in the air, the ball arcing from my fingers with just the right spin on it, I pictured myself on the stand, looking into the face of the defence attorney. I imagined myself listening to every word he put to me. When I felt my pulse increase or tension begin to tighten the muscles in my neck, I calmed myself with breathing exercises. I went over the details of my account again and again—on walks with the dogs, driving to work, washing the dishes at the kitchen sink.

Several weeks before the trial was to start, I found myself standing in front of a mirror, imagining what people would see when I was on the stand. I was wearing a T-shirt and a pair of yoga pants. Most of my clothes had that sort of comfortable, casual style. None of them would be appropriate for the trial. But I had no idea what I should wear instead. No idea how best to present myself to the people who would be judging me as much as they would Bill Cosby.

One of my friends recommended a stylist—a woman who helped dress anchors and hosts for television. This woman in turn consulted a friend who had been in the police force and was involved in hundreds of sexual assault cases. And then we went shopping. In the end, we settled on two soft, unstructured jackets—one blue and one white—and paired them with scoop-neck sweaters in the opposite colours. I also chose a pair of dressy white leather sneakers to wear with pants.

I now had my trial uniform. But there was one other way I had decided to dress myself for the upcoming proceedings.

When I had got that "truth" tattoo in the winter of 2016, I'd seen another piece of body art in the shop—a magnificent phoenix rising out of flames. I couldn't get it out of my mind. In mid-May, a few weeks before the trial was to start, I went back to the tattoo parlour to get the bird inked on my back. I explained that I wanted the flames to lick up from my waist and the mythical phoenix to ascend along my spine towards the wings that already spread across my shoulders. I wanted my entire back to serve as a canvas.

I knew a tattoo that large would take many sessions. It wouldn't be completed before I left for Philly. In fact, it wouldn't be finished until long after the jury decided whether to believe me or not. But I understood that no matter what happened in the trial, I too was going to rise from the ashes.

And I wanted to start that rebirth as soon as possible.

CHAPTER 8

THE TRIAL BEGINS

In early June, a couple of days before the trial was to start, my mother and I boarded a plane to Philadelphia. As I expected, Mom had been put on the witness list. We needed to be there early so that we could go through some final preparations with the district attorneys. As I followed my mother to our seats on the aircraft, I couldn't help thinking about her courage and strength. Here she was, on her way to participate in a huge trial while still recovering from surgery.

Over the past several years my mother had suffered from poor dental health, resulting in the loss of a number of teeth. Because of this, her speech wasn't always clear and the shape of her face was slightly altered. Her plan had been to get artificial teeth implanted over a period of time, but when she found out that she would be a witness and would therefore have to speak in public, she decided she needed to get her mouth restored as quickly as possible. Two weeks before we were scheduled to be in Philadelphia, she'd had eight implants done—a gruelling five-hour procedure that required a substantial amount of drilling through bone and suturing of gum tissue. In the days that followed, her entire face was so swollen that she was barely recognizable. She stayed at my condo so that I could nurse her with rounds of ice packs and a liquid diet. By the time we checked into our flight the swelling had gone down, but Mom was still unable to eat anything other than puréed foods. Yet she never complained; her only thought was the fight ahead of us.

When we got to Philadelphia, Mom and I checked into a small hotel in an upscale suburb called King of Prussia. It was a quiet neighbourhood, off the beaten track, and seemed to offer us the best chance of privacy. My dad and Diana were going to drive down and meet us the night before the trial began. Diana's husband, Stuart, would arrive for day two, when he was scheduled to be on the stand.

Kristen and Stewart had arranged for a car to pick us up at our hotel and take us to the courthouse in Norristown. They wanted to walk both of us through the process and let us get a feel for the courtroom. My mother and I would be in the courthouse only on the days we testified, and later, for the closing remarks and the jury deliberations. On the days we were scheduled to testify, we'd wait in the witness lounge with the victims services counsellor for Montgomery County, Erin Slight, among others.

I had seen the stately courthouse from outside, but I'd never been inside the building. Now, standing in the marble-floored lobby, I was struck by how much the place looked exactly as you might imagine a courthouse to look. The cool white stone floors stretching across the huge lobby and disappearing down high-ceilinged corridors. The curving staircases. The heavy wooden doors. It did indeed feel like a place where judgment and justice took place—where history was made.

Kristen took us to see the courtroom itself. But instead of using the main doors, she guided us down a wainscotted hallway to a single wooden door. When we walked through, we were at the front of the courtroom. The dark wood witness box and the judge's bench were directly in front of us, and the crimson carpet spread out towards the wooden seats that stretched around three sides of the room. The place was huge. Kristen suggested that I sit in the witness chair while she explained what I would see on the day of my testimony. I climbed in and let my gaze move around the room. The walls were lined with portraits of what I assume were judges. Kristen pointed to the table where she, Stewart, and Kevin would be sitting, and to the spot where Cosby and his attorney would be seated. She pointed out the jury box to my right, the press box to my left, and the seating areas for my family and friends and for the defendant's supporters. I noticed the gallery that ran along the walls, high above the dark wood panelling. People would be watching me from every angle.

The night before the trial started, my family and I gathered for dinner in my parents' suite—takeout food we'd had delivered to the hotel (mashed potatoes for poor Mom). I could tell everyone was on edge.

When we finished eating, someone grabbed the remote and turned on the TV. I looked away. I reminded everyone that I was trying not to see or hear anything about the upcoming trial. And I wasn't supposed to hear what had been said in court on the days I wasn't on the stand. I needed to give my testimony without being influenced by what anyone else was saying—be they media pundits or other witnesses. I couldn't be distracted by how the defence had treated those witnesses or what was claimed during the opening statements. I needed to stay in my own little bubble.

I suggested we get out of our rooms and go down to the lobby bar for a drink. But once there, I could sense this wouldn't be the relaxed family gathering I had hoped for. As soon as we walked in we started scanning the other tables, trying to figure out if anyone there looked like a reporter. We kept our voices low as we talked, and even once we were sipping our drinks we continued to take furtive glances around the room, afraid someone might be listening to our conversation. Eventually, we headed back to our rooms to try to get some sleep.

After I'd brushed my teeth and washed my face, I went to my suitcase and pulled out a leaflet I'd carefully tucked between my clothes. It was a copy of the one I had seen on my nonna's bureau all those years ago, with its small picture of Uncle Salvo, his story printed underneath. I propped it up against the bedside lamp. A stillness settled over me. This moment had been a long time coming; I couldn't quite believe it was here.

I slipped between the covers of the bed and positioned myself on my side, being careful not to roll on my back. My newly born phoenix was letting its presence be known—my skin still stinging and prickly whenever anything touched it, even though I'd started on the tattoo a few weeks earlier. When I left the tattoo parlour, my legs had almost given out on me. The pain was extraordinary and draining. But over the course of the five long hours, I had developed a little dance to see me through. Each time the needle began its biting path through my flesh, I'd take a deep breath and hold it for as long as I could. Then I would let it out as slowly as possible. In this way, I tried to rise above my body. As the phoenix imprinted itself on my skin, the pain did not disappear but instead became a sort of background sensation. It was almost peaceful, giving me a sense of building strength and resilience. I would need those reserves during the trial.

This is what I will be doing in a few days' time, I thought as I lay in bed. I will sit with my emotional pain, I will keep it in my body while my mental self rises above, granting me the peace and calmness I need to tell the truth.

The next morning I got out of bed, opened the curtains, and sank to the floor in the early morning light. I meditated for about thirty minutes and then got dressed to go downstairs with my family for breakfast. This is how I would start and end each day of the trial—with a short period of meditative peace and prayer. A brief but sustaining moment with God.

After breakfast, my father and sister left for the first day of the trial. On this day, the prosecutors and defence attorneys would give their opening remarks, and then Kelley Johnson would testify. In a pretrial motion, Kevin Steele had asked that we be allowed to bring in thirteen other accusers as "prior bad act" witnesses. The idea was to suggest a pattern of behaviour to refute any claim that my sexual assault was simply the result of a lapse in communication between Cosby and me—a regrettable one-time misunderstanding. In the end, Judge Steven T. O'Neill allowed only one of these witnesses. The prosecutors had chosen Kelley Johnson.

Kelley's assault occurred in 1996, making it one of the more recent. Back then, Kelley was the administrative assistant for Cosby's agent, Tom Illius, at the William Morris Agency in Los Angeles. Her working relationship with Cosby had started in 1990. Like me, Kelley initially interacted with the star by fielding phone calls for her boss. Over time, the conversations became friendly, and Cosby began asking about her family and personal life. Sometimes, he'd tell her to call him back from her own phone instead of on the company line. While the William Morris Agency had a strict policy prohibiting employees from socializing with clients, Cosby's interest in Kelley seemed fatherly, and she couldn't see the harm in continuing to chat with him, even in her off-hours. More than once, Cosby called her at home and ended up talking with her sister, who lived with her. At one point, he invited the whole family to come to one of his Las Vegas shows. And then, one day in 1996, Cosby invited Kelley to have lunch with him. He was in town, he said, staying at the Hotel Bel-Air. They could talk a little about her career.

She was so comfortable with Cosby at this point that she thought nothing of accepting. Just before she left for the hotel, however, he called her at home and told her to meet him in one of the Bel-Air's private cottages, instead of the hotel dining room. When she got to the door of the cottage, Cosby greeted her in a bathrobe and slippers, obviously not ready to head to the restaurant. That's when he told her he was having lunch sent in. When Kelley declined a glass of wine, Cosby brought her a large white pill and told her it would help her relax. He wouldn't say what the pill was, and by this point, Kelley was getting uncomfortable with the way the meeting was going. Cosby was insistent, however, so eventually she took the pill and put it under her tongue, pretending to swallow it. But Cosby demanded that she open her mouth and lift her tongue to show him the pill was gone. Thoroughly rattled, she complied and swallowed the pill.

Sometime later, she woke up on the bed, her dress around her waist, exposing her breasts and the lower part of her body. Cosby then forced her to masturbate him. She passed out again. The next thing she remembered was being in her own home with no idea how she got there.

Unfortunately, like me, Kelley had to go back to a job that demanded interaction with her assaulter. Shortly after the afternoon at the hotel, she overheard a phone conversation between Illius and Cosby in which Cosby was clearly trying to get her fired. She immediately went to the human resources department of William Morris and tried to explain what had happened. But the HR person sent her home to calm down before she could get the whole story out. In the end, Kelley took stress leave and was eventually fired.

At the time of the trial, I knew only the bits and pieces of Kelley's story that had made it to the media. But in the courtroom, twenty years later, she told her story in her own words to the whole world.

Once my father and sister had left for the courthouse, I went to the hotel gym to work out. For the rest of the day I prayed, meditated, and listened to music. Mom stayed in her room, chatting on the phone with relatives back home.

Around lunchtime, my father and sister reappeared. I was surprised. I knew the court was supposed to be in session all day. But I could tell the instant I looked at my father that he was struggling. His face was contorted with agitation and anger. As soon as he entered his room, he went straight to the bottle of Grey Goose vodka we'd brought with us. In short order, half the bottle was gone.

My sister said quietly, "I don't think Dad will be able to do another day."

"The things that man said," he muttered.

I tried to remind him that I shouldn't hear about anything that went on in court, but he couldn't seem to contain his shock and outrage. And he clearly needed to unload to my mother and sister. It was obvious he was reacting to Brian McMonagle's opening statement, which, unsurprisingly, had cast me as a liar and my mother as an extortionist. (My father and Diana hadn't stayed long enough to hear Kelley's testimony, which began after the lunch break.) In the end, I gave up trying to change the topic and went back to my room.

That night—the night before I would take the stand—I lay in bed and pictured myself staring out at the courtroom. I imagined the seats filled with spectators. I imagined the twelve jurors studying me. And I thought about what Kristen had said.

She had come to the hotel earlier in the evening to prep me for the very last time and give me a few final words of advice. She told me that I would likely be cross-examined by Angela Agrusa, and she reminded me to stay calm and focus on the truth—not on besting Cosby's lawyers.

"If one of the defence lawyers wanted to challenge you to a one-on-one basketball game, you'd go out there and kick butt, right?" she said to me. I had to agree with that. "And you would. Because that's not their game," she responded. "But remember, Andrea, *this* is." She told me not to think about the trial as a contest. I couldn't "beat" the defence. "All you can do is control the truth," she said. She cautioned me once again about overthinking my answers. And then she said, "I know this may be one of the most difficult things you will ever have to do, but we know you can do it, and we are proud of you."

Kristen's advice was sobering, but at the same time, it lifted a weight off my shoulders. The mock trial in Toronto had made it clear that lawyers did indeed have all the training and all the skill. I couldn't think about this as a game with winners and losers. If it was that, I was already the loser just by being there. Cosby had done what he wanted to me. He had won back then, and I had never truly escaped the poisonous world he'd created for me. But Kristen had reminded me once again that my truth was my power. And that power was considerable.

The next morning, I ate my breakfast quietly, got dressed in my soft blue blazer and pants, then headed downstairs to meet the car that was being sent for me.

Angela Rose and Delaney Henderson from PAVE, the sexual assault survivor group, were also staying at the hotel. They had offered to attend the trial to provide me with additional moral support. They were waiting in the lobby, along with my sister.

My father had decided that he could not bear another day of the trial. He would stay at the hotel with my mother. In truth, I was relieved. My dad had struggled to cope with the way our lives had been upended by the charges and trials. He was angry at Cosby, his supporters, and the press, but he was also deeply hurt by the things that were being said. Unfortunately, he expressed that hurt through more anger—sometimes directed at the people nearest him. I couldn't imagine how he would respond if he felt I was being attacked on the stand. I was relieved not to have to worry about that.

Angela, Delaney, Diana, Stuart, and I were driven to the courthouse in a car arranged by Detective Reape. Once there, my sister would head into the courtroom, and the rest of us would be brought to the witness lounge.

I could sense the circus-like atmosphere as soon as we got close to the courthouse. The streets had been turned into a sea of television vans and antennas. The sidewalks were full of people. I could hear the rumble of the crowd as we got closer and closer, could see a wave of protest signs rippling in the distance. I had thought the courthouse was mobbed during the pretrial hearing, but this looked like madness. Later, I would hear that despite the blazing hot temperatures, many people waited outside all day—to show their support for Cosby or their trust in his accusers, and to hear any updates from people leaving the courtroom.

Kelley Johnson's mother, Patrice Sewell, was due to testify first. She would be questioned about what her daughter had told her about the Cosby assault—and when. She was to be followed by a lawyer who'd handled Kelley's workers' compensation claim. Next was Detective David Mason from the Durham Regional Police, the man who had come to our house to take my first statement about the assault. Then my brother-in-law, Stuart, would be questioned about his role in my original complaint.

When I walked into the witness lounge, Erin Slight from Montgomery County Victims Services was there to greet me. She had been in touch with me a few months earlier, and I'd met her briefly after arriving in Philly. She'd asked if I had any questions about the process of giving testimony or attending court. Warm and reassuring, Erin told me that she would stay in the witness lounge in case I needed support.

The hours crawled by. I chatted with Stuart, Erin, Angela, and Delaney; listened to music; and spent a good deal of time playing with the therapy dog, Turks, who was brought in by his handler, Kiersten McDonald, an investigator with the Montgomery County Detectives Bureau. I would have liked to meditate, but the room was too busy, too full of people.

Lunch was brought in for us, and after we'd eaten, Stuart was called into the courtroom. And then, at around 2:30, one of the detectives came into the lounge and said that Stuart had finished his testimony and the jury was on a break. When the court reconvened, it would be time for me.

"Andrea, you're going to be fine," Kiersten said. "Just go out there and take your power back."

I stood up and put my hand in my jacket pocket, feeling for the two little stones I had put there. One was a piece of pink quartz that symbolized truth, among other things, and the other was a piece of red tiger's eye, a stone thought to aid in emotional stability and confidence. Diana had given me both before we left Toronto. Then I moved my hand to my pants pocket and ran my fingers over my other talisman: a small brass medallion with Uncle Salvo's face stamped in relief on it. Holding the disc between my fingers, I left the lounge and joined the group of people waiting to escort me down the hall. Erin, Angela, courthouse security personnel, a number of police officers, including Detective Reape—we all made a slow procession down several flights of stairs and along a few corridors. Every step we took was recorded by the photographers and reporters who crowded the hallways. When we got to the door that led to the front of the courtroom, the officers told me I would be called in by the usher when the court was fully in session. Erin and Angela left to find seats in the courtroom. We were probably waiting no more than five minutes, but it felt as if time stretched on forever. I became aware that during my long walk from the witness lounge to the courtroom, fear had crept its way in and was squeezing the breath from me. All the preparation I'd done—the visualizations, the relaxation exercises, the practice—had helped me get to this point, there was no doubt about that. But would it see me through what lay ahead? Months ago, I had felt that Cosby's defence lawyers, McMonagle and Agrusa, had given me a pretty good idea of the narrative they would try to spin. But in truth, I had no idea what traps they might lay for me, or what tactics they would use to undermine or twist my testimony. I was frightened. Then I gave myself a little shake.

I knew what I had to do. As I had when heading into a big game all those years ago, I had to return to the moment—and stay there. I couldn't think about my opponents or what plays they might make. I couldn't worry about how I might perform or the outcome of the match. Instead, I had to remain calm, relaxed, and centred. By the time the door in front of me swung open, I was breathing easily once again, my mind focused only on what was directly in front of me, only on what was happening at that very moment.

I stepped into the courtroom, aware of the thick carpet beneath my feet, the brass chandeliers lighting the windowless room. I had visualized this moment throughout the last few days, but I hadn't really been able to imagine what it would be like. As soon as I crossed the threshold, I heard the soft rumble of conversation give way to a burst of gasps and the clacking of fingers striking laptop keyboards. And then, as I walked past the jury to reach the witness stand, an eerie silence descended. The air seemed to crackle with tension. The usher opened the gate to the witness box, and I stepped in. The bailiff approached me, a Bible in his hand. Just as I'd seen so many times on TV, he told me to put my left hand on the holy book and raise my right hand. Then he asked, "Do you swear that the evidence you shall give shall be the truth, the whole truth, and nothing but the truth, so help you God?"

"I do," I said.

Of course I was going to tell the truth, I thought. It was the only thing I had ever wanted to do.

CHAPTER 9

ON THE STAND

My heart had started to hammer while I was saying my oath, so as soon as I was finished I took a long, deep breath and sat down. I planted my feet firmly on the floor, folded my hands in my lap, and tried to adopt a neutral expression. I closed my eyes for just a few seconds, and when I opened them again, I looked over to the jury briefly. Seven men, five women. Then I moved my gaze to the rest of the room.

The place was packed with hundreds of people (many more were apparently sitting in another courtroom, watching the proceedings over closed-circuit TV). Fifty or sixty reporters were squeezed into the press section. In the spectator area, I noticed a number of familiar faces. My sister and Angela Rose were sitting near the front, smiling at me. Dolores and Bebe, my lawyers from the civil suit, were there. So was Lili Bernard, holding a bouquet of soft pink gladioli. (She had made gladioli buttons for all the other supporters too, but of course I couldn't see them from that distance.) Other Cosby accusers sat near Lili. I immediately recognized Barbara Bowman, Therese Serignese, Victoria Valentino, and Jewel Allison. I could see the warmth and encouragement on the faces of these extraordinary sisters—a whole chorus of support and love. It was perhaps strange in that sober, daunting moment, but I felt a blush of happiness.

And then I turned to Kristen, Stewart, and Kevin, the people who would try to convict Bill Cosby. They too were smiling at me, and Kristen's words from the night before echoed in my mind: "We are proud of you." I locked eyes with her to maintain my focus and get ready for what was next.

And then Judge O'Neill called the court to order.

Kristen approached me, a gentle yet professional look on her face. She asked where I lived and what I did for a living. When she asked if I had a specialty in the practice of massage therapy, defence lawyer Angela Agrusa jumped to her feet to object, questioning the relevance. Judge O'Neill quickly overruled her, saying it was perfectly acceptable for the prosecutor to introduce the jury to the complainant in this way, but as soon as Kristen repeated the question, Agrusa objected again. I exhaled slowly. I had expected the cross-examination to be intense, but it appeared that even mundane questions would be challenged. It was going to be a bumpy ride.

After Kristen had me describe how I had met the accused, she asked me to identify my assaulter. Of all the questions I had rehearsed in my head, I hadn't rehearsed this one. It hit like a punch; a flood of queasiness swept through me. I realized that ever since walking into the courtroom, I had avoided looking at the defendant's table—at Cosby and his team. When I raised my eyes to him now, the sick feeling subsided. Cosby stared back at me. He looked older than when I had last seen him, certainly. But he didn't appear the least bit feeble. His expression was confident—arrogant, even. A chilly emptiness filled my heart.

"He's wearing a dark-coloured coat, brown tie, and white shirt," I said. Then I shifted my eyes away. I would do my best not to look at him for the rest of my testimony.

Nor did I look at the side of the courtroom where his small group of supporters sat. The day before, Cosby had shown up on the arm of Keshia Knight Pulliam, the woman who had played his youngest daughter on *The Cosby Show*. His four daughters and his wife, Camille, had not attended the trial that day, and they weren't there the day I testified. Nevertheless, I knew the faces on that side of the room would be hostile.

Then Kristen started to walk me through my history with Bill Cosby. I explained about the many phone calls he made to the Temple women's basketball office to follow up on the team and various matters. I described how the conversations eventually became friendly. Then Kristen moved on to review all the times I had seen Cosby socially. I described the first time he had invited me to his place for dinner, the night I had eaten alone and then Cosby and I had sat in front of the fire. That was the night he put his hand on my thigh and then took it away.

I told the court about the second time I visited Cosby's house, joining a dinner party that he was throwing for local restaurant and bar owners. That was followed by another dinner party at which the other guests were mostly people who worked at local universities. And then there was a second solo dinner with Cosby.

After that, he invited me to meet him in New York City, where he introduced me to a TV and film writer and producer named Charles Kipps, who Cosby said could talk to me about careers in television. The three of us ate dinner at Cosby's Manhattan townhouse, and then Mr. Kipps took me to the train station, and he and I continued to talk. Another time, Cosby invited me to join a group of people who were going to hear a jazz ensemble he was introducing in New York.

Then there was the trip to Foxwoods Resort Casino in Connecticut, where Cosby was performing. He had suggested I drive up to take a look around the reservation where the resort was situated. But I was working that day, and by the time I got there, it was a little too late for a tour. Instead, I looked around the casino and then joined the resort manager, Tom Cantone, and Cosby for dinner in Cosby's hotel room. After I'd returned to my own room, Cosby called me to say that he'd had some baked goods delivered to his suite and that I should come back and get a few. I had assumed he'd simply meet me at the threshold with the sweets, but when I knocked, he opened the door empty-handed and wearing some kind of long white shirt. He told me to come in while he got the pastries off the room service cart. I did, perching on the edge of the bed as he rummaged through the food. I leaned back on my elbow and let my feet lift off the floor. Cosby found what he was looking for and put it aside. Then he came over to the bed and lay down. As he did, his bare leg brushed mine. I was thinking we might talk for a bit, but Cosby closed his eyes and didn't say anything. After a few minutes had passed, I got off the bed, said good-night, and left with the croissants.

In the course of this rundown, Kristen asked me if I'd ever had any sense that Cosby was romantically interested in me, and I answered that I hadn't.

I suppose some people might wonder why I accepted all those invitations. Well, I enjoyed getting out and meeting people. I enjoyed the change of pace. The truth was, my social life in Philly wasn't exactly robust. I was missing family get-togethers. My friend group was tight but small. My closest pals at the time were my neighbours, Stine and Purna, and my girl-friend, Sheri, who lived in North Carolina. I spoke on the phone to Sheri often, but we couldn't see each other as much as we would have liked. Stine and Purna's friendship was therefore a lifesaver. But still, my home life was quiet, and I was often lonely. I would have accepted an invitation to watch paint dry—and Cosby must have sensed this.

Over the years, I've gone over those times I spent with Cosby and come to the realization that he was grooming me—carefully, methodically build-ing up my trust. I sometimes wonder if that first dinner I had with him, when he put his hand on my thigh, made him decide to play the long game with me. After that, the next few invitations were for large parties with other people. When I think about it, they were odd invitations. Why invite me to a gathering of restaurateurs—or academics, for that matter?

After those two dinner parties, he invited me to his house alone and tested the waters again by trying to undo the button of my pants. But I told him, "I'm not here for that." And so the next couple of invitations, both trips to New York City, were again for events that involved other people—I spent more time with his friend Charles Kipps than with Cosby on the first one, and I didn't even see Cosby, except when he was onstage, during the second. In fact, he made a point of telling me that the group he had assembled for that concert included a woman who shared many of my own interests. He seemed to be suggesting that part of the purpose of that trip was for me to make a new friend. If I had developed any suspicions about his intentions (which, naively, I hadn't), those kinds of invitations would have likely reassured me that his interest in me was innocent and altruistic. And then there was the evening in Foxwoods—another moment that seemed to be sending me a message: You are safe alone with Bill Cosby.

But of course, while I was on the stand, Kristen didn't invite me to speculate about Cosby's behaviour or motives. Instead, we stuck to the facts of what had transpired between Cosby and me. She asked me about the ways he mentored me, and I described how he'd encouraged me to get headshots done so that I could use them if I applied for positions in sports broadcasting. He also set up a meeting with a man named Lou Weiss, from the William Morris Agency, so that I could talk with him about becoming a sports commentator (although I wasn't seriously pursuing that line of work). Kristen then asked me if I had ever given Cosby presents. I said that I had brought him some things over the months—small gifts like Temple University hats and T-shirts—to thank him for his interest in my career and the advice he was giving. Once I brought him some incense; another time I brought him some bath salts.

And then Kristen asked me to describe the night of the assault. I explained everything that had happened between the time I arrived at Cosby's house until I walked out the door in the morning.

Talking about my assault wasn't easy. At times, my voice trembled as I spoke, and I had to work to keep the tears from flowing. The other times I'd shared the details of that night, there were only a few people in the room. It was hard to ignore the presence of hundreds and the clicking of computer keys—a reminder that my words were being recorded for thousands more to read in their morning papers. But Kristen was standing in front of me, and I could look into her face for reassurance. I also knew that I needed to address myself to the jurors and connect with them as well. I tried to look their way as often as I could when I spoke.

The jury members were all from Pittsburgh. Cosby's defence team had argued that any potential jurors from the Philly area would have heard too much about the case to be impartial. Given that Cosby was a huge celebrity and the charges had drawn national—even international—media attention, it seemed unlikely that people in Pittsburgh would have significantly less exposure. But Pittsburgh jurors would have to be sequestered in their hotel rooms after their long days in court, and this would make the experience even more lonely and trying. How likely was it that their family and friends would drive three hundred miles for the permitted weekend visits? The defence's move seemed calculated to create conditions that might make the jurors resentful of being called to serve, especially as the days wore on.

Glancing over, I could see that the jurors were all studying me intently. They looked focused and impartial, ready to listen, ready to weigh my words with respect. All except one man. Juror #3 seemed much older than most of the others. He glared at me as I spoke, the hard line of his mouth twisting in what looked like disgust. His squinting eyes and knitted eyebrows sometimes made it seem as if he was straining to hear or struggling to understand. At other times, his expression suggested distrust. I tried to move my gaze to the other jurors, but it was difficult not to feel scorned. I was stung by a small point of fear: my truth was my power, but maybe it wouldn't be enough. Maybe I wouldn't be believed.

After I'd gone through the details of my assault, Kristen asked about the night I tried to talk with Cosby after the dinner at the Chinese restaurant. She then asked about a Cosby concert in Toronto that my parents and I had gone to once I was back home. Finally, she returned to the subject of my assault and asked about Cosby touching my breasts, putting my hand on his penis, inserting his fingers in me. Did I give permission for those acts? I said no. And then it was time for Kristen to hand over the questioning to Cosby's defence attorneys.

Angela Agrusa stepped up to the witness box. I sat up straight and reminded myself to keep my expression neutral. I needed to stay calm and not get rattled by the false narrative she would surely spin.

Agrusa introduced herself and asked if I had prepared for my testimony with any consultants or advisors or lawyers other than the DAs. Were there people who'd been involved in "directing" my testimony and evidence?

I said no, but I could see that she was trying to plant an idea in the jurors' minds that my story had been manufactured or adjusted.

Next she asked whether I had made a phone call to Cosby in the days immediately before I told my mother what had happened. I had no recollection of doing that, but I said it was possible. Agrusa then handed me a copy of my Canadian phone records showing the call. When she did, I noticed that her hand was shaking. I knew she was there to test me, to challenge me, to call my story into question, to discredit me. I knew it would get ugly. But at the same time, I felt sorry for her. She seemed nervous. This was probably the biggest case she had ever worked on, and maybe ever would. It was no doubt nerve-racking knowing that all eyes were on her. I suppose she must have seen it as an opportunity of a lifetime, but I couldn't help wondering if it was a case she would come to regret. It made me realize once again how many people Cosby's crimes had touched, and how widely his contagion spread.

Staying with my phone records, Agrusa pointed out that I had gone on the internet to look up lawyers in the Philadelphia area and then called a couple of them. She made a point of the fact that the two I had called were personal injury lawyers. I responded that I knew nothing of the law and had no idea what sort of lawyer I should be calling.

Kristen and Stewart had warned me during our trial prep that Agrusa's questions would be little more than statements. She didn't want to know *why* I'd called Cosby before I called my mom, and by not asking, she was letting certain implications sit with the jury. (If I really was a sexual assault victim, why would I want to speak with my attacker?) The same was true for her questions about the lawyers—personal injury lawyers might suggest to the jury that I was looking for some sort of payout.

In court, however, I didn't think about any of that. Instead, I focused on simply answering her questions. But back at the hotel that night, I would be struck by the irony of the exchange. The day I told my mother about my assault, I had indeed gone on the internet to look for lawyers as I waited for her to return home from work. I'd launched that frenzied search because I knew that as soon as I reported the assault, I would be in dangerous territory. I had watched enough police procedurals to know that victims of sexual assault often faced a tricky legal road—especially when accusing a figure as rich, powerful, and beloved as Bill Cosby. Besides, I'd been advised again and again during my years in Philly to always protect myself. And the person giving me that advice was Bill Cosby.

In one of the first conversations we'd had once we became friendly, I'd told him about a couple of friends who were thinking of starting a busing company. During my basketball days, I'd spent countless hours on long, dull road trips, and I had suggested they think about providing some on-board entertainment systems—much like the kind found on airplanes.

"Andrea," Cosby said to me when he heard about the suggestions I'd made, "be careful. You have to protect yourself in these situations." He advised me not to get into any sort of business discussions with people without representation.

Another time when I told him that my cousin was going to stay with me in Philly for a while, Cosby cautioned me about the need to set formal terms, even with family members, so I wouldn't be taken advantage of. He said he believed in lawyers, in the importance of engaging professionals to help keep you and your interests safe.

So when I realized that I would be starting down a road studded with landmines, I put Cosby's words into action. And when I received a phone message from Marty Singer, Cosby's lawyer at the time, I ramped up my hunt for legal representation, eventually settling on Bebe and Dolores.

Agrusa moved on to the statement I'd made to the Durham Regional Police back in Canada. I was prepared for that line of questioning. She pointed out a number of inaccuracies. For example, the police had written down that I introduced myself to Cosby at a basketball game, although I was actually introduced to him by someone else. (It seemed there was no inconsistency too small to bring up in court.) Agrusa then asked if I was saying that the incorrect information in the report "must have been [the officers'] mistake." I sensed she wanted me to cast blame on the police, but I wouldn't be led into that. Instead I replied, "I can't speak for them."

Next she asked me why I had become friends with Cosby. She suggested that I had wanted to get to know him because I was interested in being a sportscaster and was looking for his help. I explained that Cosby was the one pushing the idea of a broadcasting future for me—I had had no serious interest in it before that. I didn't deny, however, that later I saw my friendship with him could be helpful in that area, and I was honest about the fact that I initially thought a friendship with Cosby would be helpful to the Temple women's basketball team.

The next inaccuracy in my statement to the Durham police was that I said I hadn't been alone with Cosby before the night of my attack. I was ready to admit that my answer had been confused. But as soon as Agrusa referred to two nights of "sexual contact"—the thigh touching and Cosby's attempt to undo my pants button, I assume—I corrected her. "Not what I would consider sexual contact, ma'am," I said. I pointed out that I had described them as "suggestive" and part of a "sexual advance." I didn't want anyone to think that this had been consensual sexual activity.

Next, Agrusa launched into a series of statements about my trip to Foxwoods casino; she used these statements as an opportunity to make more insinuations.

"You also spent time alone with him during a trip to Foxwoods Resort in Connecticut, right?" she asked.

"Correct," I answered.

"In fact, that night when you laid alone in a bed with him, there was no one else in the room, correct?"

In the mock trial preparation, Kristen and Stewart had warned me that the defence lawyers would craft their "questions" in ways that conveyed their version of events. They advised me to say yes or no and avoid launching into a story or descending into some rabbit hole that might become a trap. But I was now realizing the challenge of addressing those statements. Agrusa tucked multiple misleading ideas and outright errors into each one—along with a few words that might be true. A simple yes or no couldn't possibly address everything she was saying. I did my best to make it clear exactly what I was saying yes to and what I wasn't—like the idea that we were "in bed" together.

"The answer to the second part of your question is yes," I said.

"So again, you weren't being truthful to the Durham Regional Police of Canada," Agrusa pressed, "when you said you had never been alone with him prior to the night in question?"

"I think I've stated on the record that there was a lot of confusion trying to put a lot of the dates together."

"But you weren't confused about the fact that you were alone in a hotel room with a married man at Foxwoods Resort, correct? You knew that, right?"

"What's your question? Sorry," I said. Agrusa repeated the question about being at the resort alone with Cosby, but this time, she didn't include the business about his being a married man. Still, the criticism lingered in the air.

Agrusa also pointed to a spot in the original police statement where I had said my contact with Cosby after the assault was brief, and then she asked if I remembered all the phone calls we'd had. There were, she said, about seventy. (Kristen pointed out in the redirect that many of these were me returning calls or leaving messages with Cosby's answering service.) She noted, as well, that my statement said the assault happened on the night I met Cosby and the others at the Chinese restaurant. "I was mistaken," I told the court.

And then came the questions about my assault. While I was repeating, once again, all the humiliating and painful details, I looked towards Agrusa and caught sight of Cosby sitting at the table behind her. He was smirking at me. It made my skin crawl.

Agrusa moved on from there to return to the idea that I'd come forward in 2005 so I could sue him. She pointed out a line in the police report that said I had decided it was time to pursue a sexual assault lawsuit. I corrected her, saying that I had only been interested in pursuing sexual assault *charges*.

"Are you saying the officer made this up?"

"I'm not saying that at all," I replied.

"But you said that to the officer, right?" she snapped back.

"I answered all the officer's questions as best I could," was my response. I simply wasn't going to engage in the choices she was setting up.

There were more questions about the lawyers I'd called around the time I talked with my mother and the police in 2005, and then Judge O'Neill stepped in to say it was time to stop. After giving some instructions to the jurors, he dismissed them. Then he turned to me. He apologized if I had thought my testimony would be finished in a day, but obviously, I would have to be back the next morning. He reminded me that I was still under oath—I couldn't talk to anyone about my testimony after I left the courtroom. And with that, my first day in court was done.

The ride back to the hotel with Angela, Diana, and Delaney was quiet. I couldn't talk about what I had just been through, and I was thinking about what lay ahead the next day. The two and a half hours I'd been on the stand were more or less evenly divided between the direct examination by Kristen and the cross-examination by Agrusa. The next day, I knew, I would start off being questioned by the defence. There would be a redirect examination by the DA at the end of the day, but I would be at the mercy of Agrusa for as long as she wanted. That was a daunting thought. I had found her unnecessarily harsh; her questions were delivered with an icy edge and plenty of disparaging innuendo. But I was comforted that the proceedings were being led by Judge O'Neill. He seemed smart and patient—ultimately the process was in good hands, I was sure. I also felt huge relief just knowing that I had got through the first day of the trial. I had remained composed, and I had got some of what happened off my chest. I was one step closer to the end—the next day would likely be my last on the stand, and I now knew I could do it.

My family and I spent a low-key evening together. We had dinner in the hotel restaurant and then retired to our own rooms. Getting ready for bed that night, I had time to reflect a little more on my experience on the stand. And on Cosby himself. I realized that I had two overwhelming feelings about him. The first was disgust. Disgust that he had caused so much pain for so many. Disgust that his arrogance meant he would take no responsibility for his actions. After all, he could have taken a plea deal and avoided the trial. He could have spared so many people the time, the effort, the pain of rehashing these dark episodes of our lives. Instead, he was utterly defiant and lacking in remorse. And that prompted me to a second reaction: I felt sad. Sad for all of us who were suffering, but also for Cosby himself. He was a deeply damaged soul. His victims were evidence of that—collateral damage of a truly broken life.

As night fell, I drifted off, but sleep could not hold me in bed for long. I sat up and crossed my legs. It took forty-five minutes of meditation until I was able to press the coming day away and slip into tranquil sleep once again.

CHAPTER 10

ALWAYS FOLLOW THROUGH

On the third day of the trial, my mother joined me, Diana, and Angela at the courthouse. Where I had fought back nervousness with deliberate calm and focus, my mother, despite her still-aching jaw, was bristling with momma-bear energy.

As soon as I got into the witness box that morning, Agrusa started back in on her questioning, quickly turning to my phone records once more. She pointed out that after I had contacted the Durham police—but before I'd been interviewed by the Cheltenham police—I called someone who'd been at the Chinese restaurant with Cosby. In fact, Agrusa listed off all the people I phoned before and after I'd talked with the officials in Montgomery County, including my girlfriend, Sheri, and Linda Gordon, a Temple University administrator whom I had contacted to get my phone records.

"And [you were] trying to get your dates straight, weren't you—" Agrusa said.

"No, ma'am," I jumped in.

"—before you were interviewed by the police?"

"Not that I recall," I said.

And yet, she was right in a way—I had called one of the people who was at the dinner to find out the date of the restaurant gathering. But it wasn't because I was attempting to create a fictional timeline, as Agrusa was suggesting. I'd called because I suspected that I had mixed up the night at the Chinese restaurant with the night of my assault when talking with the Durham police. I knew my assault had happened sometime in January. When the woman told me the dinner at the Chinese restaurant had been in early March, it confirmed my suspicions and reminded me of the conversation Cosby and I had at his house after the meal. And I'd called Linda Gordon because the police had suggested that I locate any phone records that might be helpful to the case.

Agrusa then stated that I had made many calls to friends, as well as to Cosby himself, the night of the Chinese restaurant dinner.

"So the very time you had told the police that you were drugged and unconscious," she said, refusing to acknowledge that I had mistakenly conflated the two evenings, "you were on the phone for periods of time making multiple phone calls to Sheri Williams and Warren Chambers."

Warren Chambers was a man I had met at one of the Temple basketball games. He had started a company that sold therapeutic bath salts and was targeting athletes and college athletic departments. He was also hoping that Cosby might take an interest in his product and had asked me to deliver a sample when I next saw him. I explained to Agrusa that I had phoned Warren to tell him I'd done what he asked. After a few questions about that, Agrusa returned to my Temple phone records.

"So once you got hold of your phone records and saw that you could not have been passed out and unconscious on the night that you told the police that you were sexually assaulted, you changed your story?"

I explained that I never got those Temple phone records, but Agrusa didn't respond to that or give me an opportunity to remind the jury that I had already freely admitted I got the date of the assault wrong at first.

During this exchange, I'd looked over at the jury. As I spoke, I could see Juror #3 scowling at me, slumping down in his chair, cocking his head. I tried not to let it get to me, but his expression somehow stripped me bare and made me feel less than human. It was creepy and unnerving. I also noticed a number of the jurors look in Cosby's direction with sympathetic expressions on their faces. That didn't feel reassuring either. I decided that I was better off staring straight at Agrusa when I was answering her questions.

When she was finished with my phone records and the Durham police statement, Agrusa then produced my original statement to the Cheltenham Township Police Department and began to draw attention to the various amendments I had made to the notes the officers typed up. She was working hard to suggest that I was massaging my story rather than correcting it.

Kristen made an objection. She pointed out that Agrusa wasn't asking me questions about what had actually happened but instead was introducing old statements and asking me to respond. But Judge O'Neill let the defence continue in this vein.

Agrusa took me again through the two evenings I'd had dinner alone at Cosby's house prior to the night of the assault. Her descriptions of those evenings emphasized elements that might seem romantic to listeners— the wine, the fireplace, the dim lights (something I don't remember and never mentioned in any of my statements). She described how I "allowed" Cosby to touch my thigh during the first dinner.

"You said 'allowed.' I didn't—Mr. Cosby did that of his own volition," I corrected.

After she asked if Cosby was romantic with me and I said no, she brought up the hair dryer he had bought. I pointed out that he gave it to me so that I could style my hair for the headshots he wanted me to get. When Agrusa pivoted back to the night of the assault, she emphasized small details I hadn't mentioned in my first statement to the police, like my question about putting the pills under my tongue. Then she came back once again to the fact that I'd originally said the assault happened on March 16, the night I went to the Chinese restaurant.

Next she wanted to revisit the number of phone calls I'd made to Cosby after the assault in January. She pointed out one I'd made on the afternoon of February 14, Valentine's Day. "You know Mr. Cosby's a married man, right?" Agrusa said.

When Agrusa and McMonagle had talked to the press earlier in the year, I thought they were giving away their playbook. They were casting me as a liar and claiming that any sexual activity between me and Cosby was consensual. The day before, when Agrusa had asked me if I was aware that Cosby was a married man when I accepted his invitation to Foxwoods casino, I thought she was picking up on the idea of consensual sex and implying that I didn't have any qualms about hooking up with someone else's husband. But this follow-up question about being with a married man, paired with the Valentine's Day reference, finally made it clear to me exactly what kind of story they were spinning for the jury. For the first time, I understood that they weren't just suggesting we'd had sex—they were suggesting Bill Cosby and I were *lovers*.

In trying to figure out now why this distinction came as such a shock, I realize that in Cosby's own version of events, the idea of "romance" had always been invoked, but he had put a transactional spin on it. In his deposition for the civil trial, he was asked, "When did you first develop a romantic interest in Andrea?" He answered, "Probably the first time I saw her." When he was asked to describe that romantic interest, he said, "Romance in terms of steps that lead to some kind of permission or no permission or how you go about getting to wherever you're going to go." "Romance" to Bill Cosby seemed to be simply the method you used to get a woman into bed.

Now, however, his lawyers were recasting the idea of romance into something other than a road map to sexual gratification. According to them, Cosby and I were in the kind of committed romantic relationship that would have been marked on Valentine's Day. Something intimate, emotional, *real*. Or at least, they seemed to be saying, I had thought we were in this kind of relationship—I had thought we were "in love."

Despite the fact that I was well prepared to face all sorts of false accusations, I found this one strangely upsetting. When Judge O'Neill announced it was time to break for lunch, I was relieved. I needed a little time off the stand to digest that unsettling new twist.

When I got back on the stand a little over an hour later, Agrusa came back once again to how many times I had talked with Cosby on the phone

during the winter of 2004. Throughout her questioning, she kept cir-
cling back to things we had already covered. It seemed like a technique
designed to catch me off balance or simply wear me down. And it certainly
was exhausting.

While Agrusa questioned me, I kept my eyes focused on her. But any
time there was a pause, I'd look over at my friends and supporters in the
spectator area. Whenever I did, I would see Diana and Angela Rose beam-
ing back at me. Their smiles and the warm expressions on the faces of all
my other supporters conveyed so much love and positive energy that I'd
actually feel a little burst of joy, which renewed my strength. When there
were longer breaks (for instance, if the prosecution and defence met with
the judge at the front of the room or in his chambers), I would get down
from the witness box and sit near the prosecutor's table. There I would
close my eyes and meditate until I was called again. That helped to keep
me calm and centred.

Eventually, Agrusa introduced a new topic: the Cosby concerts my
family and I had attended. She suggested that I'd asked for free tickets,
although it was Cosby who had offered. She was particularly interested in
a concert we'd attended north of Toronto, the summer after the assault.
She wanted to make sure the jury knew that I had gone with my parents.
There was no opportunity for me to explain that my parents—who didn't
yet know what he'd done to me—had heard Cosby was coming and wanted
to go. (The night had been excruciating for me.) Agrusa did ask about a
gift my mother had brought for Cosby, and about the fact that we didn't
see him after the show. She seemed to be implying that I had wanted to
meet up but had been rebuffed. Nothing could have been further from
the truth.

Agrusa finished her questioning by returning to intimations of a
romance. She walked me through the list of gifts I had given Cosby during
my time in Philly. She lingered on the bath salts, even though they weren't
really from me, and the incense, which Cosby had asked me to bring him.
She also questioned me about gifts that Cosby had bestowed on me: that
hair dryer, as well as the three cashmere sweaters and the perfume.

And then, finally, Agrusa took her seat, and Kristen returned to the front of the courtroom. During her redirect, she gave me the opportunity to explain the inconsistencies that Agrusa had been so intent on exploiting. And then she went through my various police statements to show how the important details, the essential elements of my story, had always been consistent.

Agrusa had one last chance to question me.

She revisited the fact that originally I had the date of the assault wrong. She went back to the idea that I'd talked to Cosby after the assault but never *about* the assault. And then, perhaps not surprisingly, she ended her examination of me by returning to Valentine's Day 2004.

"On February 14, on Valentine's Day, you weren't having conversations or placing calls to Mr. Cosby about Temple business, were you?"

I couldn't imagine why I would have called him if it wasn't about Temple business. But I had come to court to be honest. I guess Agrusa sensed she could use that against me.

"Perhaps. I can't recall specifically, but perhaps," I said.

I would have liked to say I knew without a doubt that I spoke to him *only* about Temple business. I would have liked to produce the exact words of our conversation. But they were lost to time. All I could do was be truthful about that.

Kristen came back one last time to clarify a point, and then my time on the stand was over. I had done what I could. I had to turn the fight over to other people. I returned to the witness lounge to wait while my mother took the stand.

My mother and I didn't talk about our experiences on the witness stand while the trial was ongoing, in case we were recalled, but over the next few days I heard bits and pieces about her performance. A *Maclean's* article published a day after she testified declared, "'Canada's Mom' slayed 'America's Dad,' unleashing unrelenting maternal fury on Bill Cosby." A reporter from the *Los Angeles Times* called Mom "feisty and defiant."

© Colledge Studios Ltd.

The Albert Campbell High School women's team with coach Brian Pardo at the OFSAA Championships, 1990 in London, Ontario.

Photo courtesy of the author

"Always follow through." In action for the University of Arizona women's basketball team, 1994.

Photo courtesy of the author

On the bus, heading to the World University Games in Sicily, Italy, summer 1997.

© SeM Studio/Fototeca/Universal Images Group via Getty Images

My Great Uncle Salvo D'Acquisto, executed by Nazi soldiers after an act of selfless bravery, was an inspiration to me throughout the trials. Photo from around 1943.

Photo courtesy of the author

With Donna Motsinger
at her home in Questa,
New Mexico, August 2016.

Photo courtesy of Jim Reape

With Shannon Reape (Detective Jim Reape's daughter) and Gloria Allred, May 2017,
at the preliminary hearing, Norristown, Pennsylvania.

Photo courtesy of Angela Rose

With Mom and Diana outside the hotel in King of Prussia, Pennsylvania, June 2017.

Photo courtesy of R.M. Stineman

Celebrating at NYC Pride, New York City, June 2017.

© Dominick Reuter/AFP via Getty Images

Protesters greet Cosby on first day of second trial, April 9, 2018.

© EPA/Tracie Van Auken, via Canadian Press Images

Lili Bernard, centre, addresses the media on the first day of deliberations for trial two, April 25, 2018. On her right is women's rights advocate Caroline (Kitty) Heldman, and to her left, trauma therapist Shari Botwin and Cosby accuser Victoria Valentino.

© AP Photo/Matt Slocum, via Canadian Press Images

The prosecution team at a press conference, April 26, 2018. *Front row, left to right:* Kristen Feden, Kevin Steele, Stewart Ryan. *Back row, left to right:* Detective Jim Reape, Robert Falin (Deputy DA of the Appellate Division).

With my counsel Bebe Kivitz on my right and to my left, Kate Snow, counsel Dolores Troiani, and PAVE Founder Angela Rose in New York City, May 2018.

Photo courtesy of the author

© AP Photo/Jacqueline Larma, File, via Canadian Press Images

Bill Cosby escorted from the courthouse after sentencing, September 25, 2018.

Photo courtesy of the author

At an event for Nicole Weisensee Egan's *Chasing Cosby* podcast, Los Angeles, February 2020. *Back row, left to right:* Tamara Green, Sunni Welles, me, Eden Tirl, Victoria Valentino, Linda Kirkpatrick, Therese Serignese. *Front row, left to right:* Barbara Bowman, Janice Baker Kinney, advocate Susie Spite McKinney, Lili Bernard, Zion Bernard, Kate Kelton, and Caroline (Kitty) Heldman.

© Roger Cullman, www.rogercullman.com

Doting on Maddy at home in Toronto, fall 2019.

© Roger Cullman, www.rogercullman.com

"Phoenix Rising," a tattoo depicting my journey and transformation, by Paul Samplonius, Toronto, January 2021.

And apparently she was. When Agrusa implied that Cosby and I had been intimate and asked if I had ever shared anything about a physical relationship with him, my mom snapped, "No, because there wasn't anything to share." At another point, Agrusa tried to cast doubt on my mother's knowledge of my romantic life. She pointed out that by the time I came back from Philly, I hadn't been living with my parents for many years. My mother wasn't about to let anyone suggest she didn't know what was going on with her daughter. "I hadn't lived with her physically, but I live with her every minute of every day," she shot back.

Then when Agrusa tried to press her on exactly what time we'd left Cosby's Toronto concert, my mother lost her patience. "I find you are testing my memory about irrelevant things," she said. "Could you ask me questions that are important?"

A number of people in the courtroom would later tell me that it seemed as if Agrusa just gave up trying to get my mother to answer in any way that would help the defence. She let her off the stand at about 5:15 p.m. Mom returned to the witness lounge, and we headed out to the car to go back to the hotel.

That night, we were both exhausted but relieved. Like me, my mother had had to keep quiet about my assault since the civil trial, and I think finally having the opportunity to talk about what had happened—and even to vent her frustration and rage—felt like an enormous release.

For the next two days, Mom, Dad, and I remained at the hotel while Diana, Angela, and Delaney attended the trial. A number of witnesses took the stand.

On June 8, Purna Rodman Conare, who lived down the hall from me in Philly and had become a good friend, was called to talk about the changes in my behaviour that he had noticed during the winter of 2004. The other two witnesses that day were Detective Sergeant Richard Schaffer and Detective Jim Reape, both of the Cheltenham Township Police Department. Schaffer testified about my reports to the police. He was also asked to read aloud large portions of Cosby's police interview from 2005.

Diana would later tell me she was struck by one exchange in particular. When asked, "Have you ever known Andrea at any time to be untruthful?" Cosby had replied, "No."

After Richard Schaffer was done, Jim Reape was called to talk about his original investigation and to read out other statements that Bill Cosby and I had given him back in 2005.

On June 9, Detective Reape was recalled to the stand. Then Dr. Veronique Valliere, a clinical psychologist who ran a counselling practice for both sexual offenders and victims of sexual assault, testified about common reactions and behaviours of assault victims. Finally, Dr. Timothy Rohrig, a forensic toxicologist, was called to testify about whether the Benadryl that Cosby claimed to have given me could have caused the sedative effects I had experienced. I heard later that he testified it could, and also indicated that Benadryl is commonly used for drug-assisted sexual assault. (The defence had also provided evidence that a blue-coloured version of the drug was produced in 2004.). Under cross-examination, he allowed that someone could take Benadryl and still consent to sexual activity.

That night, Delaney, Angela, and the rest of us went out to dinner at a nice restaurant across the street from our hotel. We had been trying to stay under the radar and had to that point spent all our evenings back at the hotel. Even there we were cautious, always checking the lobby, bar, or breakfast room for reporters before we sat down. But now we wanted to mark the weekend, a few days' break from the trial. And the beginning of the end, since we expected the closing remarks to be delivered on Monday. It wasn't exactly a celebration, but it felt good to be out of hiding.

My family and I spent the rest of the weekend at the hotel, and then on Monday morning, we returned to the courthouse. We weren't sure if there were going to be any witnesses that morning, but Sergeant Schaffer was recalled to the stand by the defence. Mom and I, along with Delaney, Angela, Erin Slight, and Kiersten McDonald, waited in the witness lounge until he was finished. Then in the early afternoon, we headed into the courtroom to join the others.

It felt so different to be in the spectator area, instead of at the front of the room. I was surrounded by family, friends, and supporters. I focused on the men and women around me, and tried not to glance across the aisle at the defence's side of the room. People around me were whispering that Camille Cosby was there for the first time since the trial began. Earlier, Cosby's spokesperson, Andrew Wyatt, had told reporters that Cosby asked her to stay away because he didn't want her to be the focus of the media circus. I can only guess why she came for the defence's closing arguments. Perhaps she wanted to be there to show support for her husband. Perhaps the defence thought her presence was a good visual reminder of their assertion that I was the "other woman." (Indeed, at one point in his closing, Brian McMonagle said something about Cosby not being a faithful husband and pointed to Camille.) Perhaps they felt it helped to suggest Cosby's honesty—here he was, coming clean about an affair in front of his wife. He wasn't trying to hide anything.

The judge settled the room quickly, and McMonagle stood to begin his closing. I had to admit, he was a remarkable speaker. He started by describing a scene he'd witnessed just the night before. He'd been having an early dinner at a Shake Shack in the beautiful King of Prussia neighbourhood. He noticed a man sitting outside with his tiny daughter on his lap. The father was carefully spooning small amounts of a milkshake into his daughter's mouth. And after every spoonful, the dad gave the girl a little kiss.

"She looked at him like she was looking at God," McMonagle said. "It was the adoring eyes of a daughter to a dad." But children grow up in a blink of an eye, he continued wistfully. And pretty soon, they see that we are not perfect. "We try to be, but we're not . . . I wish I could just see that look one last time. But you don't, because we're not perfect." The emotion in McMonagle's voice sounded genuine, his words heartfelt. In less than two minutes, he had the jury in the palm of his hands.

He proceeded to acknowledge that Bill Cosby was not a perfect man either. But he was also, McMonagle said, not guilty of sexual assault. As he continued his speech, he appealed directly to the jurors, acknowledging how tough the trial must have been on them, sympathizing with the difficulties of being so far from home. He complimented their intelligence, their common sense, their sense of duty. And he aligned himself with them in subtle ways. I would later learn that at one point during the trial he described what he'd been doing when he came up with an insight into why I would change the date of my assault. He had, he told the jurors, been dining alone at the Shake Shack restaurant (again!). He was sitting outside with a burger and fries, thinking of his wife, his family. Just an ordinary guy who ate at burger joints. Missing his family, just like the jurors. At another point in the trial he asked the toxicology expert, Dr. Rohrig, what would happen if he, McMonagle, gave his wife one and a half tablets of Benadryl (the amount Cosby claimed he gave me). Would the two of them still be capable of a romantic interlude, a sexual encounter, after which his wife might fall asleep? The next day, he jokingly told the jury that his wife had not appreciated being used in his example. He seemed to be laughing at himself, saying, "I'm just a flawed spouse like everyone, like Bill Cosby."

During his closing remarks, he referenced his long-suffering wife again. He was also self-effacing about his skill as a lawyer. It had taken him longer than it should have, he said, to piece together why I had changed the date of the incident from March to January—longer than it should have to understand I had figured out that the phone records would prove I wasn't unconscious on the evening of March 16. He admitted that he was probably a little rough on Kelley Johnson during questioning. Angela Agrusa was a much nicer person, he acknowledged. It felt as if he was saying to the jury, "Hey, I'm one of you. Just a regular fellow. Flawed, sure, but still able to see when things don't add up."

His oratory was folksy and passionate, down to earth but also theatrical. He repeated phrases and words over and over again—rhetorical flourishes that created convincing drama and urgency. And he worked hard to make a connection between the jurors and Cosby—he frequently pointed to Cosby as he spoke or turned towards him, trying to get the jurors' focus to follow his own.

Everything about his tone said, "You can trust me when I tell you not to believe a word Andrea and Kelley have said," but he also emphasized that the jurors didn't have to worry too much about the details of our stories. He never even really addressed why Kelley and I would *want* to lie. Instead, he repeatedly reminded the jurors that all they needed to concern themselves with was reasonable doubt. If they had any uncertainty at all about my story, he insisted, they had to acquit. A man's "life was on the line," he repeated again and again.

McMonagle's closing remarks lasted a full two hours. I tried to remind myself that it was just a show he was performing, a tale he was spinning, but it was remarkably humiliating to listen to this warm, fatherly man tell the world what a terrible person I was. I tried to keep the dismay from showing on my face. I sat as still as possible and stared at the judge and jurors, praying that they weren't being taken in by McMonagle's charm-laced storytelling. But whenever I looked over at Juror #3, I suspected that the defence attorney's words had hit their mark. It was so sad that my life had come to this moment—a moment of watching someone twist the truth into lies just because it was his job to do so. The worst job in the world, I thought.

When Kevin Steele began his closing remarks, he was faced with the challenge of neutralizing McMonagle's passionate summation. The defence could spin fantastic stories. Kevin would have to stick to the mundane facts. He reminded the jurors that while they had heard a lot of witnesses, they could convict without considering anything other than *my* own words, the words of the victim. That alone was enough to find Cosby guilty. The truth, Steele seemed to be suggesting, didn't require embellishment or support— it didn't need the fancy verbal footwork that McMonagle had been so busy executing just moments before. But he did note that my account was in many ways buttressed by Cosby's own statements. Cosby had, for example, claimed in his statement to the police in 2005 and later in his deposition during the civil trial that he'd made sexual advances that I had shut down. So, Steele pointed out, Cosby understood that I might not consent to a sexual encounter. And yet he acknowledged that he had given me a drug to make me sleepy and then engaged in sexual activity with me while the drug was taking effect. He also admitted that he had left me passed out, half dressed and uncovered on his sofa, while he went upstairs to bed. Cosby's very words pointed to the fact that the sex act couldn't have been consensual—even if we had been lovers, as he claimed. I had been medicated far past my ability to give consent.

One point that Kevin made struck me keenly. He noted that throughout my testimony and all through my police statements, I had referred to Cosby as "Mr. Cosby." And it was true. When I have to talk of the man these days, I usually say "Cosby," but all I had ever called him to that point was "Mr. Cosby," or very occasionally, "Mr. C." Agrusa and McMonagle wanted jurors to believe that I'd carried on a torrid affair with a man I had never once in my life called "Bill" or even just "Cosby." Of course I hadn't. I'd thought of him as a mentor, an older man worthy of respect. That turned out to be the biggest mistake of my life.

Kevin did a good job of pulling the truth back into view, but McMonagle had been warmly persuasive. I just had to hope and pray that his charm had not become too lodged in the jurors' thoughts.

Once Kevin was finished, the judge gave the jurors instructions about the deliberation process. They then moved from the courtroom to the jury room to commence their work. It was 5:30. My little crew returned to the witness lounge, where we would be served dinner. At about 7:30, we were brought back to the courtroom. The jurors had asked that part of Cosby's statement to the police be read again to them. Then it was back to the witness lounge. Finally, at about 9:30, the judge dismissed the jury for the day, and we headed back to the hotel.

The next morning, Diana and my father decided it was time for them to drive back to Toronto. They'd wait for news of the verdict there. Mom and I would stay in Pennsylvania, spending our time in the witness lounge until the jurors were ready with their decision. We expected to see Dad and Diana in a couple of days.

Our first full day of waiting in the lounge was a long one, broken up by three trips into the courtroom, when the jury had questions for the judge. At one point, they asked to hear again the portions of Cosby's police statements that involved sexual activity with me. I had seen these accounts during my trial preparation, but it was still shocking and nauseating to listen to his fiction about the supposed consensual sex we'd had on a number of occasions, including the night he assaulted me. He claimed that at one of those early dinners at his house we had masturbated each other, and that later, as we said goodbye in his entranceway, he had lifted my shirt and bra to suck on my breast. For no apparent reason, he threw in, "Andrea has very flat breasts." He ended the story with the claim that I had told him to stop after a few seconds, which he did. Now these wholly fabricated and lurid details had been heard twice by the jurors, the spectators, the reporters. And of course, they were part of the public record. As sickening as that was to think about, another uncomfortable thought settled in my mind as the story was being read out to the jury: He did this to another woman. He was using old sexual memories to create details about me. What happened to this other woman?

After each session in the courtroom, the judge sent the jury members back to the room where they were deliberating, and Mom, Angela, Delaney, Erin, and I returned to the witness lounge. (Kristen, Kevin, and Stewart popped in and out.) There, I tried to while away the time, listening to music, playing *Heads Up!* on my phone, and cuddling with Turks, the therapy dog. His handler, Kiersten, provided me with just as much entertainment as her furry companion: she was a great storyteller, with good jokes and witty observations. Others spent the long hours on their phones, reading press reports and streaming news broadcasts. Occasionally, they chatted among themselves about what the pundits were saying or what was happening outside the courthouse. I tried not to pay attention, but I caught enough scraps to understand that Cosby's spokesman, Andrew Wyatt, was on the courthouse steps for most of the day, spinning the story of the trial, interpreting the case, and drawing meaning from each hour that passed with no verdict. When the supper hour rolled around, dinner was once again brought in for us, but there was no hope of going home. Finally, at 9:30 p.m., we were all called back into the courtroom, and Judge O'Neill announced that we would reconvene tomorrow. I was so relieved that the long and tedious day was over. The air conditioning for the courthouse seemed to be on overdrive, and I was both tired and freezing.

The next day of deliberation was just as long. Once again, the jurors returned to the courtroom several times to revisit portions of testimony. At one point in the mid-afternoon, Judge O'Neill had to explain to them that not all of the court transcripts had been fully transcribed to be in a readable form. That process was a lot of work for the court stenographer. He sounded a bit testy when he told them they would have to wait. It was almost 8 p.m. when the testimony they wanted to hear was ready. As the judge read it out, I noticed that many of the jurors looked weary and frustrated. Juror #3 was slumped in his chair. His eyes seemed barely open, and it was hard to tell if he was even listening. After the testimony had been read, the judge sent the jury back and McMonagle asked for a meeting in chambers. Kristen and Stewart later told me that he'd asked for a mistrial, saying that Juror #3 had clearly been sleeping as the testimony was read. This was evidence, he said, that the jury members were exhausted and their deliberations had become non-productive. The judge pointed out that the jurors had not said that—if they were willing to continue, they could continue. Then he recalled them to send them home at 9 p.m.

Everyone was back at the courthouse bright and early the following morning. When we got to the witness lounge, I headed for one of the sofas, my heart sinking as I felt the icy grip of the air conditioning close in on me. I had woken up congested, and now my head was beginning to pound. And I wasn't the only one who was uncomfortable. Everyone seemed on edge— even Kevin, Kristen, and Stewart. Tension rippled through the lounge. It was hard not to feel as if we were beginning to get caught in a torturous loop.

At around 11:30 that morning, we were all called back into the courtroom. Just a few minutes earlier, the foreperson had given the judge a note saying that the jury was deadlocked. As Judge O'Neill announced this, my heart dropped. All around me, I saw stricken faces. Some people gasped; others started to sob. McMonagle, however, was far from dismayed. He pounced on the news, arguing that since the jurors had now been deliberating for the better part of three days—at least thirty hours—it was time to declare a mistrial. Once again, Judge O'Neill refused, pointing out that the jurors had not declared themselves "hopelessly deadlocked," so the deliberations were not at their end.

Each day so far, I had said a little prayer for the jury. When we returned to the lounge now, Delaney, Erin, and I joined hands and prayed together. It seemed as if the jurors were worn out and beginning to lose hope of coming to an agreement. I asked God to give them the strength to continue their work and come together to reach some resolution.

A short time later, one of the staff from the prosecutor's office came into the lounge. She was carrying a mini over-the-door basketball hoop and a small ball. I laughed and jumped up from the couch. We went out into the hallway and hooked the hoop on the lounge door. While Delaney, Erin, and a few others looked on, I took shot after shot at the tiny net. Having a ball in my hands made me immediately happy, just as it had when I was a kid, and the repetitive motion was soothing. The ten minutes I spent playing out in the hall was just what I needed—a moment of lightness and silliness to break the sombre mood before we returned to the lounge. Someone had taken some videos of me sinking baskets, and I decided to post one to my Twitter account. Underneath the video, I typed, "Always follow through." A little reminder to myself that we weren't done yet.

The basketball was a lovely break, but the day seemed eternal despite that. It was close to ten o'clock by the time we arrived back at the hotel that night. As soon as I got into my room, I ran myself a hot bath. I needed a quick way to bring some warmth back to my frozen limbs and clear my aching sinuses. As I sank down into the water, I felt tears well up in my eyes. The jurors had been deliberating for forty hours, and it seemed very possible that they would never reach a unanimous conclusion. I had never seriously considered that this could all end in a mistrial, but it was beginning to seem like a real possibility. As the water lapped around me, I had a good long cry. When my tears were spent, I pulled myself up out of the tub and let my feelings of disappointment and sadness disappear down the drain with the bath water. Tomorrow would be a fresh start. There was still room for hope. I slept well that night.

Day ten of the trial was a repeat of the previous three days. My team moved back and forth between the witness lounge and the courtroom over and over and over again as the jury asked to hear one portion of testimony after another. And each time we descended the marble staircase from the witness lounge to the main-floor courtroom, our steps were accompanied by the clicking of cameras. How many photos could they possibly need of us walking up and down the stairs? I wondered.

The jurors looked increasingly tired and frustrated as the day wore on. (By the evening, Juror #3 did indeed appear to be sleeping through the readings.) McMonagle repeated his request for a mistrial at every opportunity—in open court and in frequent meetings in the judge's chambers, I was told. At one point, he argued that jurors were asking to hear every bit of testimony all over again—that the deliberations were essentially turning into another full trial. Kevin Steele explained to me that by late evening, after over fifty hours of deliberation had been clocked (the trial itself had lasted only thirty-two hours), Judge O'Neill said he was willing to grant a mistrial—but only if the DA agreed. Kevin refused.

As nerves frayed and exhaustion overtook those of us waiting inside, things were also getting testy on the courthouse steps. Since the beginning of the trial, protestors on both sides of the case had shown up daily to wave signs and shout slogans. A group from the National Organization of Women (NOW) had been outside in the early days, trying to draw attention to the problem of drug-assisted sexual assault. A number of protestors were demanding the elimination of the statute of limitations for sexual assault. Many others had come to demand support for victims and ask that Cosby's accusers be believed. On the other side, many of Cosby's supporters carried signs claiming the charges were the result of systemic racism. But during the deliberations, the crowds got even bigger. At one point, the podium that was meant for the anticipated verdict announcement broke under the weight of all the microphones that had been leaned against it. One man brought a reclining chair to the foot of the steps so he could be comfortable while he waited. Perhaps not surprisingly, given the lengthy days spent in sweltering heat, this growing crowd became increasingly agitated.

Indeed, after the trial was over, I would hear that at the end of the third day of deliberations (June 15), Linda Kirkpatrick, one of Cosby's victims, lashed out when she overheard his spokesperson chatting happily on a cellphone about how well things were going. Linda reminded the woman that Cosby had raped her. And Lili Bernard and Jewel Allison, who are both African American, got so frustrated with the claims of racism that they stood on the courthouse steps and addressed the pro-Cosby protestors, pointing out that they too were his victims. (Lili would later do several powerful interviews about how a third of the accusers were women of colour whose truth was being denied by claims that the trials were racist.) Their anger was no doubt fuelled by the conjecture that Andrew Wyatt was broadcasting. He was pumping up the Cosby supporters by saying that the lengthy deliberations were proof their man had been "vindicated."

"This deadlock shows the 'not guilty' Mr. Cosby has been saying the entire time," Wyatt crowed. "He is just happy to know that he has twelve people of his peers who understand the facts of this case don't add up."

That drew furious rebuttals from Gloria Allred and others.

News of all this had apparently reached Judge O'Neill's ears. I heard from Kristen that in a June 16 meeting with the defence team and the prosecutors, the judge voiced concerns about what was happening outside the courthouse. In fact, the judge had raised the issue with them the evening before as well. He'd noted that while there was a publication ban on the trial, he couldn't stop Wyatt from opining as long as he wasn't reporting on what actually happened in the courtroom. But the judge clearly didn't like it. In the meeting the following morning, he returned to Wyatt. He was concerned about the implications of his claims. Did Wyatt think the lengthy deliberation meant that a not-guilty verdict was coming? Or was he saying that even a mistrial was a vindication? And if the latter, did his employer, Bill Cosby, understand what a mistrial really was? Did he understand that he could be tried again? Judge O'Neill insisted that Cosby return to the courtroom so that he could put these questions to him, even as his case continued to be debated in the jury room.

Finally, at the end of another very long day, Judge O'Neill sent the jurors back to their hotel, then he met again with both sides in his chambers. Kristen later told me that there had been a discussion about calling in Juror #3 to ask if he really had been sleeping. The judge suggested that if he had, he could be dismissed. But McMonagle wasn't interested in that option. A mistrial was the only thing that would satisfy him.

It was June 17, day eleven of the trial. The jury had been deliberating for four and a half days. As we took the morning drive to the courthouse once again, I suspected that it would all soon be over. It was hard to imagine that the jurors had much more energy left.

Sure enough, just before 10 a.m., we were called back into the courtroom. When we took our seats, Judge O'Neill told us that the jurors were still deadlocked. Then he called them in. I watched as they moved into the jury box and found their seats. Every one of them looked utterly depleted. I knew this was not what they wanted. They had sacrificed seventeen days of their lives and spent countless hours debating the case and reviewing the evidence. I was sure they weren't happy that they had come to no conclusion.

Once all the jurors were seated, Judge O'Neill asked the foreperson if they were indeed deadlocked.

"Yes," she responded.

Then he asked the jurors themselves if they felt that the jury was "hopelessly" deadlocked. One by one, they each answered yes.

McMonagle immediately moved for a mistrial.

Judge O'Neill thanked the jurors for their hard work—fifty-two hours of deliberation, he pointed out, saying it was "probably one of the more courageous acts, the selfless acts, that I have ever seen in the justice system, frankly."

And then, to a sombre, hushed room, he announced that he was granting the mistrial. He thanked the jury members for their service, gave them a few instructions, and let them go.

As I sat watching the jurors file out of the courtroom, I wondered how many people were thinking, It's all over. Judge O'Neill must have been wondering the same thing. Once the jury was gone, he pointed out to those of us who remained—Cosby and his team, the reporters and spectators, my family and friends and supporters—that a mistrial wasn't a victory for either side. He reminded everyone that the defendant would remain charged and on bail until the DA decided what to do next. He then turned to Kevin. "I don't know if you have such a decision or not, Mr. Prosecutor."

I knew exactly what Kevin's response would be. The day before, he had come to the witness lounge and asked me to join him in his office. Once we got there, he told me that he thought there was a good chance a mistrial would be called. He would try the case again, but only if I was willing. How did I feel about embarking on a second trial?

I'd felt a lump rise in my throat. A mistrial wasn't a loss, but even so, it meant the only way to achieve justice was to put my life on hold once again. And what if a second trial ended with a not guilty verdict or another mistrial? How long would I be caught in this harrowing cycle? I took a few deep breaths to calm myself.

I could have asked for time to think about it. I could have met with Dolores and Bebe, my family, Angela and Delaney, my many supporters. But I knew, ultimately, this decision was mine. It's not important if things don't turn out in your favour, I reminded myself. What's important is to speak up, to ask for justice, again and again and again.

And anyway, Kevin had just told me that he, Kristen, and Stewart were ready for the next battle.

If they were in, I was in, I told him.

So when the judge asked Kevin if he had made a decision, there was no hesitation.

"We have, Your Honour. We will retry the case."

As people began to file out of the courtroom, I stood and walked to the side. There, I embraced the shocked and grieving women who had come to support me: Lili, Victoria, Jewel, Linda. Angela, Delaney, Dolores, and

Bebe joined us. We stood huddled together, our arms around each other, until the courtroom was almost empty.

And then I said my thanks and goodbyes, and the women headed outside to face the press.

Dolores spoke on my behalf to reporters, assuring them that I believed justice would eventually be done. "We are confident that these proceedings have given a voice to many victims who felt powerless and silenced," she said. Gloria Allred also addressed the cameras, expressing her hopes for "round two."

Meanwhile, Andrew Wyatt and other members of the Cosby team also talked at length to reporters. One young woman read a statement from Camille Cosby. Mrs. Cosby described Kevin Steele as "heinously and exploitatively ambitious." She called Judge O'Neill "overtly arrogant" and accused him of collaborating with the DA. She described "the counsel for the accusers" as "totally unethical," and much of the media as "blatantly vicious entities that continually disseminated intentional omissions of truth for the primary purpose of greedily selling sensationalism at the expense of a human life." All the while, Bill Cosby stood behind her, looking smugly sober as Andrew Wyatt nodded and fist-pumped the air.

Then it was Wyatt's turn. "Mr. Cosby's power is back—it's back. It has been restored," he said. "The jurors, they used their power to speak . . . So the legacy didn't go anywhere. It has been restored." He also claimed the mistrial was a victory for Black America.

Of course, I only heard about all that later. In the moment, I exited the courthouse the same way I had come in—through a small door tucked around the side of the building. Mom and I then got into the car that was waiting there. As I sat in the back seat, looking at streets dampened by steady rain, I tried to rise above my disappointment. And yet as strange as it may sound, I was disappointed more for the others than I was for myself. I certainly had not been on this journey alone. I thought about Kristen, Stewart, and Kevin; Dolores and Bebe; Angela and Delaney from the women's survivor support group; and Erin from victims services. They had all worked so hard. I thought about my family members, who had sacrificed not only their time but also their anonymity and their peace of mind. Most of all, I thought about the more than sixty women who had laid their souls bare, had sacrificed their privacy and dignity, and had seen their reputations battered. And it didn't stop there. So many women had never been able to come forward with their own experiences and were hoping this case would restore their faith in the justice system. So many people would be disappointed. My heart broke for them.

And then I let those thoughts go. We weren't done fighting. We'd simply had a practice run. There was more left to do.

Always follow through, I thought. Always follow through.

CHAPTER 11

#METOO

When Mom and I stepped off the plane in Toronto, it was as if someone had unplugged my battery. All the nervous energy, the adrenaline, the hope that had seen me through the days of the trial simply evaporated. I was bone-tired and unable to imagine how I was going to bring myself back to life.

So when I received a call from my friends Purna and Stine, inviting me to join them in New York City for Pride Weekend, I quickly said yes. I needed something joyful to stave off the numbness that was creeping over me. If I couldn't celebrate a legal victory, I could at least celebrate something else of immense importance—the recognition and growing strength of LGBTQ+ rights.

I had marched in plenty of Pride parades in Toronto, but I had never joined the crowd where it all started, never followed in the footsteps of the men and women who had raised their voices and fought for equality and justice in the Stonewall riots. As I walked arm in arm with Stine and Purna through Greenwich Village and into Midtown, I chanted and sang, my voice blending with those of thousands of others. It felt good to be an anonymous marcher in a sea of proud and passionate people. I tried to absorb as much of the positive energy of the day as I could.

Once I returned home, however, I found it hard to hang on to those feelings for very long. I went back to my massage therapy work, but a few more clients were no-shows. They don't trust me now, I thought. They think I'm a liar.

As the cool, wet summer unfolded, I found myself increasingly unable to rise above my own grey moods. I was thinking about the trial. I was dwelling on painful thoughts. I was sleeping badly again. And I was letting doubt creep in.

The night after the mistrial was declared, Mom, Dolores, Bebe, and I had all gone out for dinner in Philadelphia. My mother was despondent. The thought of another trial had her almost in tears. "I just don't think I can do it again," she said. We talked it through as we ate, and by the time the evening was over my mother had reclaimed her maternal protectiveness and was vowing to support me for as long as it took.

But now, weeks later, I was the one wondering if I could go through it all one more time. My doubts weren't helped when I learned in late August 2017 that Cosby had switched up his legal team. His defence was now going to be headed by a California criminal lawyer named Tom Mesereau. Mesereau had successfully defended Michael Jackson on child molestation charges back in 2005. He'd also represented boxer Mike Tyson when he was investigated for rape in 2001 (the charges were dropped), and actor Robert Blake when he was charged with the murder of his wife, also in 2001 (he dropped off the case after a preliminary hearing). In the Cosby case, Mesereau would be joined by Kathleen Bliss, a former federal prosecutor in four different states, and a number of other local attorneys.

What I had read and heard about the Michael Jackson case made it clear that Mesereau was not above using unseemly methods to get the results he wanted. It sounded as if he'd badgered and manipulated the two vulnerable and traumatized young accusers in court to make it appear as if they and their families had been looking for a financial payout after their friendship with the star ended. But I wasn't worried about how I would weather that sort of cross-examination. I was a mature woman with a strong, supportive circle, and I'd been speaking my truth over and over again for the past several years. I wasn't going to be knocked off course by a tricky interrogator. What I was disheartened about was how the change in legal representation would affect the timing of the second trial. It had originally been scheduled for November 2017. But now Judge O'Neill agreed to postpone it until at least March 2018, presumably to let Cosby's new legal team prepare. I had another seven months of limbo to endure before we could fight my case again.

And so, one morning in late summer, I hit bottom. Lying in bed, unable to rouse myself even to eat breakfast or make myself a cup of tea, I realized that I was not looking forward to the day. I wasn't looking forward to anything. The future seemed bleak. What's the point? I thought. What am I doing here? Maybe it would be better if I had never existed.

Maddy began to shift on the bed. I could hear Cassie shuffling in the hallway outside my door. I pulled myself out of bed to get their morning meal ready. As I moved about my condo, I realized I couldn't go on like this. I needed to pull myself out of my stupor. So I dove back into the teachings of Paramahansa Yogananda.

"Do not acknowledge defeat," the guru wrote. "To acknowledge it brings greater defeat. You have unlimited power; you must cultivate that power—that is all . . . Your trial may be great, but your greatest enemy is yourself—your ego." That was certainly true—I was standing in my own way. And my ego had put me there. I had let myself forget that the second trial, and the stressful months it would take to get there, was something I needed to do, not only for myself but for all the other women who couldn't. This isn't just about you, Andrea, I told myself.

I was also reminded that in thinking about the outcome of the first trial or worrying about the outcome of the second, I was only making myself miserable about things that were simply not in my hands. Yogananda had words of wisdom about this, too: "The person attached to the fruits of his actions suffers as a result of his attachments. He performs all actions concentrating on the fruits of actions and is elated by success and cast down by failure. Through non-attachment, the same person, even though he lives in the world, experiences even-mindedness whatever the outcome of his efforts. How sad it is to see the suffering people go through when they base their expectations of happiness on other people, or on circumstances over which they have no control."

I was in God's hands. I knew this, but I had temporarily let that truth slip from view. Now I pulled it back into sight. I also realized that it was time to lean on my friends as well.

I reached out to Donna Motsinger more frequently, and went to visit her in New Mexico in February. We talked a lot about God and our spirituality, about growth and change. She always gave me good advice about how to build up my spirit, how to avoid looking back, how to move on. And before any conversation or text exchange finished, she would slip into "mother mode," insisting that I find myself a nice girlfriend. I would usually fire back that I was too busy for sex and love. But I adored her relentless matchmaking urge.

And then, while I was busy shoring up my spirit, the world seemed to shift on its axis just a bit.

On October 5, 2017, the *New York Times* printed an explosive story in which journalists Jodi Kantor and Megan Twohey reported that actors Ashley Judd, Rose McGowan, and a host of other women had been sexually harassed or assaulted by Hollywood producer Harvey Weinstein. Five days later, Gwyneth Paltrow and Angelina Jolie came forward with their own stories of sexual harassment at the hands of Weinstein.

But the floodgates *truly* opened after actor Alyssa Milano shared on Twitter a suggestion made to her by a friend: "If all the women who have been sexually harassed or assaulted wrote 'Me too' as a status, we might give people a sense of the magnitude of the problem."

Of course, Milano did not coin the phrase "Me Too." That was the work of Tarana Burke, a sexual assault survivor and activist who created the non-profit organization Just Be to empower black girls. In 2006, Burke had introduced the phrase "Me Too" on Just Be's MySpace page in the hopes that women would share their stories to raise awareness of the pervasiveness of sexual assault and harassment.

While Burke's work was invaluable, Milano's suggestion added jet fuel to the movement. Thousands and thousands of women around the world began to post using the "MeToo" hashtag, and many included accounts of their own experiences. Soon came more reports of abuse by powerful men. By November, US broadcasters Matt Lauer and Charlie Rose had been fired from their jobs after multiple women told harrowing tales of sexual harassment, and actor Kevin Spacey found his own reputation in ruins.

Sadly, none of the revelations surprised me. Listening to the stories of Cosby's many accusers had made me realize how easy it was for rich and famous men to use that power to commit serial sexual assaults, especially when they worked in the entertainment industry. These influential men spent most of their time in environments that provided them with plenty of contact with young women. And they had associates and employees who could act as go-betweens, as well as representatives and lawyers who could clean up after the damage was done. In Cosby's case, he had asked a number of agents to send him models, some still in their teens, for him to "mentor." The agents did so, although at least one of those models claims she told her agent that she was subsequently assaulted.

The stories from Cosby's accusers also bore witness to the role played by friends, employees, and other people in aiding and abetting assaulters. One of Cosby's "helpers" came forward to tell his story in November 2014, after the Buress video had taken off. Frank Scotti, who had worked as a facilities manager at NBC when *The Cosby Show* was on the air, told the New York *Daily News* that for years, groups of young models were sent to the studio. Cosby would look the women over, pick one, then task Scotti with standing guard outside his dressing room door while the star "interviewed" her for a role on the show. Scotti was also asked to arrange an apartment (through Donald Trump's brother) that Cosby could use to meet up with another woman. And it was Scotti who delivered monthly payments to eight or nine women over the course of years, on Cosby's behalf. (Scotti was given cash and told to get money orders issued in his own name.) Eventually, all the dirty work became too much for Scotti. "I felt sorry for the women . . . It bothered me . . . You've got all these kids, every time ... I used to like him, but that's the reason I quit him after so many years—because of the girls."

In my case, a representative from the William Morris Agency tried to broker a meeting between Cosby and my mom and me in Miami to discuss paying for my schooling and therapy. Dolores and Bebe later theorized that this trip may have been a ploy to entice us to cross the border into the US so that Cosby could then accuse us of extorting him. In 1997, he'd got Autumn Jackson, a young woman who claimed to be his daughter, charged with extortion. The woman's mother had had an affair with Cosby, and Cosby had been paying her and Autumn until Autumn dropped out of college and Cosby cut her off. When the young woman tried to blackmail him by threatening to reveal that she was his out-of-wedlock child, he asked her to come to see him in New York City, where she was promptly arrested. Dolores and Bebe thought he might have been planning to invent a similar story about me—and would have had law enforcement waiting for us in Florida. Fortunately, we'd turned down the offer to be flown to Miami.

As the #MeToo movement gained momentum, some people questioned why the public was now paying so much attention to accusations of assault when the women who'd made complaints about Cosby in 2005 and 2006 had been ignored or dismissed.

Perhaps people were more willing to believe Weinstein's accusers because he was not a household name the way Cosby was. He may have been behind the star machine and partly responsible for the careers of many actors and actresses, but he wasn't a beloved star himself. He certainly wasn't America's Dad.

Whatever the reason, it really did feel as if a profound shift was taking place. And with that shift, I knew that going ahead with a second trial was the right thing to do. It would be worth the heartache and pain. In the courtroom I was telling my own story, but I was also bearing witness to the pain of Cosby's other victims. I was fighting for justice for them. The #MeToo movement made me realize just how potent that symbolism was. It wasn't just the sixty-plus women I was representing—it was thousands of men and women who were now telling their stories, often with no hope for justice or redress. Those of us who *could* fight for some form of justice were representing multitudes—and demanding accountability for those who'd sexually assaulted others in recent days and in decades past.

That knowledge was like wind beneath my wings. It moved me outside of my trauma, lifting me into fresher air. I was also buoyed by the wave of healing that was beginning, the conversations people were finally having—the men and women acknowledging the breadth and depth of the problem of sexual harassment and sexual assault. Before I met Cosby, I had never really taken account of the subtle yet consistent ways women are often demeaned and sexualized. The dirty joke. The sexual innuendo. The unwanted touches or looks. But I had come to understand that this was the toxic culture that set the stage for larger acts of aggression and exploitation. Now it seemed that huge numbers of men and women were ready to acknowledge this—and to work against it.

And all that gave me tremendous hope. Were people more willing to believe us now? Had the reports about Weinstein and all the other powerful men given credibility to the idea that Cosby drugged and abused countless women? I suspected they had.

Amid all this social agitation, the Cosby criminal case ground along. And just as they had with the first trial, Kevin, Kristen, and Stewart kept me informed about the endless motions and legal ploys that Cosby's team was using to slow the advent of the second trial. On several occasions, the defence delivered thousands of pages of phone records, flight schedules, and itineraries to the DA's office. The prosecutors regarded those tactics as a way to distract them and take up enormous amounts of their time. But these document dumps would have consequences that Mesereau and his colleagues could not have imagined.

Not surprisingly, the defence submitted a number of pretrial motions asking that the case be dismissed. In one, Cosby's lawyers accused Kevin Steele of prosecutorial misconduct for discussing the possibility of prosecuting Cosby during his campaign for district attorney. Mesereau and his team also argued that Judge O'Neill should recuse himself because his wife was a social worker and advocate in sexual assault cases. (During jury selection, they also raised the idea that the judicial process was inherently racist.)

In yet another motion, the defence argued that the statute of limitations had expired. They suggested that the alleged assault happened before December 30, 2003—in other words, more than twelve years before charges were laid. But before the civil trial in 2005, I'd worked out that the assault had to have happened in the first two weeks or so of January. My cousin had come to stay with me in Philly on January 22, 2004, and I knew Cosby's attack had occurred before then. In the first trial, McMonagle and his legal team had raised the issue only to point out that I had originally got the date wrong—"proof," they said, that I'd made it all up. But Mesereau was focusing on the confusion around the date to suggest that the case didn't fall within the statute of limitations. The fact that I couldn't pin it down more precisely now seemed as if it could make us vulnerable.

But none of these motions were granted. The defence did, however, win a couple of key decisions that suggested this trial might unfold quite differently from the first.

Prior to the first trial, McMonagle had asked that a woman named Marguerite (Margo) Jackson, a Temple University academic advisor, be put on their witness list. Judge O'Neill rejected that motion on the grounds that her testimony would be hearsay. When faced with the same request in the second trial, however, he agreed to let her take the stand. He had apparently changed his mind about the hearsay.

We knew the story Jackson was going to tell because it was already out. After two days of deliberation in the first trial, Andrew Wyatt had taken his regular place on the courthouse steps and declared, "This court has not given [Cosby] a fair and impartial trial." While he claimed that Cosby still had confidence in the jury, he said the judge's decision to disallow a key defence witness, Marguerite Jackson, proved the trial had been rigged. He then read a statement from Jackson to the assembled press. In it, she claimed that I'd once roomed with her on a road trip for the Temple women's basketball team. After watching a TV news item about an alleged sexual assault by a famous man, I had supposedly told her that I could accuse a high-profile person of doing the same to me and then launch a civil suit to get money from him to use for tuition and to open a business. She said she was shocked when a year later, I did just that.

It was, of course, complete fiction. ("The slander doesn't stop," Dolores had told the press at the time.) I rarely shared a room when I travelled with the team, and I had certainly not shared one with Jackson. In fact, I'd had so little interaction with her that I hardly remembered her. But Judge O'Neill's new ruling meant she could spin her story inside a courtroom.

The proposed witness list also included another surprising name: Robert Russell. Unlike Marguerite Jackson, Robert was clear in my memory.

I had met Robert seventeen years earlier, in 2000. I was back living in Toronto after two years of playing pro ball in Italy, and I'd taken a job at Nike's flagship store in the Yorkville neighbourhood while I tried to figure out what I wanted to do with my life. One day, Robert had come into the store to look at shoes, and we ended up talking about sneakers, running, and sports. He began to drop in on a regular basis, and whenever I was free, we'd chat. I would occasionally take my break or lunch when Robert showed up at the store, and we'd sit outside on a big rock in a small public square and laugh and talk. I discovered that he was something of a free spirit. He didn't appear down and out—he was a snappy dresser and always neat and well-groomed—but he was essentially homeless. He had no cellphone and, because he bounced between shelters and other temporary living spaces, no landline either. He relied on pay phones whenever he needed to reach someone. It was an unusual way to live, and perhaps it should have raised a few red flags for me. But I was young and trusting, and determined to respect his privacy and simply enjoy his company and his conversation.

Robert loved athletics as much as I did, but I soon realized that he didn't have the luxury of working out in a nice gym. At the time, I had a membership at a very exclusive place, and I invited him to join me there as my guest. It was nice having a workout buddy, and I could tell Robert loved the experience. He was always enthusiastic and positive, but I wondered how many other people he had in his life. After a few months, I decided to invite him to my parents' place for one of our regular Sunday dinners. He hit it off with my mom and dad, and the family dinners that followed were also a great success.

After we had known each other about six months, however, things got a little strained. I had an idea for a small business that would provide health and wellness presentations and seminars: Supernova Communications, I was calling it. I shared this idea with Robert, and he wanted to get involved. But that was a tall order given that he didn't have a phone, a computer, or any resources. I created a business plan and found an angel investor. Robert, who loved to draw, provided a sketch that I turned into a logo. But no sooner had I launched the business than I realized that I couldn't really run an operation like that without a skilled partner. I shut it down. I could tell Robert was disappointed, but in truth, I had never really been able to see a role for him in the enterprise.

After the business letdown, Robert seemed intent on finding some other sort of close connection with me. He began to talk about astral projection. Despite all the spiritual seeking I'd been doing, astral projection—the idea that your soul, or astral body, could leave your physical body and travel through the universe—was too far-fetched for me. But Robert kept pushing me to explore it with him. He said he had taught others, and he wanted to teach me. His insistence started to make me uncomfortable. It felt like a sort of psychic invasion—as if he was trying to get inside my head. I stood my ground.

With that, our friendship began to fade, and I saw less and less of Robert. Around the same time, on a trip to North Carolina, I met Sheri, who would become my long-distance partner for the next ten years. And through Sheri, I met Dawn Staley, who hired me for the position at Temple University. About four or five months after I last saw Robert, I moved to Philadelphia, and our friendship receded into the past.

Now, in 2018, Robert had reappeared. And he was saying that when he knew me in Toronto, I had a drug problem—an addiction to magic mushrooms and marijuana. He claimed that I had talked about setting up a man for extortion, and that I had been fixated on becoming a million-aire. Robert's "theory" was that I was coming after Cosby because I had run through my settlement money and wanted more. He also portrayed me and my family as hard-core racists. My mother, he said, had vowed never to allow a person of colour in her house, and he compared her to Hitler. He claimed I had lost a boyfriend to a Black woman, and this had spurred my family to seek revenge against African Americans. He called us a "dark" family and said he had decided to part ways with us long ago.

I was heartbroken when I learned that Robert had resurfaced and was spewing such a viciously fabricated story. His claims made me realize how badly Robert had been wounded by the evaporation of our friendship, and how bitter he remained. I suspected that the years had been hard on my old acquaintance. And unhappiness about the way his life had unfolded might have made the prospect of playing an important role in the trial of a famous man pretty appealing. But I still couldn't understand how the kind, sweet man I remembered could have come up with such a ridiculously false narrative. And then I saw a photo of him in the papers during the pretrial phase, when the lawyers were meeting with Judge O'Neill about their wit-ness lists. Gone was his soft, gentle expression. His eyes looked hard and empty, his face as stiff and soulless as a marionette's. I couldn't help think-ing that Cosby's people were pulling his strings.

Judge O'Neill ruled that Robert Russell could testify—but only about his claim that I had told him I was interested in getting a job at TSN, the Canadian sports specialty channel. The defence clearly intended to use that to argue I'd befriended Bill Cosby so that he could help me become a broadcaster. (In truth, it was Cosby who had kept trying to push me in that direction.) Judge O'Neill said in his ruling that the rest of Robert's stories had the potential to unfairly prejudice the jurors, even if they were rebutted. We knew that we could marshal many character witnesses who would emphatically counter Robert's lies, but I was grateful that we didn't have to.

Robert's fantasy story, however, was not going to be kept quiet. Almost as soon as the judge had made his ruling, Andrew Wyatt took to the courthouse steps again. He loudly shared Robert's falsehoods and claimed that Judge O'Neill's ruling proved the trials were corrupted by racism. A number of news outlets repeated the slander, and one shady "news" organization conducted an extensive video interview with Robert following the trial. (The hate mail we received after this prompted my mother to contact the police.)

But the prosecutors for my case scored a few victories of their own. The defence had tried to keep out of the second trial the portions of the civil deposition where Cosby talked about Quaaludes, but the judge said no. Judge O'Neill also ruled that the defence couldn't bring in Bruce Castor, the former Montgomery County DA, as a witness or focus on his refusal to prosecute in 2005. (Castor hadn't appeared in person at the first trial, but McMonagle had relied heavily on his decision not to prosecute and the various statements he'd made justifying that decision.) And perhaps most importantly, this time the judge decided to allow the prosecution to call five "prior bad act" witnesses, instead of just one. That meant that five women who had been assaulted by Bill Cosby would be able to tell their stories in a courtroom for the first time. Judge O'Neill did, however, place one restriction on the witnesses: their assaults had to have taken place in 1982 or later. That limited the prosecutors to less than half of the nineteen women on their list.

While all these legal manoeuvres were playing out, Bill Cosby briefly re-entered the public sphere. He had kept a low profile before the first trial, but shortly after the mistrial, Andrew Wyatt had announced that Cosby was planning to do a series of town hall presentations over the summer. Apparently, he wanted to talk to young people about how certain behaviours might open up a person to accusations of sexual assault. I was shocked by the arrogance of this—Cosby was once again putting himself out there as a moral and ethical leader. And I could just imagine the tone-deaf, inadvertently self-damning things he might say. I guess his lawyers could imagine them too, because in short order, Angela Agrusa announced that the lecture tour wouldn't take place. Wyatt then claimed the story about the town halls had been false all along.

But by January, it seemed that Cosby could no longer resist stepping out before the cameras. Perhaps feeling that he should drum up a bit of support in light of the #MeToo movement, he posted pictures of himself at a barbershop and a café on his social media accounts. Then, on January 10, 2018, he invited a cadre of reporters and cameramen to join him while he dined in an empty Italian restaurant in Germantown, Pennsylvania. "We're ready," he said to the journalists about the trial.

A few weeks later, he gave a small performance at LaRose Jazz Club in Philadelphia, walking in on the arm of Andrew Wyatt. He posed for photos with fans and friends, and then took to the stage to tell stories and jokes. His performance was met with warm laughter and applause. A lone protestor stood vigil outside.

At the end of February, however, a family tragedy quieted Cosby's personal PR campaign. His daughter Ensa, only forty-four years old, died of renal failure.

I have written here about the pretrial legal wrangling, about Cosby's public appearances, and about his daughter's death to try to reflect the events that were swirling around this case as the second trial came into view. But at the time, I was only vaguely aware of all this. The prosecutors kept me informed, and friends and family told me about things they'd heard. But these bits of news were on my screen only briefly before I turned my eyes away. With Ensa's death, I certainly felt for the Cosby family, but Yogananda teaches that death is simply a release from earthly attachments, a spiritual deliverance. My strong belief in this has always made me react to people's passing in a less mournful way than most. But I was also doing my best not to think about Cosby and the trial. I needed to stay positive and even-keeled. Even though I had long ago forgiven Cosby for what he'd done, I knew that I wouldn't find that balance with one foot in *his* world.

"You are sent on earth to witness earthly experiences—heat and cold, disease, war, famine, pain and suffering—as unaffectedly as you would watch a motion picture," Yogananda once wrote, describing the peace that comes with freeing yourself from attachments. I wasn't sure I could master that level of detachment at this point in my life, so instead I tuned out all news and noise about the trial and about Cosby.

I tried my best to live in a world of my own making. The winter was a fairly cold and miserable one in Toronto, so I escaped the snow with a trip to the Caribbean in February. As the winter began to fade, I took my bike out to the hilly country roads that threaded around my parents' new home in an area outside Toronto. I pushed myself towards personal best times on each ride. The cycling cleared my mind, allowed me to take in the beauty of nature, and gave me an extraordinary emotional boost as I felt my body grow stronger and stronger with each hill I climbed.

I went for weekly massages to work out any stress and stiffness that crept into my muscles, but I knew that my spiritual well-being was even more important than my physical health. I went to the SRF temple regularly and tried to take part in group meditation as often as possible. I had always found meditation more powerful when surrounded by others. But even when I wasn't at the temple, I worked on being mindful and chasing away negative thoughts whenever I felt them slip in.

I also had two long, long sessions to complete the phoenix tattoo, one in January and another in March. Once the bird was finished, I had the tattoo artist add three phrases:

Love melts all blockages.
Forgiveness brings peace.
Service is the purpose of life.

When the work was done, a beautiful colourful image of transcendence covered my back and lifted my spirits.

———

In the weeks before the trial was set to begin, I talked often with Kristen, Kevin, and Stewart to review and prepare. I was reminded that while I could try to forget about the trial for periods at a time, the prosecutors could not. They were as positive and supportive as always, but I suspected that they were tired. While Cosby had been able to hire seven new trial lawyers (all of whom were supported by large legal firms and a host of other lawyers), the DA's office had limited resources. And Kristen, Kevin, and Stewart were supposed to be working on other cases as well as mine. With the number of pretrial motions that the defence had filed, they'd had to rely on their colleagues to take over some of their other work. Sergeant Richard Schaffer, Detective Mike Shade, and others were helping them sort through the document dumps, and the appellate division drafted some of the motions they had to file in answer to the defence's petitions. But Kristen, Kevin, and Stewart had still put in twelve-hour-plus days for many months.

It wasn't just the sheer volume of work that had been weighing on them. Once the trial was over, Kristen talked openly about the particular stress she had felt going into the second round. What will it mean for society if we lose? she'd asked herself. This hadn't been on her mind during the first trial, but with more Cosby accusers on record and all the women coming forward in the #MeToo movement, she was keenly aware of how many people would be following this new trial, looking to see if justice was in fact possible in cases like these. Another mistrial or a not guilty verdict would be devastating, and would send a truly terrible message to the world. This case—my case—had become much more than a simple legal proceeding.

That said, Kristen, Kevin, and Stewart never once complained to me about the extraordinary amount of work they were doing. In fact, they made it clear what an unusual gift it was to retry a case. After a mistrial, it was rare for a new trial to go forward—because the complainant does not want to go through the experience again or for a host of other reasons. They were excited about getting a second chance to fight for justice for the people of Pennsylvania.

During our conversations, they advised me to prepare for a lot of questions about a supposed financial motive for my accusation. It was, after all, a favoured approach for Mesereau in sexual assault cases. They also warned me that he was old school when it came to handling sexual assault complainants. I should expect questions about what clothes I'd been wearing, whether I'd had anything to drink, and if I'd done anything to encourage the man.

I would soon learn that Kristen, Stewart, and Kevin were right. The defence attorneys had no intention of changing with the times. They would embrace all the cruel, misogynistic, abusive tactics of the past. No fiction would be too outrageous, no attack too personal.

It was fortunate that I didn't really comprehend what lay ahead of me. Indeed, the security of knowing I'd weathered the first trial helped me retain my emotional strength. And whenever I flagged a bit, I reminded myself that I was truly blessed to be living in a remarkable transformative moment. A moment when women's voices were being raised—and listened to in a way they had never been before. When Cosby had performed his show in Hamilton, Ontario, after the Buress video went viral, protestors showed up with signs saying "We believe the women." Now, I was hearing that refrain again all around me.

I found myself wondering, Was it possible that the new jurors would add their voices to that powerful chorus?

CHAPTER 12

A NEW APPROACH

When Mom, Dad, Diana, and I approached the doors of the hotel, I was struck by a sense of déjà vu. Ten months earlier, we had walked across the carpeted lobby floor with the same mix of apprehension and hopefulness. And with the same questions about the future.

This time, however, I had a leash in my hand. During the last trial, I had found Turks, the therapy dog, a great comfort. But of course, I could play with him only when I was actually at the courthouse. I had missed my own dogs, Maddy and Cassie, during the long days at the hotel—and I had worried about them. So this time I had driven to Philly with my family, and we'd brought the dogs with us. And this time, as we walked into the hotel, there were familiar faces to greet us.

"Andrea!" the receptionist called out as soon as she saw us. "Welcome back! We've got everything ready for you."

During our previous stay, we'd got to know the hotel staff quite well. They had been warm and accommodating. This visit promised to be no different. By the time we had our room keys in our hands, a number of employees had told us how they'd been following the case in the intervening months. "You're so brave for doing this," one of them said. "We just hope you have better luck this time."

Later that night, while we relaxed with a drink in the lounge, the bartender echoed the welcome. "Thanks for fighting the fight," he said as he handed me my glass of iced tea. All this positive energy made me feel lighter—and eager to get back into court. Let's get her done, I found myself thinking.

Unfortunately, I was going to have to hit the brakes.

During the first trial, only two witnesses preceded me. This time, I would have to wait until six women had testified before I would be called to appear. Five of these were the "prior bad act" witnesses. Kelley Johnson would not be one of them. Kristen, Stewart, and Kevin felt that since her testimony in the first trial was readily available to the new defence lawyers, they might be able to prepare a line of attack that could weaken her effectiveness. Instead, they chose Janice Baker Kinney, Heidi Thomas, Chelan Lasha, Janice Dickinson, and Lise-Lotte Lublin.

I had met Janice Baker-Kinney at Jennifer Litton Todd's Virginia home after the Women's March in February 2017, and I knew the story of how she met Cosby in 1982 when she was a young bartender at Harrah's Hotel and Casino in Reno, Nevada. The four other women had also already spoken publicly, and all four had been featured in a *New York* magazine cover story about Cosby's accusers. I was, however, only vaguely aware of them and didn't read their accounts until after the trial. If the defence attorneys planned to accuse me of colluding with them to create similarities among our narratives, I could honestly say that I didn't know their experiences. But of course when I did learn them, I wasn't surprised to discover that all our stories echoed each other in one way or another.

Like me, Heidi Thomas got to know Cosby when the comedian offered to mentor her. She was twenty-four years old, living in Denver, and trying to break into the acting world when her agent informed her that Bill Cosby was interested in helping her. The agent didn't explain how the comedian had become aware of Heidi, but shortly after their conversation, Cosby called her home. He talked with her parents for a while and then arranged for Heidi to come down to Reno, where he was doing a show at Harrah's Hotel and Casino. There, he would give her some coaching to prepare her for auditions.

When Heidi got off the plane, a driver was there to meet her. He took her to a house on the outskirts of town, where Cosby was staying. When she entered the sprawling home, Cosby greeted her, then told her to get into some comfortable clothes and join him to begin the training session. The driver showed her to "her room." She was surprised, as she'd assumed she'd be staying at the hotel.

When she got back to the living room, she performed a monologue she'd been rehearsing. Then Cosby handed her a script. The character he instructed her to play was supposed to be intoxicated. Heidi admitted she had never been drunk, but she said she'd seen plenty of drunk people at college. Cosby told her, however, that she should have a drink to get into the role. He handed her a glass of wine. One sip was all it took. Her memories of the next four days exist only as tiny fragments. She knows that after swallowing the wine, she passed out. She woke up at one point as Cosby was forcing his penis into her mouth. At another point, she remembers Cosby saying, "Your friend is going to come again." She doesn't remember being driven to the airport or greeting her mother and father as she got off the plane back in Denver.

Several months after that weekend, she flew out to St. Louis, where Cosby was performing, hoping to find out what had happened to her. Cosby rebuffed her, making it clear that he was no longer interested in being her "mentor." She did, however, get someone to take a picture of her with Cosby. He wasn't very happy about that.

Chelan Lasha was just fifteen years old in 1984 when her stepmother, who worked for a production company that had ties to Cosby, contacted the comedian, hoping he might help Chelan move forward in her modelling work. He responded by inviting the girl and her grandmother, whom she lived with, to a taping of one of his shows. Over the next couple of years, he befriended Chelan's grandmother, and several times he had dinner at their

Las Vegas home, always bringing treats for Chelan, her sister, and the rest of the family. Then, in 1986, he invited Chelan to the hotel where he was staying to have some photographs taken for her portfolio. Despite having a bad cold, Chelan was excited at the prospect of taking this next step in her career, so she headed over to the suite of her family friend.

When she got to the room, a camera was indeed set up. But before the shoot began, Cosby gave her what he said was an antihistamine to help with her sneezing and coughing. He also pressed several glasses of Amaretto on the girl. In no time, she felt woozy. Cosby took her into the bedroom and put her on the bed. He lay down next to her and began pinching her breasts and rubbing up against her. Then something warm hit her leg. The next thing she remembered was the sound of clapping hands and Cosby's voice: "Daddy says wake up. Daddy says wake up."

Janice Dickinson was one of the most well known of Cosby's accusers when she went public with her complaint. In 1982 she was already a successful model, but she was hoping to make the transition into acting. So when her agent told her that Bill Cosby had expressed an interest in helping her, she was eager to meet him. They first met and talked in Manhattan, and then Cosby asked her to fly to Lake Tahoe, where he was doing a show, to continue the discussion. When she got there, he had arranged a session for her with a musician and composer who would later do work for *The Cosby Show*. After she demonstrated her singing abilities to the men, she and the musician attended Cosby's show and then joined him for dinner. During dinner, Janice told the men that she wasn't feeling great—she was suffering from menstrual cramps. Cosby handed her a blue pill, telling her it would help. She started to feel light-headed shortly after she swallowed it. Once dinner was finished, the musician left and Cosby told her they would carry on talking about her new career up in his room. When they got there, she was feeling weak, so she sat on the bed. She was in a stupor and having trouble talking. Cosby changed into a bathrobe and then made a phone call. When he was done, he came over to the bed and got on top of her. She found that she couldn't move, couldn't do anything to stop what was happening. She felt a pain between her legs and then passed out. When she awoke, she was in her own hotel room, alone, and she was naked from the waist down. She noticed semen on her legs, and her anus was hurting.

Janice confronted Cosby sometime later, but he behaved as if he had no idea what she was talking about. She also tried to write about the assault in her 2002 memoir, but her publisher's legal experts made her remove the passages.

Of the five women, Lise-Lotte Lublin provided the most recent account, although it still preceded my assault by fifteen years. Like so many of his other victims, Lise-Lotte, then twenty-three, was put in contact with Cosby by her modelling agency. Her career aspiration was to be a teacher, but when Cosby invited her to his Las Vegas hotel to talk about expanding her modelling work, she was happy to accept.

That first meeting was fairly uneventful. As the months unfolded, however, Cosby stayed in touch. He got to know the rest of her family, often calling her mother, who was in the psychology field, to chat. He even once introduced Lise-Lotte as his daughter when they were out. When he invited her to meet him at his Las Vegas hotel a second time to talk about her modelling future, she went without a thought.

When she got there, much to Lise-Lotte's confusion, Cosby suggested they practise some improvisation. Even though Lise-Lotte told him she didn't drink, he insisted she have one and then another to loosen up for the work. After the second drink, she started to get dizzy and was having trouble making out what Cosby was saying to her. He told her to come over to the couch and sit between his legs. She was struggling to stay standing, so she did. While she tried to figure out what to do, he began to stroke her hair. She soon realized she could no longer get up on her own. After that, she can recall only brief mental pictures of various parts of the hotel suite. Then nothing. When she woke up, she was in her own bed at home. Two days had passed.

Those were the histories the jurors would hear before I described yet another iteration of Cosby's predation and abuse. But before any of us got a chance to tell our stories, Dr. Barbara Ziv, a forensic psychiatrist and an expert in the patterns of behaviour of both sex offenders and victims of sexual abuse, was asked to provide context for our experiences.

In the first trial, the prosecutors had called on an expert to speak as well. Unfortunately, that expert, clinical psychologist Veronique Valliere, was not as effective as Kristen, Stewart, and Kevin had hoped. For one thing, she and Kristen had struggled to keep things general—the defence objected repeatedly when their discussion got too close to the specifics of my own situation. And then during cross-examination, the defence alleged that Dr. Valliere was not impartial, citing a post she had made on Facebook after Cosby was charged. "Victory. Case goes on," she had written.

But in preparing the witness list for this second trial, Kevin had suggested another reason that Dr. Valliere's testimony might not have helped the jurors understand what Kelley Johnson and I were telling them. Between my testimony and Dr. Valliere's, the jurors had listened to two and a half days of other witnesses. And four days had passed since they'd heard from Kelley Johnson. Kevin pointed out that they were being asked to retroactively apply any new understanding they had gained from the expert. It was simply unrealistic to assume that they would be able to revise their first impressions, to see things through a different lens.

This time around, Kevin suggested they put Dr. Ziv on immediately following the opening remarks so that she could educate the jurors about the common behaviours of sexual assault victims *before* they were asked to judge the credibility of our accounts. Kristen and Stewart were surprised by this suggestion. The conventional practice in sexual assault cases was to put the complainant and any "prior bad act" witnesses on first, followed by other witnesses. But they agreed that Kevin's suggestion made a lot of sense.

By all accounts, Dr. Ziv was a powerful witness. She explained how the trauma of sexual assault commonly led to inconsistent details, confused chronologies, and delayed reporting. She pointed out that in cases where alcohol or drugs were involved, memories could be very hazy, which often contributed to a victim's reluctance to come forward. She noted that a shocking 85 percent of sexual assaults are perpetrated by someone the victim knows. Because of an overwhelming desire to forget about the assault, to pretend that it never happened, or to understand why it happened, victims often try to normalize their relationships with their attackers. It is the *rule*, not the exception, Ziv told the jury, for victims to reach out to their assaulters. She also explained that most victims don't fight back: it's extremely common for them to describe themselves as "frozen" in fear while under attack. This fear and confusion also often prevents them from leaving the scene of the crime right away.

But Dr. Ziv also stressed that people's reactions after being sexually assaulted can vary widely—from carrying on as normal to shutting down completely or engaging in acts of self-harm. Some victims even become extremely promiscuous, she noted, in a desperate effort to regain control over their own sexual activity. There was one trait, however, that all sexual assault victims shared, Dr. Ziv said. "I would challenge you to find one victim of sexual assault, one—I've been doing this a long time. I don't know that I can name one victim of sexual assault who is not humiliated by the fact that they have been sexually assaulted, who doesn't blame themselves in some way, and who is not deeply ashamed of it."

She concluded her initial testimony by emphasizing just how hard it is for victims to talk about their experiences, to open themselves up to questioning and judgment, to risk losing control over the narrative and their privacy.

During cross-examination, defence lawyer Kathleen Bliss tried to twist Dr. Ziv's words and mockingly questioned her research, but the doctor stood firm. The stage was perfectly set for Heidi, Chelan, Lise-Lotte, Janice Baker-Kinney, and Janice Dickinson to tell their stories.

My sister had decided that this time around, she would attend the trial only when Mom and I were testifying. So all four of us—Mom, Dad, Diana, and I—stayed at the hotel as the early days of the trial unfolded. Once again, I was trying to insulate myself from the news, but my family was paying close attention to the trial, and bits and pieces of information drifted through to me—including the fact that crowds of protestors and supporters were outside the courthouse again. I learned that on the first day of the trial, a woman had leapt over a barricade near the entrance and pulled off her shirt. Across her bare chest she had written the names of a number of the accusers, the words "Women's Lives Matter," and the name of a women's activist group. And that evening, Lili Bernard held a vigil outside the courthouse for Cosby's victims.

When the "prior bad act" witnesses had their days in court, I reminded my family that I didn't want to hear anything about their testimony. I had, in fact, turned off my phone as soon as we'd arrived in Philly. But at the end of the third or fourth day of the trial, my mom and sister came into the room Diana and I were sharing, excitement in their eyes. "Andrea, you'd be so proud of the women," Diana told me. "It sounds like they are really standing up for themselves. Really fighting back."

I was so glad to hear that.

While the dogs, the friendly hotel staff, and the brave women who preceded me were providing plenty of positive energy, I couldn't deny that being back in the midst of this very public trial weighed on me and everyone else in my family. My mother was itching to get back in the courtroom. ("Oh, they are really going to be in for it," she'd joke about facing the lawyers. "I'm so much better prepared than I was last time!") But like me, she found the waiting a strain. And I could tell that my father and sister were worried about us. Almost every evening, we headed down to the hotel lounge to have a drink and unwind, but in truth, we spent much of our time together trying *not* to talk about what was at the top of everyone's mind—which was its own kind of stress.

At night, Diana or I would take the dogs out for a walk, and then I would meditate for a while before we crawled into our separate queen beds. Cassie would settle on the floor while Maddy curled up beside me. I usually drifted off easily, but I didn't stay asleep for long. By two or three in the morning I would be awake again, trying to figure out where I was. As awareness edged in, I'd lie on my back and listen to the dogs' snuffling and my sister's soft breathing. Sometimes, I would think about what a strange situation I was in. It was as if I'd been cast in some kind of never-ending play about good and evil. The last time I was in a courtroom, I had felt as if I'd stepped onto a stage, under glaring lights. Everyone seemed to be playing a part, strutting about, reciting lines, trying to cast a spell over the audience. And no matter how hard I had tried to hold on to reality, the room had swirled with artifice and pretense. When I thought about being in that theatre again, I had to wrap my arms around Maddy. I needed the comfort of something real. Maddy was real. Real and loving and good. My God was real. My gurus. And dear Uncle Salvo, whose picture stood on my bedside once again.

At other times, my eyes would flicker open in the darkness and I would lie quietly, wondering who else was awake at that hour. Were Heidi, Janice, Chelan, Janice, and Lise-Lotte stretched open-eyed on their own hotel beds, wondering what they were doing so far from home? Were they worried about the moment when they would see in the flesh the man who had haunted them for so long? Did they rehearse their testimony, going over it again in their minds in the hope that no one would be able to diminish their words?

What about Kristen, Kevin, and Stewart? Was one of them at the kitchen sink right now, drinking a glass of water and thinking about how the defence might come after our witnesses? Was one of them pacing a bedroom floor, trying to guess what the defence witnesses might have to say?

What about the jurors and Judge O'Neill? Or Mesereau, Bliss, and the other Cosby lawyers? How many were wide awake like I was, borrowing from the coming day?

I would close my eyes and spend a few more moments saying a silent prayer for all of them. Then I'd rise from the covers to meditate, clearing my mind for sleep once again.

The evening before I was scheduled to testify, my family and I went out to the Capital Grille across from the hotel for my belated birthday dinner. While we were there, Kristen texted to say that she needed to meet me for a few last-minute preparations. When I arrived back at the hotel, she shared some surprising news: Cosby's lawyers had almost casually mentioned that they intended to introduce the actual financial terms of the civil settlement I had made with him. They had already given Kevin, Kristen, and Stewart the figure. It was the first time the prosecutors had heard what I'd been paid—until that moment, only Cosby, his lawyers, Dolores, Bebe, and I knew.

Kristen was uncertain exactly how the defence planned to use this information. After all, the money had been paid long before I agreed to go back to court—twice—for criminal proceedings that would certainly not provide any further financial gain. But it did seem to confirm that Mesereau's standard approach in sexual assault cases was to claim the accusers were only after money. I had been expecting that accusation. But now I would have to address it while millions of dollar signs hung before the jurors' eyes. Another piece of my privacy gone. I could just imagine the headlines that would follow the news that Cosby had given me a small fortune.

After Kristen left, I went up to my hotel room, hoping to get to bed early. When I arrived, Cassie and Maddy were dancing about, desperate to get outside, even though they had already had their evening walk. It was pouring rain. Diana put her coat on without a word of complaint and disappeared out the door with the dogs.

Perhaps because of our unfamiliar surroundings, or maybe just the tension that hung in the air, the poor dogs' digestive systems were scrambled. Despite being taken out several times in the evening, they were nudging Diana with their wet noses almost as soon as we snapped the lights off. All through the long night, I woke again and again to the sound of paws scrabbling against the floor and the sight of Diana with two leashes in hand, heading back out into the driving rain with the pups. In the morning, she and I both laughed at Maddy and Cassie's strange intuitiveness. Even though they lived with me and usually approached me whenever they wanted anything, they seemed to know that I had a big day ahead and that they should leave me to get a bit of rest.

———

The next morning, the ride to the courthouse with my sister and Delaney Henderson from PAVE was eerily familiar. So too was the sight of the crowds outside the courthouse, although this time they looked a bit larger and perhaps even more boisterous.

Inside the courthouse, reporters once again lined the hallways. Erin Slight from victims services greeted us in the witness lounge. Turks, the service dog, was there too. And I had my stones and my brass medallion of Uncle Salvo tucked safely in my pocket.

This time, I didn't have to wait long before I was called. The proceedings were to start at 10 a.m., and I was the first witness of the day. By about 10:15, I was sworn in and sitting in the witness chair.

As soon as I settled, I looked out at the gallery. Delaney and Bebe were there. Lili Bernard had committed to attending the entire trial once again. (But this time, she was without her glorious pink gladioli. Among the defence's many pretrial motions was one requesting that the court-room be "flower-free." Judge O'Neill had acquiesced to this strangely petty request.) Other Cosby survivors, including Victoria Valentino and Therese Serignese, were there too.

A sea of familiar, supportive faces. I was so grateful. And also amazed. I would be up on the stand for a day or two, and then would be back for closing statements and deliberations. But many of the survivors, like Lili, were going to sit through every day of the proceedings—once again. I marvelled at their commitment and their bravery. Each time I'd heard someone speak of her own sexual assault—whether it was another Cosby survivor or a Weinstein accuser or any other victim now emboldened to share her experience—I felt my own dark memories sweep over me. My heart would race, my stomach would clench, and I'd fight to catch my breath. Lili and the other survivors had likely experienced the same reactions as they listened to the stories of the five "prior bad act" witnesses. And now, for a sixth time, they would feel those same emotions as they listened to me. What's more, I knew they would be filled with indignity and outrage at the defence team's every effort to dismiss us.

I smiled at my friends and then looked over at the jurors. I knew they were all from the local area—Mesereau and his team had not requested a Pittsburgh jury this time. These jurors appeared on average to be slightly younger than the last group, and there was certainly no equivalent of Juror #3, as far as I could tell at first glance. (After the first trial, one juror gave an interview to the *Philadelphia Daily News*. "She was well coached," he was quoted as saying. "Let's face it: She went up to his house with a bare midriff and incense and bath salts. What the heck?" I had never worn a midriff top around Cosby, and I didn't go to his house with those bath salts from my co-worker. But I guess whichever juror this was—and I suspected it was Juror #3—hadn't been listening to me.)

By contrast, these twelve men and women appeared focused and attentive. There was no way to tell what they were thinking, but I did get the feeling that they were ready to listen.

And finally, I looked over at the defence table. You couldn't miss Tom Mesereau. With his shock of long white hair and his cool expression, he was striking—and unnerving. And I recognized the older blond woman with the team as Kathleen Bliss. There were also a couple of unfamiliar faces. And then Cosby.

The man looked no less defiant than he had at the last trial. There wasn't a trace of remorse or apology on his face. But he seemed changed in other ways. More tired. More grizzled. Despite his bravado at the Italian restaurant, his recent family tragedy and the months between the two trials had clearly been hard on him.

Kristen started her questioning by asking me to tell the jury how much I'd been paid in the civil settlement. I did. She asked if I had any pending lawsuits against Cosby. "No," I answered. And then she cleverly shifted focus to the financial implications of participating in this criminal proceeding. Was I being paid to be here? No. Did I have to take time off work to be here? Yes. Would I be compensated for lost wages? No. She didn't get into the cost of gas, flights, and hotel rooms for me and my family, but the implication was clear. If I was out for money, why would I be doing this? I'd already received a settlement. The trial would only bring costs, not windfalls.

Then Kristen said to me, "Ms. Constand, why are you here?"

"For justice," I replied.

Kristen paused for a moment, letting those words linger, before she moved on to ask me about my work, my basketball career, and my home life.

Earlier, she had told me that she would spend more time introducing me to the jury than she had done during the first trial. This time, the prosecutors wanted the jurors to get a better sense of who I was and what made me tick. They wanted them to feel as if they knew me to some degree. And they wanted them to understand that like everyone else, I was a flawed human. Someone who might make mistakes with memory but wasn't a liar.

As Kristen questioned me, a large photo of my teenage self appeared on the screen at the front of the courtroom. She handed me a copy to look at. During the testimony of the five other victims, the prosecutors had shown pictures of the women with Cosby, taken around the time of their assaults, to prevent the defence from arguing that he didn't know them or had never met them. They didn't have to do that with me, of course. In Cosby's deposition, he'd admitted to interacting with me. But since the jurors had seen pictures of the other women's younger selves, Kristen, Kevin, and Stewart decided that they should also see me as I was before my life took a dark turn.

In the photo, I'm standing in my basketball uniform, long brown curls falling past my shoulders and disappearing far down my back. My smile is wide and relaxed. I can see the joy in my face, and the anticipation of all the good things life could offer me. I remembered this photo well. It was taken at the provincial championships. I was so proud to be representing my district, and so eager to get out onto the court with my team.

What a striking contrast I now was to that young woman. Of course, I was so much older—thirty-one years, in fact. And in getting ready for the trial, I'd chosen to let my age show. I had stopped colouring my hair months before, and patches of grey now bloomed from my temples. That morning, I had put on a bit of mascara and a touch of pink lip gloss, but that was as far as I went. I wanted to look like myself. I wanted everything I did in that courtroom to be honest. I had been wearied and weathered by what happened to me. That was the reality.

Of course, everyone ages, and had I never been assaulted, my hair might well have looked much the same at forty-five. But when I looked at that photo of my youthful self, I recognized the subtle changes in my expression over the years. I don't know that I've ever smiled as readily since my assault. I've lost the easiness of expression, the softness of innocence. Sitting on the stand that day, I was still a positive person, but now that attitude took work. It came from a conscious decision to see the best of life; it was the result of constant emotional and spiritual work. In my teens and twenties, however, joy, hope, and enthusiasm came to me without thought or effort. They had pulsed through my veins like blood.

Kristen began to question me about my job at Temple and about travelling with the women's basketball team. I responded to a series of queries and confirmed that I'd had my own room on the road trips, and that I knew Marguerite Jackson's name but had never shared a room with her.

We moved on to how I had met Cosby and how we had become friendly. Kristen walked me through each occasion I'd spent time with Cosby outside of work. And then, of course, I had to recount every painful detail of the night of my assault. I had told this story dozens of times, but it never got easier.

Kristen's final questions were about the toll the criminal proceedings had taken on me and my family. She concluded by asking me a number of pointed questions about whether I had consented to any of the sexual events that took place at Cosby's house that January night in 2004.

And then it was time for Kristen to step away. Time for me to come face to face with Cosby's famously ruthless defence attorney.

CHAPTER 13

SCATTERSHOT

Tom Mesereau stood up and approached me. He introduced himself and gave me a few instructions about how to answer his questions. Then he handed me the Durham Regional Police report on my assault.

"Have you seen that document before?" he asked. His tone was cool. Clinical. I kept my expression as neutral as I could. But something about Mesereau's air of detachment unnerved me. I'd thought the first trial had prepared me for anything a new defence team might throw at me. Now I wasn't so sure.

Despite my nerves, Mesereau's first questions felt like familiar terrain. He hammered away at the inconsistencies between my statement to the Durham police and my later statements, including details such as whether I'd introduced myself to Cosby or had been introduced by someone else. Like Agrusa in the first trial, he also made an issue of my attempt to contact lawyers before I spoke with the police.

Then he asked who had done the rooming assignments for the Temple women's basketball road trips, and whether I'd ever roomed with anyone. I knew that line of questioning was heading to Marguerite Jackson, but Mesereau didn't continue. Instead, he asked whether I'd entered Cosby's house by the "back door." When I said that I had, he returned, "You knew he was married, correct?" His tone was flat, yet there was no mistaking the contempt of his words.

The next questions were focused on the times Cosby had touched me and my drive up to Foxwoods casino. Mesereau asked once again if I knew Cosby was a married man. He returned to the business of my going in the back door of Cosby's house, then boomeranged to Foxwoods and to my "laying [sic] on the bed" at the hotel. And then he lobbed something new at me. He asked if I'd made it "a point" to wear the cashmere sweaters Cosby had given me whenever I met with him. When I answered no, he pointed out that in my civil deposition, I said I'd worn a grey cashmere sweater when I went to his house that night in January.

He discarded the sweater talk quickly and switched tacks again. Now he was mentioning my phone records. In one of my early statements to the police, I stated that on the night of my assault, I called from the street outside Cosby's house to let him know I'd arrived. The hunt for that call became a huge focus for the defence—during my cross-examination and eventually in Mesereau's closing remarks. In truth, I have no clear memory of that call. And I suspect I might have been mistaken when I said I'd phoned. I admitted that to Mesereau and the court. Later, I understand, Cosby's personal chef—a defence witness—took Mesereau and Bliss by surprise when he commented that the gate was most often left open, so there would have been no need to ring Cosby. Nevertheless, now Mesereau was grilling me about phone calls, implying that any day when I hadn't called the Elkins Park house in the early evening was clearly not a date when I could have been at Cosby's home. He was suggesting that the evening I was referring to had to have happened outside the statute of limitations.

This was an argument that had been made in pretrial motions, but not one I thought I would have to tackle in court. Before I really had a chance to digest the idea, however, Mesereau had pivoted to talk about what he called the "three sexual contacts" I'd had with Cosby and the various times I'd seen him outside of work. The next thing I knew, he was asking me if I'd ever seen Cosby's wife, Camille, at any of these events.

"Did you ever ask him where she was?" Mesereau's tone was cool, but I could hear the sneer in his voice.

"No," I said.

"Did you care?" he shot back.

Having implied that I was callously willing to be the other woman, Mesereau then asked a few questions about job opportunities I had looked into while at Temple, before heading off in another unexpected direction.

Had I ever taken sexual harassment and sexual assault training at Temple? he asked. I had no memory of anything of the sort, but I admitted it might have been part of my employee orientation. He produced a form showing that I'd attended a seminar on the topic.

"And you don't recall anyone teaching you that in a case of sexual assault, you must report immediately? You don't recall that?"

I was working hard to stay in the moment, to answer the question asked and only the question asked, so all I said was no. But later, I would be amazed at how odd his argument was. He seemed to be suggesting that my assault couldn't have been real because I hadn't followed guidelines I'd been given in an employee orientation seminar. Even there on the stand, I was beginning to realize that Agrusa's cross-examination in the first trial had been a breeze compared to what lay ahead.

Agrusa had been brittle and snippy. I'd been a little alarmed by her abrasiveness, but she hadn't really got to me. Her chilliness was tempered by obvious self-consciousness. The way she looked at the jury or around the room as she spoke hinted that like me, she felt she was being judged on her performance. Her shaking hand as she passed me documents suggested that she wasn't at all sure she was making the impression she hoped for.

There was no such touch of humanity with Mesereau. He was steely and dispassionate, yet I was learning that despite the dry demeanour, Mesereau could be a crafty manipulator when he was trying to work me into a trap. He would twist words, try to get me to agree to misstatements, load questions and assertions with innuendo. And he had other tricks up his sleeve, too.

After the questions about the seminar, and then another odd moment when he handed me a Temple employee orientation handbook and drew my attention to a passage that cautioned against getting personally involved with trustees or members of the board, he asked if I knew a woman in Arizona named Sarah Ross. I'd known someone with that first name, but her last name wasn't Ross. The woman I believed he was referring to was a supporter of the University of Arizona women's basketball team. At the end of my time at university, she had let me stay with her and her son for a month while I finished a course. She was newly separated and struggling emotionally at the time. Once I moved to Europe, I completely lost touch with her.

As I tried to figure out why Mesereau would be raising this old acquaintance, he asked if I had ever done drugs at her house. I was stunned. At the time, I was a dedicated athlete, trying out for WNBA teams. I would not have been doing drugs. But before I could answer, Kristen objected to the question. She had been objecting ever since Mesereau brought up the woman's name. She wasn't on the witness list, and we had no idea of her possible relevance. The judge sustained this objection and suggested a sidebar so the lawyers could consult with him about this line of questioning. But before Mesereau moved to the judge's bench, he leaned towards me and said, under his breath, "She's a wreck because of you, you know."

It was soft enough that the court reporter didn't catch it, but Mesereau looked over at the jurors as he spoke. He seemed to be hoping they had caught his words.

His accusation was like a penknife slipped quickly between the ribs— furtive enough to go unnoticed by others but meant to wound nonetheless. It did indeed give me a start, but the discussion at the bench allowed me a moment to wash it from my mind and regain my focus. When Mesereau came back, he asked no more questions about the woman and moved on to another topic.

Thinking back on the exchange later that evening, however, I realized how much digging, how much travelling, how much money had gone into trying to find skeletons in my closet. All they had come up with, it seemed, was another unhappy person, like Robert Russell, who had once known me and perhaps felt that I'd abandoned the friendship. Someone who was willing to cook up a disparaging story for her own purposes. It was disheartening to think about how far Cosby's toxic net had spread, and how many people he'd preyed on, directly or indirectly. And it made me worry that sexual assault victims would never be safe from slander and character assassination when they faced rich and powerful abusers. Indeed, Harvey Weinstein had hired an Israeli firm with offices in Tel Aviv, Paris, and London to investigate and follow his victims. (Journalist Ronan Farrow had broken that story in a *New Yorker* magazine article that appeared shortly after the *New York Times* piece about Weinstein was published.) Now it seemed Cosby had done much the same thing. With those sorts of tactics, it wasn't surprising that so few women had come forward about rich and influential men over the years.

The next few questions were also a surprise. Mesereau asked me about Supernova Communications, that short-lived company I had tried to get off the ground. He suggested that when I shut it down, I hadn't bothered to pay back my angel investor and instead bought myself a car with his money. I responded that I'd leased a Volkswagen Beetle after I started working at Nike—with the money from my salary.

Next he asked me if I was qualified for my job at Temple. Had I prepared spreadsheets or budgets before? I didn't have to answer that because Kristen objected. Mesereau, however, continued on about the job. It required three years of administrative experience, didn't it? I hadn't a clue and couldn't imagine where he was going with this.

And then, seemingly out of nowhere, Mesereau said, "Do you recall being involved in a pyramid scheme at Temple?"

Once again, I was lost.

He then produced an enormous stack of papers and drew my attention to an email regarding a company called 10in10 BIZ. The name did ring a bell, and I had vague memories of receiving a few emails about the company and forwarding them to friends.

Mesereau read out one of the emails I had forwarded—it suggested that people pay sixty-five dollars to join the company. He pointed out that I had signed it "Regards, Andrea."

When I looked at the email, I could see that I had done that, but I knew the words were not mine—I had copied text that someone had sent to me. I had a memory that this was a project my girlfriend, Sheri, was into, and that I had been helping her out.

Mesereau asked me to agree that I had sent a lot of emails on the subject. I said I didn't know how many there were. I couldn't remember much about any of it.

He flipped to another page in the huge pile of papers he was holding. He wanted me to read another email. I tried to focus on what Mesereau had shoved under my nose, but the task felt daunting.

Judge O'Neill obviously felt the same. He noted that there were almost one hundred pages of emails in the evidence package and Mesereau couldn't expect me to read through them while I sat on the stand. He suggested we take a break, or if Mesereau preferred, he could give me the papers to look over on the weekend and we could come back to them on Monday.

Much to my relief, Mesereau agreed to the latter suggestion. He asked me a few more questions about the company, however, before he let me go.

What was my role in it? he wanted to know.

"Nothing," I said. "I had a job."

"But you're raising money in this email, correct?"

I told him I had never made any money from it—as far as I could remember, I was just forwarding emails from a friend.

And with that, my first day on the stand was done.

I spent a quiet weekend at the hotel, reading through the emails, working out, and walking the dogs. We had dinner with Dolores and her husband one evening, and I talked briefly to Bebe on the phone, but I was careful not to discuss my testimony or the questions I'd been asked with either of my lawyers.

Sure enough, as soon as I got back on the stand on Monday morning, Mesereau began grilling me about whether I'd talked with my lawyers over the weekend. I suppose he was trying to plant the idea that they had been coaching me, but I could honestly say that we hadn't talked about the trial at all.

That opening salvo was followed by more questions about Cosby's marital state, about the gifts I'd given him, and about my Foxwoods visit (including, of course, assertions that I had been lying on the bed with him). And then Mesereau asked if I'd read through the emails on the weekend.

The seventy-five emails had indeed refreshed my memory. My girl-friend, Sheri, had got involved in some sort of group-buying business that could get members phone cards and other services at a discount. I'd given her the sixty-five dollars and had forwarded the email to one or two friends. I'd even called it a pyramid business, though in truth, I had no idea what that term meant at the time and had used it inaccurately. (I hadn't realized pyramid schemes were a way for their creators to collect money by recruiting members who paid entry fees but rarely saw any return on their investment.)

After I'd sent the first email, I continued to pass along any info coming from the company to the people I'd contacted. I rarely read those emails myself or thought much about this "business." I was too busy with my Temple job to pay it any attention.

But now Mesereau was trying to make it sound as if I was out there fleecing as many friends and acquaintances as I could. He pointed out that one of the emails suggested I was a "bronze level" member of the organization. It was true that one of the emails mentioned that, but I don't remember seeing it at the time or having any idea what it meant. Mesereau, however, was pointing to it as a sign of my success with the company.

"But you don't know why you were promoted—you just know that you were promoted?" he asked.

"No, I don't know anything about that type of stuff," I answered. "I was an athlete my whole life. I was just helping a friend."

"Did you think you would become a millionaire?"

"No."

"Why not?"

"Because I didn't think about it."

Given Mesereau's tactics in the Michael Jackson case and the fact that he had wanted the world to know how much Cosby paid me, I had expected him to label me a gold digger. But the accusation that I'd been running a pyramid scheme and was some kind of con artist (my sexual assault accusation just another sting I was running) was a whopper no one on the prosecution team had seen coming.

Mesereau's next financial argument was perhaps a little more predictable. He made an issue of the fact that I had cooperated with the DA's office even though I'd accepted $3 million from Cosby. I made a point of correcting him.

"It was a little bit more than that, sir, and you know that. That's not the correct amount."

"$3,380,000, right?" he said.

"That's right," I replied.

He was trying to use the money to make me look bad, but I wasn't about to downplay the sizable payout Cosby had given me. I hadn't asked for that amount. I wasn't going to be apologetic about accepting it.

More questions about phone calls and Valentine's Day and the night at the Chinese restaurant followed, then Mesereau closed his cross-examination by finally asking me about his upcoming witness. Did I know Marguerite Jackson? Had I ever roomed with her? Had I ever told her about a plan to fabricate a sexual assault accusation to get money?

By the time I got off the stand, I was a little astonished at all the theories Mesereau was putting out there. Agrusa and McMonagle, by comparison, had kept their fiction fairly straightforward: Cosby and I were lovers, and after our relationship was over, I made up an assault story for revenge as well as a payout. Mesereau's approach felt more scattershot. Like Agrusa and McMonagle, Mesereau was suggesting that I'd engaged in consensual sex with Cosby—he tried to play up the luridness by repeatedly mentioning the back door and invoking Cosby's marital status—but the twist in the story was that I was a longtime grifter, unhappy in a job I wasn't qualified for and looking for a big score. All the while I was in romantic pursuit, I was setting Cosby up, playing him for a mark.

At the same time, Mesereau spit out a host of other seemingly unrelated theories. I was a drug user. I couldn't be a sexual assault victim because I'd attended a seminar about sexual harassment and hadn't followed the advice given there. I wasn't an honourable person because I had agreed not to pursue criminal charges, and now I was. And if all else failed, the night in question was outside the statute of limitations.

Mesereau was supposed to be a big LA legal genius, and yet I couldn't help feeling his defence was haphazard and desperate. I wondered how many jurors thought the same.

It was a huge relief when I was finally dismissed from the stand in the middle of the afternoon. As my mother was being sworn in, I made my way back to the witness lounge, accompanied by police officers. Before we got very far down the hallway, though, Scott Ross, one of Cosby's private investigators, stepped up to me. He had a piece of paper in his hand. "Sorry to do this, Andrea," he said. "Good luck."

He had given me a subpoena to appear as a defence witness. Mesereau wanted to call me back to the stand later in the trial. Perhaps after Marguerite Jackson had appeared. Maybe to grill me about her claims.

I smiled warmly at Ross. Before I left the courtroom, the prosecutors had told me this was likely to happen. But for some reason, I was quite certain I wouldn't be back on the stand. I believed my time as a witness was done. I actually felt a little chuckle bubble up in my throat. Yes, indeed, Mesereau was throwing everything out there. But this wasn't going to stick.

Once again, I waited in the witness lounge while Mom was on the stand. I was a little worried about her. She'd been vibrating with energy and confidence going in—ready to fight for her child, and certain that if the defence lawyers treated her roughly, she'd be able to come back at them tenfold. But

I had just seen how hard Mesereau worked to unnerve me, to provoke me. Would my mother be able to maintain her defiance if Kathleen Bliss dug into her in the same way?

A couple of hours later, I had my answer. Mom walked through the door of the lounge, red-faced with anger. "What bullshit!" she was saying.

In the first trial, Mom had been irritated by Agrusa's aggressive questioning, but Bliss had outraged her. The string of expletives didn't stop for some time. Bliss, I later learned, had suggested that I bought my parents a house with the settlement money, and that they had supported me in the civil suit because they too were looking for a payoff. She'd also hammered at the idea that my mother didn't know what was going on in my life in Philly, challenging her with falsehoods that she presented like facts. Did my mother know that I had taken advances on my Temple salary? Did she know that the university had sent a collection agency after me? Did she know that I was struggling at work and probably would have been fired from my job had I not quit?

Bliss provided no support for any of her claims, prompting Judge O'Neill to remind the jury at one point that statements embedded in questions were not evidence and should not be considered as such.

But the lies had clearly shocked Mom. She pushed back hard. And from the sounds of it, Bliss let her own temper fly as well. When my mother said she didn't recall something, and then added that she didn't see what the question had to do with anything, Bliss fired back, "You're not here to debate with me." Then she turned to the judge and demanded that my mother be instructed to answer the already answered question.

The cross-examination only got testier after that. At one point, my mother got so flustered by Bliss's tone that she blurted, "Why are you asking me in that voice?" Once again, Bliss asked the judge to admonish my mom. She then refused to repeat the question and demanded that my mother's comment be stricken from the record first. The judge ignored the request and asked Bliss to proceed, but her next question was phrased in such a condescending way that it raised both an objection from Kevin Steele and a reprimand from the judge. "Again, it is amazing, Ms. Bliss, that you ask this witness not to do what she did to you and then you come right back and—I'm not going to referee between the two of you."

The cross-examination ground on in that vein for a long time: Bliss badgering my mother, Kevin raising objections, my mother attempting to straighten the defence's slanted narrative, the judge jumping in to move the testimony forward. Finally, Bliss ended her cross on a cutting and intensely personal note.

"Mrs. Constand, you love your daughter, obviously—both of your daughters—very much. Is that right?"

"Definitely."

"And you and your husband raised them to be good girls, isn't that right?"

"Definitely."

"And so is it fair to say that it would have broken your heart to know that your daughter Andrea was having an affair with a married man?"

My daughter didn't do that, my mother responded.

"You didn't raise your daughter to have an affair with a married man, did you?" Bliss continued.

She wasn't about to let my mother have the last word.

"I have no further questions," she said before she walked away.

Despite my confidence that I wouldn't be called back to testify again— that the subpoena was simply a tactic to rattle me and the prosecution—I couldn't help feeling stressed about the week that stretched ahead. There would be several days of prosecution witnesses. Sergeant Richard Schaffer from the Cheltenham Township Police Department and Detective David Mason from the Durham Regional Police would be on the stand. So would my friend Purna. They would be followed by Judith Regan, Janice Dickinson's publisher, and Detective Jim Reape. (My brother-in-law, Stuart, was not called this time.)

In the first trial, the defence had called just one witness. Sergeant Schaffer, who had testified as a prosecution witness, was called back to be questioned by McMonagle about the notes he had taken while interviewing me. Calling few or no defence witnesses is not unusual, since the law insists that a person is innocent until proven guilty. But in this second trial, the defence attorneys had drummed up a healthy roster. Not only would there be a brief appearance by Robert Russell and a no doubt much longer one by Marguerite Jackson, but Cosby's team was also calling another Temple employee, presumably to shore up their claims that I knew Marguerite and might have roomed with her on a trip. In addition, they intended to call an assistant from the William Morris Agency and one from a promotional company that worked with Cosby. Cosby's personal chef was also on the list, as was a medical expert who would counter Dr. Rohrig's testimony about the effects of Benadryl.

It didn't sound as if these witnesses could do a great deal to strengthen the defence's arguments. The two assistants simply explained how carefully Cosby's itineraries were kept and insisted that he didn't use an answering service in New York. (The defence was arguing that calls I made to the New York number were proof that Cosby was at his Manhattan townhouse in the first two weeks of January. But I used that number often, even when he was in Philly.) The chef volunteered during cross-examination that everyone used the back door at Cosby's home. (So much for me using it to "sneak" into the house.) And in Stewart's cross-examination of Marguerite Jackson, he got her to admit that she had made two affidavits—the second of which was a collaborative effort with Kathleen Bliss. Bliss had even suggested that Jackson add the words "money is a great motivator" to explain why I might lie about the assault. Stewart was also able to dismantle her claims about my extortion plans by pointing out that she had submitted absolutely no expenses for travelling with the Temple women's basketball team in 2004, when she supposedly roomed with me. (The only travel expenses she filed were in 2003.) And the medical "expert" the defence produced was so poorly qualified to talk about drug toxicology that Stewart's cross actually had jurors chuckling.

But Kristen suspected that these appearances had less to do with what the witnesses said and more to do with stretching out the time between my account and those of the five other accusers so that the jurors might forget the similarities between our stories when they started their deliberations.

In the end, closing arguments didn't finish until more than a week after my final appearance on the stand.

But it wasn't only the inclusion of extra witnesses that promised to lengthen this trial. During my two days on the stand, there were frequent breaks so that the DAs and defence attorneys could meet with the judge to go over what material could or could not be raised in court. Kevin, Kristen, and Stewart later told me that I had glimpsed only the tip of the iceberg. While Cosby had seven lawyers with him in the courthouse, many more were back at their law offices generating motion after motion to put before the judge. Most of these were arguments that he should reconsider decisions he had already made on previous motions—like the one about not allowing material from the Castor suit to be raised. But all of them needed to be read and considered by the judge and the prosecutors. Some required Kevin, Kristen, and Stewart to file their own motions in response. They told me they had never seen anything like this tsunami of requests in the midst of an ongoing trial, and that it didn't bode well for a speedy process—which was probably the whole point.

All of that added up to many days before we would get to closing arguments. And then I would have to be in Philadelphia once the deliberations started—and who knew how long they would last?

I didn't think I could wait it out. Nor could I continue to watch what the waiting was doing to my family. The civil suit and the first trial had both been tough on them. But now—with Cosby's PR people airing Robert Russell's story about my parents being vicious racists and Bliss suggesting that my civil settlement had bought them a home—their reputations were being shredded in an even more intense way. And they were obviously struggling with that.

During the weekend between my first and last day of testimony, Dolores and her husband had invited my dad to go golfing with them. Diana and I would get together with them for dinner at the end of the day. (Mom wanted to spend a quiet evening alone at the hotel.) It sounded like a perfect plan. I had all those emails to read through, but the rest of my family would be hanging out in the hotel without much to do. Golf would be a great distraction for Dad, and the dinner was something for Diana and me to look forward to.

But as soon as my sister and I got to Dolores's house for a quick drink before dinner, we realized that things had not worked out the way we'd imagined. Apparently, the food facilities at the golf course had not been running, but the bar service was going full steam. The day was warm; my dad was thirsty. One beer led to another. By the time we got to the restaurant, Dad was swaying towards the table, his judgment and restraint left somewhere back on the links. It was abundantly clear to everyone that we weren't going to have a long, quiet dinner, working through several courses and slowly sipping nice glasses of wine. Instead, we ordered the quickest meal we could think of—pizza—and stuffed a few slices into my father as soon as it arrived. Then Diana and I hustled him out the door. When we got him back to his hotel room, Mom was apoplectic.

The following morning, my father left a voicemail apology for Dolores and her husband. My mother had calmed down, but she was obviously still rattled by the fiasco. I knew she also felt bad for my dad, however, as did Diana and I. We were all struggling, but my mother, sister, and I seemed to have more ways of coping. Alcohol was one of the few things that helped my dad release the enormous tension he was feeling. But that obviously created its own problems.

Once Mom and I had finished our days in court, I just couldn't see the point of lingering in Philadelphia any longer, especially given the friction that comes with living in cramped quarters under extraordinary stress. We had a quick chat about it, and then we all packed up our cars and headed back to Toronto with my poor suffering dogs.

I was relieved at the prospect of sleeping in my own bed again, relieved by the thought of being back on familiar soil. It would be a short burst of calm and normalcy before I was once again pacing the witness lounge, trying to quiet my nerves as the jury sat in a room somewhere nearby, deciding whether or not to believe me.

CHAPTER 14

THE MOMENT

Once home, my family followed the news coverage of the trial while I picked up bits and pieces from them. There were reports of things that happened in the courtroom, but once again the liveliest stories were coming from the courthouse steps as Andrew Wyatt and another Cosby spokesperson, Ebonee Benson, spun their version of events. In the early days of the trial, Gloria Allred, who represented three of the women who testified to Cosby's prior bad acts, addressed the media as well, often getting into heated exchanges with Wyatt and Benson. Lili Bernard and Victoria Valentino also tried to provide a counterpoint to their fantastic claims. By mid-trial, however, the daily scenes had become so raucous that Judge O'Neill barred Cosby's team from the courthouse grounds (although their move down the street didn't quiet things at all).

Four or five days after I'd returned to Toronto, I flew back to Philadelphia by myself to hear the closing arguments and wait for a verdict from the jury. Delaney shared a room with me at the hotel, and we planned to attend the closings and deliberations together. But I had decided to do this just a bit differently from the last trial, when I had taken my place in the spectator area.

The defence had made a highly unusual request to present closings from *two* lawyers: Mesereau and Bliss. I was certain that they would be a tag team of low blows. Even though I hadn't been in court when Heidi, Chelan, Janice, Lise-Lotte, and Janice testified, I'd heard that the defence attorneys had blamed and shamed the women. They had besieged Chelan Lasha with questions about a decade-old minor criminal conviction and left her sobbing on the stand without so much as a Kleenex while they took long sidebars with the judge. They'd ruthlessly interrogated Janice Baker-Kinney about her past drug use and current prescription for antidepressants, desperately trying to create the impression that she was a drug abuser. They'd accused Janice Dickinson of being unabashedly promiscuous. Indeed, their blame-the-victim tactics had permeated the entire trial. They had even asked Cosby's personal chef what I was wearing when I came over to the house, and if I drank while I was there.

The women, I understood, had bravely stuck to their truths. Chelan Lasha, despite her distress, had fought back against defence accusations that she'd come forward because she thought she could get money if there was a settlement fund for survivors. (Chelan was represented by Gloria Allred, who had asked for such a fund.) At one point, Chelan even turned to Cosby and challenged him directly. "You remember, don't you, Mr. Cosby?" she spat out. Cosby had only smiled back at her.

Janice Baker-Kinney was especially powerful when she passionately but unapologetically explained her current use of antidepressants. She'd had to turn to them, she said, after two devastating losses: the passing of her mother, followed by the sudden and unexpected death of her husband.

Janice Dickinson didn't mute her fury for a minute, and she refused to let Mesereau suggest that she hadn't included the rape in her memoir because it wasn't true. "Today I'm under a sworn Bible!" she reminded him.

I was proud of these women, but I suspected that the defence's closing arguments would be a repeat performance of this heartless treatment. I had certainly had a taste of it on the stand. And I understood that Mesereau had raised other theories in his opening statement that he hadn't bothered to ask me about in court. I had gone to the restaurateurs' dinner at the Cosby house, he suggested, because I was keen to meet people with money. At the dinner with the academics, I heard about the donations Cosby had given and concluded there were big bucks to be made off him. I pursued him relentlessly. I waited a year to make my accusation so that I had time to destroy all evidence of my real relationship with him.

But most outrageously, Mesereau claimed that I had taken advantage of Cosby's grief over the 1997 murder of his son, Ennis. "He was lonely and troubled, and he made the terrible mistake of confiding in this person what was going on in his life," Mesereau had said after describing how "brutal" the trials were for his legally blind client.

In reality, Cosby had never once talked to me about his son. Yet Mesereau was eager to exploit a *real* family tragedy to engage in character assassination. I had no doubt he and Bliss would raise similar vicious false-hoods about me and the other witnesses in closing. I didn't want to spend a minute more in the presence of that sort of negative energy.

This time, I decided I'd sit out the closing arguments in the quiet of the witness lounge.

It turned out to be a good idea. In his closing, Mesereau apparently focused on the twelve supposed lies I had been telling, lobbed his "con artist" pitch once again, and went through a numbingly tedious review of phone records and itineraries to argue that if it happened at all, the events couldn't have happened within the statute of limitations. He also claimed that if I'd really been attacked that night, I never would have been wearing the sweater Cosby gave me. (Of course, I hadn't yet been assaulted when I put on that sweater. And if I were really trying to seduce Cosby, I probably would have put on some sort of tight-fitting top instead of bulky wool. But I suppose Mesereau meant that wearing the sweater was a way of trying to tell Cosby I was romantically interested in him—which was quite a stretch.)

Mesereau's closing might have been dry, but Kathleen Bliss had already built a bonfire when she opened the closing arguments. Her incendiary remarks were filled with slander and misogynistic contempt. She began by asking the jurors to consider how unfair it was for Cosby's accusers to be "digging up stuff" from three decades ago. She acknowledged that there had been horrible crimes in the country's history, but that there had also been "horrible, horrible periods of time where emotion and hatred and fear overwhelmed us—witch hunts, lynchings, McCarthyism." And then, having lumped all of Cosby's accusers in with this kind of "mob rule" (with its intimations of racism), she began to get specific.

I was a liar, a scammer, and "not a good girl," she said. My mother was "angry" (as if that were a bad thing) and "a phony." Heidi Thomas had come forward for the fame she'd always craved. Chelan Lasha was a convicted liar, hungry for money and the talk-show circuit. Lise-Lotte Lublin, who couldn't even remember what had actually happened to her, was also after fame—she "just wanted to be part of it." Janice Baker-Kinney was a drug user who was all about "party time," and she and I had colluded at the Women's March to create our stories.

Bliss saved her most vicious remarks, however, for Janice Dickinson. She was a "failed starlet" looking to sell books and get attention. Bliss brought up details about Janice's sexual past, going so far as to say, "I mean, it sounds as though she's slept with every single man on the planet . . . Is Ms. Dickinson really the moral beacon that the women's movement wants?"

Bliss even accused Detective Reape of doing shoddy police work. And before she concluded her remarks, she made sure to reinforce a common misconception about sexual assault. Bliss invoked her former career as a prosecutor to claim that real rape victims were always consistent about the details and gave the authorities facts that could easily be checked.

I would later hear that Bliss's "blame the victim" approach had at times caused jurors to roll their eyes or even flinch.

After Bliss and Mesereau had finished their remarks, there was a short break, during which I returned to the courtroom. Even though I'd missed their performance, I could see the effect it had had on Kristen as soon as she began to speak. A blazing passion to set the record straight echoed through her words.

She started by explaining the emotional trauma I had suffered, but she quickly turned the defence's "con artist" argument on its head. The "con" in the term, she noted, refers to "confidence." The con artist works to earn his targets' confidence so that he can take advantage of them. The real confidence man, she said, was Cosby. He was the one who had created a sense of trust before abusing his victims.

Kristen then reminded jurors that in his civil deposition, Cosby had admitted to his sexual interest in me. These were hardly the words of someone who was interested in "mentoring" a young person, she pointed out. She also noted that his deposition clearly showed he understood the effects of central nervous system suppressants like Benadryl and Quaaludes. He had even admitted that he didn't like taking them himself because they made him sleepy.

But one of the most remarkable moments in the trial occurred when Kristen turned to the "utterly shameful" way Bliss had treated the five women who'd testified about their assaults. She pointed out that all five had taken responsibility for their own actions. But she said it was appalling that they had been questioned about Cosby's marital status. "How dare she [Bliss] accuse these women and say, 'Well, you knew he was married.' That's an obligation that *he* holds. That is not something that should be used to assassinate the characters of these women. They shouldn't be responsible for his sexuality."

At those words came the sound of laughter. *Bill Cosby had just laughed.* Kristen spun around towards him, pointing her finger.

"And he laughs, but there's nothing funny," she said, her voice vibrating with shock and anger. "There's nothing funny about what's going on here."

The words hit hard, crackling through the room like an electric current. And if Cosby and his lawyers had hoped his callous disrespect would be forgotten as the summations continued, they were out of luck. Kristen's visceral, heartfelt response seemed to make everybody pause and consider the real meaning of that laughter.

The rest of her closing focused largely on the other victims who had come forward in this trial; they were human beings, she stressed, with families and lives that were only going to be disrupted by their participation. She implored the jurors to think about the emotional and psychological costs these women bore when they relived their assaults, faced their abuser, and endured the harsh treatment of his lawyers. She reminded them of the privacy they had lost and the vulnerability they had accepted.

And finally, she returned to the idea that I was a con artist.

"You think a con artist is going to come in here and say, 'Yeah, I was sexually assaulted, but then I went home, showered, and went to work'? Do you think that's a con? *That's* an assault victim."

Kristen had done a brilliant job of appealing to the jury's empathy and emotional understanding of events. When Stewart began his closing remarks, he shifted direction slightly, addressing their reasoning and common sense. He started by explaining the concept of "vital interest." A defendant, he said, always has a stronger interest in the outcome of a case than anyone else, and therefore a stronger motive to be deceptive. Looked at through that lens, Cosby's admissions in the deposition from the civil suit could be seen as a way for him to acknowledge just enough guilt to look credible and yet not enough to be charged with a crime.

Stewart went on to talk about Mesereau's claim that Cosby had paid me because he had wanted to resolve an "annoyance." Why would anyone pay millions of dollars to get rid of a nuisance? Cosby hadn't paid Autumn Jackson to stop her from bothering him. He'd called the cops and had her arrested.

Next, Stewart picked apart the defence's insistence that phone records "proved" Cosby was in New York City, not Philly, when I said the assault took place. In fact, those very records showed that the short calls I'd placed to the New York number (obviously voicemails) were immediately returned from Cosby's Philly or Massachusetts number. What's more, in Cosby's deposition he himself said that my mother had first contacted him in 2005 by leaving a message with his New York answering service.

And then Stewart did something truly amazing with the thousands of pages of phone records and travel itineraries that the defence had dumped on him and the other prosecutors back in the winter—he showed the jurors that Cosby had had no business trips from January 5 to 10. He also pointed out that I had phoned Cosby's New York number on January 6. Then there were calls from that number to the Elkins Park house. Why would the answering service be calling the Cosby house if no one was there? Finally, Stewart reminded the jurors that the defence had made a big deal of my nightly phone habits. Evenings were when I'd touch base with my family and friends. The defence had argued that I'd changed the date of my assault from the night of the Chinese restaurant meal to an earlier time because I knew phone records would show I'd made a number of calls into the wee hours on that night. I clearly hadn't been passed out for eight or nine hours. But Stewart instructed the jury to look at my phone records for the night of January 6. There was a highly unusual thirteen-hour gap between that night and the next day. I had not made a single call to family and friends that evening.

I was stunned when I realized what the prosecutors and detectives had managed to do. They had taken all those documents that the defence had dumped on them before the trial and used them to pinpoint when I was assaulted. I later learned that they had confirmed the date before the second trial began but had kept quiet about it, knowing that if given the time, the defence would manufacture some new tale to try to cast doubt on it. And then in his closing remarks, Mesereau had gone through all those phone records again, insisting that the evening at Cosby's place I'd described couldn't possibly have happened in January. Listening to that, Stewart decided to pounce. And so, sitting there in the Montgomery County Courthouse at the very end of my second trial, I finally learned the date of my sexual assault: January 6, 2004.

In the aftermath of my attack, I hadn't wanted to think about that date. And so, for fourteen years I had been unsure of when exactly my life had changed forever. And now I knew. I finally knew. I was shocked at how important that felt. My truth was my power, Kristen had told me. And now I had another little piece of that truth in my grasp.

After dropping that bombshell (perhaps it was only a bombshell to me), Stewart began to take apart the remainder of the defence's narrative.

He reminded the jury of what an unreliable witness Marguerite Jackson was. And he asked why she would emerge twelve years after I had first accused Cosby and only three months before the first trial. He pointed to the words Kathleen Bliss had encouraged her to add to her second affidavit: "money is a great motivator." (Shortly after Wyatt read her statement on the courthouse steps, Jackson had started her own music production company.) Stewart also chipped away at the testimony of a number of the other defence witnesses before turning to what he called Cosby's "consciousness of guilt." He pointed out that Cosby's actions suggested he was acutely aware of the wrong he had done. The two-hour phone call with my mother. His refusal to say what drug he had given me because, as he told the police, he thought he was being recorded. (What was the problem, Stewart asked, if all he'd given me was Benadryl?) His unprompted offer to pay for my school and any counselling I needed.

The defence had suggested that I waited a year to accuse him so I could first destroy forensic evidence. But what forensic evidence would there have been, Stewart asked, since Cosby and I both agreed that we didn't have intercourse? The only real evidence would have been the pills he gave me—and he had admitted to my mother that those were still in his possession in 2005. (He'd gone up to the bathroom to look at them during their phone call.)

That's when Stewart returned to the true import of the money Cosby had paid me. The defence had introduced the settlement amount to try to suggest that money was my motive for "lying." But Stewart deftly turned that information against them. The defendant's admission about the drugs meant something, he said.

"The defendant paid over $3 million in the hopes that the district attorney's office would never hear those words," he said. "Not just about Andrea Constand in this case, but... about his general familiarity with central nervous system depressants, his signature crime. The defendant, I would suggest, knew that if anybody—be it law enforcement or someone else he had sexually assaulted—understood what he had done, what he admitted to doing, that it wouldn't just be Andrea Constand. The defendant *knew*."

The implication was clear: Why would Cosby give me more than twenty times the amount I had asked for if he wasn't buying something he felt was crucially important? He had given me and other women drugs. He *had* to keep that quiet. Stewart's words sent shivers down my spine. I could feel the presence of Bill Cosby's other victims—in the courtroom, in the country.

Stewart ended his remarks with a forceful plea to the jury. "The defendant spent years and years and years building that bank of trust and reputation," he said. "He used it every single time he sexually assaulted these women. He used it against Andrea Constand. He has attempted, through . . . individuals who speak for him, to use it with each and every one of you. The time for the defendant to escape justice is over. It is finally time for the defendant to dine at a banquet of his own consequences. It is time for each and every one of you to stand with Andrea Constand and look that man in the eye and tell him the truth about what he did. It's time for each and every one of you to find the defendant guilty."

Stewart's closing remarks had been interrupted many times by objections from the defence lawyers. It was a testament to his clear and convincing arguments and powerful oration that the frequent interruptions did not weaken the impact of his words. As Stewart walked back to his seat, I looked over at the jurors. I had glanced at those twelve people from time to time during my own days on the stand, and I had always been reassured by the openness of their expressions, the intensity of their gazes. I saw the same receptiveness throughout the prosecutors' closing arguments. Kristen and Stewart had spoken passionately and persuasively. These words were not a performance—they were real.

I couldn't know what the jurors would decide, but at that moment, with Stewart's words still floating through my mind, the outcome of the trial seemed strangely unimportant. It was as if the world had again shifted in some much more significant way. The days I had spent in court had seemed like theatre. The curtains opened in the morning and closed at the end of the day. But now the final curtain had dropped and the stage had melted away. Deception and artifice were gone. And in their place, a terrible but honest reality had appeared.

———

The next morning, Delaney, her dog Oliver, and I went down to the hotel lobby for breakfast. Warm oatmeal, toast, tea. The breakfast room wasn't crowded, but I still felt as if tension hung in the air. Every time I overheard a snippet of conversation or bit from the TV, people seemed to be talking about the Cosby case. Everyone was wondering how long the deliberations would last and what the outcome would be. I scratched Ollie behind the ears and took a deep breath. I reminded myself of Yogananda's wisdom about the danger of focusing on things you couldn't control and the risks of attaching yourself to worldly events. The jury would make its decision and life would go on. I had to be at peace with whatever happened. And yet I couldn't help feeling hopeful. No matter how hard I tried to rise above that attachment, I found myself returning to the same thought: Please let there be at least one conviction out of the three charges. That would be enough.

When Delaney and I arrived at the courthouse that morning, Erin, Turks, and his handler, Kiersten, were waiting for us in the witness lounge. The jurors were getting their instructions from the judge. By about 11:30, they were settled in the jury room to begin their deliberations.

In what seemed like a replay of the first trial, the jurors returned to the courtroom several times to ask questions of the judge. They said they wanted to hear Cosby's statement to the police again, as well as Marguerite Jackson's testimony. But their very first question was the one that particularly struck me. "What is the legal definition of consent?" they wanted to know. This was something the first jury had never asked.

Judge O'Neill's response was enlightening—and troubling. "That cannot be answered," he said. "You have the legal definitions of the crime. If that definition does not contain a definition of consent, then the jury will decide what consent means to them."

That the sexual assault laws offered no guidance on how consent might be evaluated was a strong reminder of how difficult these cases could be to prosecute. And yet the very fact that the jury had wanted to grapple with that question seemed encouraging. I felt another surge of hope that carried me through the day. By the time Delaney and I were back at the hotel late that evening, I felt sure that a verdict wasn't far off.

The next morning, Delaney, Erin, Kiersten, Turks, and I were back in the witness lounge. At about 10:30, the jurors asked to hear Jackson's testimony one more time. A few hours passed. Lunch was brought in. And then at about two o'clock, Stewart showed up in the doorway and announced that we needed to return to the courtroom. The jury had reached a verdict.

Delaney, Kristen, Kevin, Stewart, the detectives, and I all gathered outside the witness lounge. Then we started towards the courtroom. I don't really have a memory of walking down the staircase or of passing the photographers and reporters who were surely there. But there are plenty of pictures of that procession. (When I first saw a few of them, I smiled to see that I was wearing my white blazer. I had come to think of it as my lucky jacket.) I do remember seeing Sergeant Richard Schaffer standing at the entrance to the courtroom. When he noticed me, his face lit up in a big grin. Stewart was barely suppressing a smile as well. Everyone seemed to feel that the speedy decision was a good sign, and I felt myself pulsing with hope.

Once we were seated in the courtroom, Judge O'Neill asked that the jurors be brought in. He proceeded to ask them a few questions and give them some instructions. It must have taken only a few minutes, but time seemed to stretch on, the tension in the room mounting with every second that passed.

I reached out and took Delaney's hand.

And then the court clerk stood up and addressed the jury. "In the Court of Common Pleas of Montgomery County, Pennsylvania, Criminal Division, in the issue joined between the Commonwealth of Pennsylvania and the defendant, William H. Cosby, Jr., docketed at CR-3932-2016, as to Count 1, aggravated indecent assault, how say you?"

The jury foreperson was on her feet. "Guilty," she said.

I squeezed Delaney's hand, my heart thumping against my ribs.

"As to Count 2, aggravated indecent assault, how say you?"

"Guilty."

I squeezed Delaney's hand again.

"As to Count 3, aggravated indecent assault, how say you?"

"Guilty."

I could barely believe what I had heard. It was like watching three sevens come up on a slot machine.

I gave Delaney's hand one last long squeeze as the courtroom erupted in gasps and cheers and tears. Kristen, Kevin, and Stewart turned in their seats to smile at me. I could see the satisfaction and relief on their faces.

Judge O'Neill called for order.

I looked over at the defence table. Kathleen Bliss was slumped in her chair. Mesereau was stone-faced. I couldn't see the faces of any of the other lawyers at the table. They were all looking at the floor. Cosby, however, was staring straight ahead, looking grim.

As much as I wanted to bolt from my seat to hug the women around me and to call my family to let them know the remarkable news, I had to sit still for a few more minutes. The prosecutors had one more item to raise with the judge: where Cosby would be residing during the months it would take for the judge to decide on his sentence.

Kevin asked him to revoke Cosby's release on bail.

"The defence came in here from the beginning and said that $3.38 million was a paltry sum to this individual," he argued. "This is somebody who has unlimited wealth. I don't think any amount of bail can assure his presence under these circumstances." Kevin also stressed the seriousness of Cosby's crimes and the need to do a sexually violent predator assessment.

But Judge O'Neill pointed out that Cosby had not gone missing in the two and a half years since he'd been charged. What exactly were the prosecutors worried about?

"Flight," answered Kevin. "He's got a plane. We've heard all about—"

Before he could finish his sentence, Cosby had jumped to his feet. His voice rang out across the room.

"He doesn't have a plane, you *asshole*!"

The air filled with the sound of gasps and clicking computer keys.

I couldn't help feeling a small beat of satisfaction. *This* was the man I had come to know. Through two long trials he had sat quietly, speaking hardly a word, hiding behind his public persona, masking his true self. And finally, here was the real man—arrogant, entitled, unremorseful, profane.

In the end, Judge O'Neill upheld Cosby's bail agreement but demanded he wear an ankle monitor whenever he left his home.

And then the trial was over. Cosby, at long last, had been convicted for what he truly was: a rapist and a villain.

As I stood up to leave the courtroom, I looked at the sea of smiling faces that surrounded me. I'd long ago accepted that my truth was my power. And now that truth was a public truth—a truth that might give strength and courage to the other women who had raised their voices with mine, to the other people who'd had their power ripped from their lives. My heart lifted at the thought.

CHAPTER 15

GETTING IT RIGHT

After the verdict, I walked out of the courtroom with my arms around Delaney and Dolores. Kevin, Kristen, and Stewart were steps behind me. I felt as if I might burst with happiness. I knew the dismal statistics for sexual assault cases. Estimates are that in the US, only a quarter to a third of all assaults are reported to police. Less than 5 percent of all assaults result in an arrest, and only 0.5 percent end up in a guilty verdict. So against incredible odds, we had won. I had never wanted to think of these trials as contests with winners and losers, but in the end, I couldn't help feeling that way. This was the biggest fight of my life, and my team had been victorious. I almost had to pinch myself to make sure it was really happening.

In the witness lounge, it was noisy, joyous pandemonium. I tried to find a quiet corner and dialled my parents' number. My mom answered the phone.

"Did you hear the news?" I asked her.

She and my father had had CNN on all day. Her voice was ringing with happiness and relief. "I'm so proud of the jury," she said. "They finally got it right!"

Later I would see video of Lili, Therese, and others emerging from the courtroom, hugging and crying tears of elation and relief. I would have loved to join them, but once we had finished making our phone calls and thanking and congratulating each other, my happy team had to prepare for the press conference that Kevin would hold in a few minutes. Bebe was going to speak to the media on my behalf. I felt as if I had already said every-thing I wanted to say. I was ready to recede from public view.

The night of the verdict, I headed to the hotel bar after dinner for a nightcap. I spotted a number of Cosby victims who had been in the court-room, including Sunni Welles, Chelan Lasha, and Lise-Lotte Lublin. The women were surrounded by family and friends. Everyone was in high spir-its. We ended up outside, in the hotel courtyard, circled around a blazing firepit. We laughed and sang and occasionally broke out into giddy chants of "Guilty, guilty, guilty!" Our raucous celebration continued well after the bar shut down. Finally, not many hours before the sun would come up, we drifted back to our own rooms, happy but spent.

As I lay between the crisp, cool sheets that night, I found myself bliss-fully unable to fall asleep. Uncle Salvo's leaflet was propped up on the night table, the little medallion beside it. He'd never had a shot at justice. His utterly selfless act saved others, but his murder was never addressed. I had always tried to follow his example by thinking of my duties to others, by fighting for what was right, but I had been blessed to see justice deliv-ered where he had not. It almost felt as if achieving this bit of justice was a small way of honouring Salvo's sacrifice.

As I stretched out, my phone vibrated steadily. I tweeted out my thanks to the jury members, and then began responding to all the texts and mes-sages that were pouring in. Those notes of congratulation and celebration continued to arrive even after I had returned to Toronto, and as they did, I had time to reflect on what our legal victory might mean for others.

It was certainly a vindication for many. An emotional and psychological one, to be sure—a sign of hope for other sexual assault cases. (Kevin had talked movingly about this when we were together in the witness lounge after the verdict.) And it certainly seemed to suggest that the changes set in motion by the #MeToo movement might continue their forward momen-tum. But I knew it might also have some more immediate ramifications for some of Cosby's other victims. He was still embroiled in a number of defamation lawsuits. When his accusers had gone public with their stories, Cosby's team went on the offensive, slandering many of the women in the process. Janice Dickinson and three others had filed individual defamation suits, while Tamara Green, Therese Serignese, Linda Joy Traitz, Barbara Bowman, Joan Tarshis, Angela Leslie, and Louisa Moritz filed a joint suit. (Strangely, Cosby was trying to make the provider of his homeowner's insurance pay the legal fees for many of these lawsuits, which would turn into its own legal battle.) A few of these cases had already been dismissed, but I suspected that Cosby's conviction would help those whose cases were ongoing. (Indeed, in April 2019, he settled the group suit, and the following month, he dropped his countersuit against those seven women. And then in July 2019, Cosby's insurance company settled Janice Dickinson's suit without his approval.)

In the days after my return home, I made sure to connect with the two wonderful women who had come into my life in the past few years: Barbara Bowman and Donna Motsinger. They were both overjoyed by the verdict. Barb found it almost too much to believe. Donna didn't miss the opportunity to make a case, once again, for romance. "Now you can put it all behind you," she said, "and find a girlfriend."

I knew that many of the people in the Facebook group were posting about the verdict, but I didn't check the site regularly. A number of the Cosby victims, including Victoria Valentino and Lili Bernard, went on news shows to talk about what the verdict meant to them. And four of the "prior bad act" witnesses—Heidi, Chelan, Lise-Lotte, and Janice Baker-Kinney—met up in New York City for a celebratory dinner. But I chose not to do any media or public appearances. What I wanted more than anything was to be at home, return to work, walk my dogs, bike in the country, have family dinners again—just dive back into my life.

And despite all the celebrations, I knew that this chapter would not truly be closed until Cosby was in jail. I did feel safer knowing that he was now a convicted sex offender and his name would be added to the state registry. Also, he was under house arrest while awaiting sentencing, which wouldn't happen for months. The chances of him assaulting anyone in that time weren't high. He was older and frailer and had poorer vision than when I knew him. His method, however, was never to wrestle a woman into submission. He'd simply get her to ingest something and let the drugs do the rest. Still, I truly believed the only thing that would render him unable to prey on women was incarceration. But we would have to wait five months to see if that would happen.

In the meantime, my mother, father, sister, and I were invited to write victim impact statements for Judge O'Neill to consider when making his sentencing decision. That seemed like a fairly straightforward task—until, that is, I sat down to write.

When I woke up in the very early morning of January 7, 2004, I didn't know where I was. It seemed like a strange and foreign place, a strange and foreign world.

I looked about me. I realized that I was at Bill Cosby's house. I was on his couch. My bra was up around my neck. My pants were undone, my blouse twisted around my torso. I felt weak and fuzzy as I pulled myself to sitting. Unsteadily, I dragged my bra down and zipped up my pants.

When I got up and moved into the hallway, he was standing there. Offering breakfast. A blueberry muffin and tea. A perfectly normal breakfast. I sipped the tea. I was thirsty.

I needed to go home. I had to take a shower, brush my teeth, get ready for work. An ordinary day ahead of me. I would eat the muffin in the car. Save time. I wrapped it carefully in a paper napkin.

I said goodbye to the man in the bathrobe. Left the house, got in my car. I drove home. I cleaned up, put on my work clothes. Just my ordinary routine. Just an ordinary day.

But it wasn't. I had fallen asleep in one world and woken up in another. Everything looked the same, but nothing was. *I* wasn't. It would take me a full year to admit that, to accept it. That's what I was thinking about as I sat in front of my computer, trying to write my victim impact statement.

Over the past fourteen years I had recounted my history with Cosby to the authorities many times. In all those years, I'd never really described in detail how I had changed after that night. Or what exactly Cosby had taken from me. And so I struggled to put those thoughts on paper.

My former girlfriend Kristin offered to help me. It was a lovely gesture, a bittersweet way of reconnecting, and a reminder that she remained my loving and sensitive friend. Our relationship was one of the many things that had been damaged by Cosby's attack. And it wasn't the only one I'd lost. Sheri and I had parted in 2005, shortly after I told my mother what had happened. I hadn't told Sheri about the rape until that moment, and she was devastated that I had kept it from her for an entire year. I tried to explain that I'd been living in denial, hoping to forget everything, but Sheri felt my inability to share my pain was a sort of betrayal—or at least an indication that our relationship was not as strong as we had thought. We would try to get back together a number of times over the years, but my past was like a pile of rubble that always put distance between us in some impassable way. My conversations with Kristin about what I wanted to say to the judge were invaluable. She was able to draw my feelings from me and has a way with words. But those conversations also brought to mind all the losses.

In my statement, I tried to capture, just as I have in this book, what a blessed life I had led before the assault. I tried to convey the extraordinarily loving family who had supported me in everything I did. I talked about the great fortune I had with basketball and with the job I enjoyed so much at Temple.

And then I wrote of the trauma I'd experienced during the assault and throughout the long legal process that followed. Among other things, I described how agonizing it was to sit across from Cosby during the civil litigation. To see him smirking as I was forced to recount what he had done to me. To watch him make jokes and chuckle as his lawyers sneered and belittled me. To hear him offer his version of events—with me and other women—smugly, unapologetically recounting his sexual exploits.

As I wrote of those things in my statement, I made a decision. Bill Cosby had been victimizing me for fourteen years. For the two criminal trials, I'd had to make myself vulnerable once more, had to let him witness my pain. But I simply wasn't going to let him into my life that way again. I would give my statement to the judge, but I wouldn't read it aloud in court, where Cosby would be sitting in front of me, watching and listening.

On a chilly, wet day in late September 2018, Mom, Dad, Diana, and I drove once more to Pennsylvania and checked into the hotel in King of Prussia. As we headed out to the first day of the sentencing hearing, I felt a small tremor of anxiousness. The hearing would be a two-day process. It would begin with the testimony of a clinical psychologist who had been assigned to assess Cosby and recommend whether he should be designated a sexually violent predator. Then our victim impact statements would be presented, and the prosecutors and defence attorneys would make their arguments about sentencing.

We knew that the Pennsylvania sentencing guidelines for a single count of aggravated indecent assault was a minimum of three years and a maximum of ten in a state correctional facility. Cosby had been convicted of three counts, and if the sentences were applied consecutively, he could face thirty years behind bars. But I had been told this scenario was extremely unlikely—his sentences would almost certainly be served concurrently. But even three to ten years in jail was not guaranteed. There were a variety of ways to apply the sentencing guidelines. We couldn't know if Cosby would be sent to a state penitentiary or get a slap on the wrist—like a few years of house arrest. During his five months out on bail after the verdict, Cosby had celebrated his eighty-first birthday with a number of friends at his home. Apparently, a five-piece jazz band was hired for the occasion—their playing got so loud that the police paid a visit after receiving a noise complaint. Cosby would always be a convicted sex offender, but that wouldn't stop him living the high life, even if confined to one of his palatial homes. That would be hard for so many of his victims to bear. Kevin intended to argue for five to ten years in a state facility.

On Monday, September 24, 2018, my family and I, Dolores and Bebe, about eight or nine of Cosby's other victims, and a crowd of spectators and reporters gathered in the courtroom to hear the testimony of Dr. Kristen F. Dudley, who had led the Pennsylvania Sexual Offenders Assessment Board study of Bill Cosby. Cosby was there too, of course, flanked by his public relations man, Andrew Wyatt, and his new lawyer, Joseph P. Green, Jr. (He'd fired Mesereau and the rest of his legal team immediately after the guilty verdict came down.)

Cosby had declined to be interviewed for the assessment, so Dr. Dudley had had to rely on his deposition, his police statements, and the trial transcripts to reach her conclusions. For someone to be designated a sexually violent predator, that person has to have exhibited predatory behaviour and have a mental abnormality or personality disorder that makes him highly likely to reoffend. Dr. Dudley explained in detail the factors that went into determining both of those things. She concluded—indeed, she was adamant—that Cosby's behaviour *was* predatory, and that he displayed an interest in or obsession with unusual sexual practices (in his case, sex with non-consenting women).

The defence tried to call her diagnosis into question during the cross-examination, but Dr. Dudley remained firm: Bill Cosby met the criteria to be designated a sexually violent predator. Now it was up to the judge to decide whether to apply that designation or not.

Once Dr. Dudley had finished her testimony, it was time for the victim impact statements to be presented. Although I wasn't going to read mine, I was still called to the stand to see if I had anything else to add. Once in front of the court, I said, "Your Honour, I have testified. I have given you my victim impact statement. The jury heard me. Mr. Cosby heard me. And now all I am asking for is justice as the court sees fit. Thank you." And then I returned to my seat and my mother took my place. Her first words brought a lump to my throat.

"In my life, I have suffered some major traumatic events," she said. "One [is] the loss of my father when I was fourteen years old, and the other is the drugging and sexual assault that my daughter Andrea endured in 2004 by Bill Cosby." My mother described the pain she'd experienced, knowing what had happened to me and seeing me suffer. She also talked about the stress caused by the media harassment, and by being named in the breach-of-confidentiality lawsuit Cosby had filed against me and my lawyers in 2015. She talked about the effect all that tension had on her health—she'd recently been diagnosed with four brain aneurysms and Parkinson's disease. And she talked about the consequences that had come from the disclosure of the value of my civil settlement: some of her friends and family assumed that she and my father had benefited financially and had begun to treat them differently. But what struck me most keenly was when she told the court that Cosby's lawyers had insisted that she and my father sign the non-disclosure agreement in my civil settlement—effectively silencing her voice. She could not share her pain with her friends or family, or even with a therapist, although she would have loved to seek professional help. She also talked about how the stress of those first few years had forced her to quit a job she loved (and cost her a pension), as she had no way to explain to her co-workers why her behaviour had changed so much. I was reminded of how isolating this whole experience had been for my parents.

When my mother was done, it was my father's turn. My heart ached watching him take his seat in front of the crowded courtroom. For a man who had such a hard time expressing his emotions, I knew this was an act of great bravery and love.

He began by talking of that fatherly love, saying, "We live and breathe Andrea's discomforts every day." He also talked about his inability to sleep—an affliction he had only been able to address with a prescription for anti-anxiety medication—and the toll the trauma had taken on his concentration and mental health.

He ended his statement movingly: "We support every aspect of her life and encourage her to try and move into a safer space mentally and physically . . . Thank you to all who have supported and believed in my daughter Andrea. I hope the future will brighten for her and relieve her and our family of some of our anxieties."

When my sister read her statement to the courtroom, I smiled at her descriptions of what I was like as a young person and how close we had always been. But then she described how shocked and disappointed she was to see the version of me that came back from Philly. The fun-loving, laid-back, spirited sister she had been so looking forward to spending time with seemed to have disappeared. Instead, she found me "frail, timid, nervous, weak, and reclusive."

Nothing of what my mother, father, and sister said in their statements came as a surprise to me. And yet their words made me reflect on how much Cosby had cost my whole family. My parents had spent years in pain—years they would never get back. And while my father so movingly expressed his hopes for my future, I knew that his own recovery from the emotional and psychological damage might take more years than he actually had left. I could see the diminished vitality in both of my parents, but my father had lost his wonderful sense of humour as well. I wasn't sure he'd ever get it back, despite my prayers to Salvo to restore my family's well-being.

Cosby's lawyer, Joseph Green, addressed the court next. He implored Judge O'Neill to ignore all the advocacy and "noise" surrounding the case when making his sentencing recommendation. And he noted that Cosby would be seeking an appeal of his conviction. Then he made his argument for why Cosby shouldn't be sentenced within the standard guidelines of three to ten years. He recounted Cosby's difficult childhood, his military service, his desire to become a teacher, his undergraduate and graduate degrees, his change of career paths. All impressive. All beside the point, I thought to myself.

Green detailed Cosby's poor health. And he stressed that the "misconduct," as he called it, took place primarily in the eighties (referring, I suppose, to the admissions Cosby had made in his deposition). Green also asserted that I had asked for and been given the multi-million-dollar settlement. Even at this point, the defence was implying that I had been after Cosby's money.

In his sentencing memorandum, Kevin had apparently discussed Cosby's outburst at the end of the verdict. "He doesn't have a plane, you asshole." Now Green tried to explain how Cosby's frustration at what he saw as Kevin's political use of his case in the DA election led to that reaction.

When Kevin got up to address the court, he made a powerfully persuasive case for a sentence of maximum confinement. He began by underlining Cosby's utter lack of remorse, noting that he "seemingly doesn't think he's done anything wrong." He reminded the judge of the predatory nature of the attack—the mentorship, the planning, the building and betrayal of trust. And he pointed out the absurdity of Green's argument that Cosby "should get a pass because it's taken this long to catch up to what he's done."

Kevin's final point sent a chill down my spine: house arrest was simply not appropriate, he said, for a man who had used drugs to render his victims helpless. Cosby wasn't too old or too feeble to do to someone else what he had done to me—if he was given the opportunity. And house arrest would almost certainly give him some opportunity.

It was the middle of the afternoon when the court was finally dismissed. It was not as long a day as many I'd spent in the Montgomery County Courthouse, but it was so filled with emotion and anticipation that in some ways it felt like a lifetime.

Listening to my family's victim impact statements was tough, but there had also been profound moments of connection. During one of the breaks, Nicole Weisensee Egan, the reporter who had doggedly covered the Cosby allegations since 2005 (first for the *Philadelphia Daily News* and later for *People* magazine), approached me. I recognized her from both trials— we had occasionally made eye contact and said our silent hellos during those days.

"It's been a long time," I said to her.

She smiled and nodded. And then she asked, "Have you ever met Tamara Green?"

I hadn't, but of course I knew her. Tamara was the very first woman to go public when I tried to get criminal charges laid in 2005. After Bruce Castor, the Montgomery County DA, announced there would be no charges, Cosby did that interview with the *National Enquirer*. In it, he had complained about Tamara Green's story intensifying the scandal that my allegations had started. "My problem is with some media," he grumbled, "and how it appeared that Miss Green was allowed to be a 'wrecking ball.'"

Tamara Green was brave, outspoken, feisty—and I had always thought she should be proud of Cosby's attempted slur. She might indeed be a "wrecking ball," but the best kind of wrecking ball—one that destroys a broken and dangerous structure. She eventually became one of the twelve Jane Doe witnesses in my civil trial, and I was overjoyed to finally have an opportunity to thank her for everything she had done.

Nicki called Tamara over, and we immediately flew into each other's arms. When we let go, I said, "You've been in my life for some time. It's nice to finally meet you."

We stood there for what seemed like a long while, looking into each other's eyes, both lost in our thoughts. Tamara had been my own personal #MeToo movement back in 2005—the first person to stand beside me and give me strength. I was suddenly aware of the bracelet on my wrist. A band of smooth jade beads. A string of little green "balls." I pulled the bracelet over my hand and put it into Tamara's. "This is meant for you," I said. "Because you are the wrecking ball."

I told her that jade brings its wearer peace, friendship, and luck. I wished all of those things and more for her. She slipped the bracelet on immediately and smiled.

The second day of the sentencing hearing began with another short cross-examination of Dr. Dudley by Cosby's lawyer, followed by the defence's own expert witness, who supported Green's argument that Cosby was too old and infirm to be a threat. After his testimony, Stewart made the Commonwealth's argument that Cosby should be designated a sexually violent predator.

The judge then declared a short recess while he considered all the evidence and arguments, and announced that he would return shortly with his decision about Cosby's status—and his sentence.

When we gathered back about fifteen minutes later, Judge O'Neill began to speak. His words were raspy, and he apologized about losing his voice. Then he announced that the Commonwealth had made a clear and convincing case that Cosby should be given the sexually violent predator status. The judge was designating him as such, as well as placing him on the lifetime sexual offender registry.

All around me, I could hear people releasing their long-held breaths. It was a sound of satisfaction. Bebe turned to me and smiled. "This is good news!" she whispered.

Judge O'Neill reminded Cosby of his right to speak, or allocute, but he declined. Stewart then addressed Cosby directly, outlining what being on the registry would mean once he was released, including the fact that he would be required to keep the Pennsylvania State Police informed about his residences and his work status. Cosby stared at him intently the whole time Stewart was talking. It looked like he was fuming. After several minutes, he had a question. He wanted to know if he would have to inform the state if he was staying in another city for a single night.

I wondered if he was already planning his comeback tour.

Green then launched back into his arguments that Cosby should serve his time under house arrest, with Kevin giving his rebuttals. Next, Judge O'Neill carefully walked Cosby through his post-sentencing rights. By 12:15, it was time for a break. We would not hear the sentencing decision until after lunch.

While we waited for court to resume, I tried to centre myself and remind myself that no matter what the judge decided, I would have to accept it with equanimity and peace. I needed to find the stillness within me and to trust in God. But I was more than ready to head back into the courtroom an hour and a half later.

Judge O'Neill began his remarks by going through the various sentencing options available to him. "I have concluded," he said, "that probation, partial confinement, [or] county intermediate confinement is simply not appropriate." He was ordering total confinement in a state facility. I sighed with relief. Now we just had to see if the judge was going to make Cosby serve at least the minimum recommended term.

Judge O'Neill carefully outlined the factors he'd considered when coming to his sentencing decision: the seriousness of the crime, the impact on the victim, and the likelihood of reoffending. "[The] evidence is overwhelming that it was planned predation, a planned assault—the giving of the pills, the unconsciousness or the unawareness, the lack of consent," he noted. "Your own words in your deposition testimony made it clear to the fact finder that in your own mind, you had no verbal consent. You heard no verbal consent. You claimed her silence was consent. That is not the law. The jury found that she was silent because she was unaware or unconscious because of the intoxicant you gave her. Your version of consent was implicitly rejected by the jury. That is what underscores just how serious this crime is."

Judge O'Neill then explained that he had opted for total confinement precisely because he believed it was likely that Cosby would offend again if given the chance. And he noted that equal justice under the law required him to treat Cosby no differently than he would any other convicted sexual assaulter. I'm sure I was not alone in feeling that those words would have a strong impact on the victims of powerful men like Harvey Weinstein.

Judge O'Neill was not, however, without compassion for the convicted man who sat before him. He quoted a fellow judge who had referred to the Old Testament in another sentencing decision: "'Fallen angels suffered most from the torture of their fall from glory and plummet from grace, beset with the constant and unyielding knowledge of abandoned magnificence, and consumed with the certainty that what was once can no longer be. And of course, the higher the ascent, the sharper the fall. The more precious the gift, the more shameful its loss.' I recognize that impact upon you, Mr. Cosby. And I am sorry for that."

And then the judge offered his empathy to me and my family. He talked about my victim impact statement, saying, "It was nothing short of powerful . . . [It] puts meaning behind the true gravity of the offence."

Judge O'Neill described some of the things that most greatly affected him: "The person she was before, confident in the life ahead of her, the nightmare of the assault, the traumatic aftermath, the shame, the self-doubt, the confusion, the alienation from family and friends, feeling alone, unable to trust, pain, anguish, nightmares, consumption of guilt . . . Mr. Cosby, you took her beautiful, healthy, young spirit and crushed it."

The judge then looked directly at me. "I don't know whether the defendant read your statement. I did. I heard the very clear impact on your life."

Just then, one of the chandeliers began to flicker. The judge and I both raised our eyes to the ceiling at the same time. When Judge O'Neill looked back down, he continued to talk about the devastating impact Cosby's crime had had on my "extraordinary" family.

I was hanging on every word he said, comforted by his understanding, eager to hear his decision. But later, when I had a little time to think about that moment in the courtroom, I would see the flickering light as a kind of sign. It was as if the very human and genuine connection the judge had made to me and my story—his acceptance of my truth—had sent a little volt of electricity through the room. And it had run through me, too. A small burst of spiritual power that was going to light my path forward and ignite my new life and my healing.

And then, finally, Judge O'Neill said, "Thirty-four months. Thirty-four long months since this criminal complaint was brought. It is time for justice in a court of law. Mr. Cosby, this is all circled back to you. The day has come; the time has come."

I held my breath. I suspect everyone around me did the same. The moment had come.

"It is the sentence of this court, based upon the reasons set forth, that you be sentenced to not less than three years nor more than ten years in such state correctional institution as shall be designated by the Deputy Commissioner for Programs, Department of Corrections, and sent to the state correctional institution at Phoenix forthwith for this purpose."

There was a wave of murmurs from those gathered in the spectator area. The judge had not reduced the years from the guideline range.

Cosby would be eligible for parole in three years, but only if he admitted guilt and could prove to the parole board that he was remorseful and had done psychological work to avoid reoffending. That seemed an unlikely scenario.

I turned to the women who were sitting behind me: Lise-Lotte Lublin, Janice Dickinson, Stacey Pinkerton, and Chelan Lasha. (Lili Bernard, Therese Serignese, and Victoria Valentino were a few rows back.) Lise-Lotte was the closest. We reached out and embraced. I could see that some of the women were in tears. Cosby appeared to be unmoved. Of course, it was too much to hope that his lawyers would let us finish the case here. Instead, they asked for Cosby's bail to be extended until his transfer to prison. The judge denied that. Then, incredibly, Green went for a Hail Mary—he suggested that the tape recording my mother had made of her second phone conversation with Cosby was "inauthentic." He wanted the judge to read a report they had commissioned by an audio expert, in the hopes that Cosby's sentence would be postponed and he could remain out on bail while they put in a motion for an appeal based on this new "evidence." Kevin Steele called the request nonsense and said he had prepared a legal memorandum for the judge in anticipation of just such a manoeuvre from the defence. The judge took the document and left the courtroom for a few minutes so that he could look it over.

While the judge was in his chambers, I noticed that Cosby's spokesman, Andrew Wyatt, was looking over his shoulder, glaring at me. I refused to look away and stared back at him for a good twenty seconds or longer. I hoped that my expression conveyed my thoughts. I wasn't ashamed. It was time to put the shame back where it belonged, back on the man who had behaved shamefully—and all the people who had helped him.

When Wyatt turned away, I could see him chatting with Cosby and Green. Cosby was chuckling while removing his jacket and tie and rolling up his white shirtsleeves. The court had not yet been adjourned, but it seemed as if he was preparing himself for handcuffs. It was a surreal picture. The man who had smirked and smiled all through the trial—who had been smiling even through the sentencing hearing—appeared to be merrily preparing for his new life as a prisoner. And yet I knew that even though the trials had often felt like elaborate performances, the theatrics had concluded with the guilty verdict. This was just Cosby's short encore appearance. No matter how many efforts his lawyers made in the future, no matter how many scenes they staged, this moment was Cosby's last bow. He would now disappear behind the curtain. I was grateful.

Cosby's final moments in court elicited other reactions, too. I noticed that Janice Dickinson, who was now sitting quite close to me, seemed to have caught Cosby's eye. She burst out laughing. "Who's laughing now?" she said. A court officer scurried over to tell her that if she did that again, he'd have to ask her to leave.

When Judge O'Neill returned, he invited Cosby and his lawyers to partake of their right to appeal the verdict, but he refused to postpone Cosby's incarceration. The defence had managed to delay his removal by an hour or so. But by about 2:45 p.m., it was over. The judge asked us to leave the courtroom while Cosby was readied for his transport from the courthouse. We were not going to be allowed to watch the handcuffs be put on him. A few minutes later, Bill Cosby was led out of the courtroom with police officers on either side and his cane held between his shackled hands. His progress was captured by dozens of photographers. I, however, would not see this happen. Nor would I see Lili, Victoria, Therese, and the others as they stood in the hallway watching this long-awaited spectacle. I wouldn't see Cosby survivor Sunni Welles and sexual assault advocate Bird Milliken doing a celebratory dance in the rain outside the courthouse to Van Morrison's "Gloria." And I'd not hear Gloria Allred's address to the media as she stood under an umbrella with Chelan, Lise-Lotte, and others, talking about the significance of Cosby's sentence. Yet I'm not sorry about missing any of that.

As I had prepared to leave the court for the last time, Detective Jim Reape approached me. "There are a few people who'd like to meet you," he said.

Jim led me into a small room down the hall from the courtroom. There, six or seven of the jurors—including the foreperson, Cheryl Carmel—were waiting for me. When I walked through the doorway and saw those men and women who had listened to my story almost six months earlier, I was overwhelmed with emotion. I started to cry. One by one, they came up to me and introduced themselves. As we hugged, I heard the same words over and over: "We always believed you, Andrea."

Of course their verdict told me they had come to the conclusion that my testimony was credible. But there was something about hearing the words "We *always* believed you" that knocked the wind out of me.

During the trial, when Kristen had asked why I was there—in the court-room, at the centre of a criminal case—I had said, "For justice." That was true. I had wanted to see Cosby held to account for all the pain and dam-age he had wrought. But the jurors' words made me realize something else. While I had cooperated with the DAs because it was the right thing to do, what I wanted more than anything was to be *believed*. I think this is what every one of us needs—sexual abuse survivors, certainly, but also all those whose reality is not recognized or understood by others. When our truth is denied by people around us, it creates a wound that can be as grievous as any trauma. Making sure that abusers can't continue to abuse is, of course, of the utmost importance for the safety of individuals and the good of soci-ety. But for those of us who have already been victimized or marginalized, our bruises can never fully heal until our truths are accepted and believed by friends and strangers alike. In delivering their verdict, the jurors had given me the gift of seeing justice delivered. In sharing their feelings with me in person, they were giving me an even greater gift.

That evening, my family and I joined Dolores, Bebe, and Tamara Green for dinner at the Capital Grille. The food was excellent; the wine flowed. Tamara entertained us with stories about her trip to attend the sentenc-ing—a trip that had started out in an RV, driving along the interstate from her Southern California home, and ended up with the broken camper van abandoned in rural Tennessee and Tamara on a plane to Philadelphia. We talked about the extraordinary verdict and sentencing, but we also shared completely unrelated stories about our lives—and our plans for the future.

We joked and laughed and enjoyed each other's company, our effervescence and joy heightened by the feeling that we had come through something difficult and life-changing together. Our experience, while it began in a painful and troubling place, had brought us all a measure of hope for the future and a renewed faith in people's ability to see the truth and bring about justice. It had proven that while the struggle between darkness and light is the very essence of our lives, if we stand up for what is right and support each other, we can brush away some of the shadow and help the sun shine a bit more brightly in our small corners of the world.

COMING HOME

On a day in mid-April, about a year after the second trial had ended, I once again found myself in a crowded public space surrounded by people. But this time, there was no tension or anxiety in the air. Instead, the large convention room was humming with a sense of joy and celebration. I was there to join about forty other Self-Realization Fellowship members who, like me, were being initiated into Kriya yoga.

The impersonality of the convention room had been softened with large bouquets of flowers and pictures of Jesus Christ, Paramahansa Yogananda, and other Kriya yogis. Friends and family of the initiates were filling the stands on each side of the room. I moved into the sea of smiling, happy faces and took one of the chairs that was lined up in front of the flower-strewn stage. I had been practising Kriya yoga for ten years, and this rite of passage marked a new stage in my mastery of its meditation techniques, my alignment with my guru, and my spiritual union with God.

When the ceremony started, we went one by one up to the stage. There we were blessed by a Kriya monk, said a prayer, and delivered a piece of fruit and a flower to a sacred bowl that stood on the platform. Then each initiate was taught the most sacred of meditation techniques. We were now committed to mastering this technique over our lifetimes.

Once we had returned to our chairs, the Kriya monks moved among us on the auditorium floor, gently tossing flower petals over our heads. We rose to collect those that had fallen around us to take home to our own sacred altars. The flower petals represented the many blessings we'd been given.

It was a day of deep bliss and profound meaning for me. The ceremony honoured my growing spiritual unity with God and my journey into myself. And it was the perfect way to mark my movement forward.

I knew that I had to turn my focus inward once the sentencing was behind me. The drama had restarted with the Buress video, and then the two trials had again traumatized me. For four years I had worked hard to keep myself emotionally and spiritually afloat. But I was treading water all the time; even my most strenuous efforts simply prevented me from sinking. Now I needed to work on true inner liberation, to rewrite my destiny. I asked God and Salvo once more to light the way. I was looking forward to looking forward.

When the civil suit concluded, I had tried to put Cosby and the past behind me. I'd tried to forget about all of it. Now I knew that wasn't the way to become the person I was meant to be. Moving forward meant putting the pain behind me but embracing—and building on—all the good that had come out of my experience. It's tempting to say that everything I went through made me stronger. But it's impossible to imagine the person I might have been if my life's path had been different. Yet I've certainly learned about my strengths and my own character. I've developed a greater capacity for compassion and forgiveness. I've learned that when faced with difficult decisions in life, it's important to do the right thing, no matter how frightening. It's in uncomfortable moments that true growth happens. If we don't walk through storms, we will never escape them. We will never heal. Perhaps most importantly, I now know that peace and comfort never come from an external event, like a trial or a verdict. If we want to heal ourselves, we must look inside. And I've come to know the importance of finding our purpose in life. To have purpose and to follow that purpose is a great gift.

Once I returned from the sentencing, I threw myself back into my massage therapy work. As I wrote in my victim impact statement, "I like knowing that I can help relieve pain and suffering in others. I know that it helps heal me too." And I've found new ways to continue working for others. There are a number of legal initiatives that have gained momentum because of the Cosby trial and the cases of other serial sexual assaulters, like Harvey Weinstein. I've tried to support these efforts in any way I can.

One area of law that is being addressed is the statute of limitations for sexual assaults. In the United States there is no statute of limitations for murder, and yet forty states still have some time limit on prosecuting felony sex crimes (anywhere from ten to twenty-one years). In the early 2000s, after the revelations about the sexual abuse of children by Catholic clergy, twenty-nine states extended the statute of limitations in cases of child sexual assault, and fifteen eliminated the time restriction completely. Lawmakers had finally recognized that victims often don't come forward until well into their adult lives. But as Dr. Ziv so effectively explained, delayed reporting is extremely common for adult sexual assault victims as well. The Cosby case was a great illustration of that. Of the more than sixty known victims, only a few spoke of their assaults to anyone other than family and close friends before 2005. And those who did were ignored by those they spoke with. (Joan Tarshis told a reporter of her assault in the early eighties, but he chose not to write about it. In 1996, Victoria Valentino gave a videotaped interview about her assault for an article in *Playboy* magazine about the lives of models, but that story was never published. Janice Dickinson tried to tell of her assault in her memoir but was stopped for legal reasons. And yet another victim, Lachele Covington, reported her 2000 encounter with Cosby to the NYC police at the time, but no charges were laid.) As a result of statute-of-limitations laws, out of sixty-plus accusers, I was one of the very few whose case could actually be prosecuted.

Eliminating all statutes of limitations for sexual assault won't help these Cosby victims—when states get rid of the restrictions, crimes that have already passed the limitation period don't become eligible for prosecution. Yet the Cosby and Weinstein cases showed the world the extraordinary number of victims that can result when the legal system is unable to go after sexual assaulters because of delayed reporting. And a number of Cosby survivors have been at the forefront of the movement to extend or abolish the statute of limitations. In 2016, Beth Ferrier, who was one of my Jane Doe witnesses in 2005, and Heidi Thomas, who testified at my second trial, successfully lobbied to have Colorado's statute extended from ten years to twenty. Chelsea Byers, the executive director of the Campaign to Abolish Statutes of Limitations on Rape and Sexual Assault in Los Angeles, was one of several people trying to draw attention to the issue by protesting outside the courthouse during my second trial. Another was statute-of-limitations activist Bird Milliken, who, with Byers, presented Pennsylvania lawmakers with a petition signed by ninety thousand people demanding that the state extend its statute. And the work continues.

Cosby's trial also provided some fuel for those activists working to create legal definitions of consent. Joyce Short, a former trader and business executive and the founder of the Consent Awareness Network, is lobbying to have all states introduce a legal definition of consent for sexual assault crimes. As Joyce has written, "Codifying a legal definition for consent helps society clearly understand what constitutes the crime of sexual assault and enables our judicial system to hold sexual predators accountable by law." At present, however, only 24 percent of American sexual assault penal codes provide any sort of guidelines to determine whether consent has taken place. Jurors are left to make those often challenging determinations themselves. (Canada's Criminal Code does include a definition of consent to sexual activity.) Joyce invited me to act as a sponsor for her proposed amendment to Pennsylvania's Crimes and Offenses legislation that would introduce the following definition: "Consent is freely given, knowledgeable and informed agreement obtained without the use of force, duress, coercion, deception, fraud, concealment, or artifice."

One of the profoundly comforting things about the Cosby case is that it has contributed to changes in prosecutorial practice. Kevin Steele's inspired decision to put Dr. Ziv on the stand early in my second trial has other prosecutors rethinking how they can best use sexual assault expert witnesses. In Harvey Weinstein's January 2020 trial, the New York City prosecutors put actor Annabella Sciorra on as their first witness. She was followed by two others who corroborated her testimony. And then, on the third day of the trial, Dr. Ziv did the same thing for the Weinstein jury that she had for the Cosby jury. The five remaining sexual assault victims in Weinstein's case testified *after* Dr. Ziv. Weinstein was ultimately convicted of one count of criminal sexual act in the first degree and one count of rape in the third degree.

Unfortunately, other legal efforts are not as inspiring or hopeful for sexual assault survivors. On Tuesday, June 23, 2020, the Pennsylvania Supreme Court granted Cosby the right to appeal two issues in the second trial. His lawyers argued that the portions of his civil depositions in which he discussed giving women Quaaludes shouldn't have been admitted into testimony since Cosby had spoken freely only because he thought Bruce Castor had offered him an immunity deal. The defence also argued that the five "prior bad act" witnesses should not have been allowed as their stories were too old and too different from my own.

After that ruling, Cosby's public relations team returned to the idea that the charges against him grew out systemic racism. Referring to the spring 2020 protests against police shootings and brutality, Andrew Wyatt said, "America and the world is witnessing the twenty-third day of protests regarding the abuse and murder of Black people, not just at the hands of corrupt police officers; but these extremely vital and important protests are exposing the corruption that lies within the criminal justice system . . . As we have all stated, the false conviction of Bill Cosby is so much bigger than him—it's about the destruction of ALL Black people and people of color in America."

Cosby's appeal was heard on December 1, 2020. If it's successful, his conviction could be overturned.

———

I try not to think about the prospect of another trial. Instead, I focus on being still, staying in the moment, and leaving the future in the hands of the universe. If there is a time when I have to make a decision, I will pray and meditate. I will let God and Uncle Salvo guide me. In the meantime, I maintain my belief in the justice system. No matter what happens, I am certain in every fibre of my being that the jurors got it right that second time.

Throughout the two trials, both lead defence lawyers, McMonagle and Mesereau, said that the jurors had a man's life in their hands. Both made references to Cosby's poor health, his blindness, his advanced age. I suppose they would argue that they were trying to remind the jurors of the importance of their decision. But really, what role did Cosby's health have in the insistence that the jurors could convict only if they felt certainty "beyond a reasonable doubt"? No, McMonagle and Mesereau weren't simply asking the jury members to do their duty. They were asking for mercy. *A man's life is on the line.*

When I think of those words now, I'm struck by everything they leave out. Because it wasn't just one life that was on the line—it was over sixty. Sixty-plus women that we know of—and probably many more as well—had unwittingly found themselves in peril. Bill Cosby put them there. Then, in his dressing room or at a club or in their own homes, Bill Cosby acted as judge and jury to decide what their future would hold. He decided how their lives would be forever shaped. And there can be no doubt about this— Bill Cosby showed no mercy.

I don't wish suffering on Cosby. I am not someone who hopes to see him die in his prison cell. I work hard to find space in my heart for forgiveness and to release any bitterness that might creep in from time to time. And yet in the brief moments when I now think about him, I'm amazed by the way he has responded to the guilty verdict. In a November 2019 phone interview with Black Press USA, he said, "When I come up for parole, they're not going to hear me say that I have remorse." But if he admitted guilt, participated in rehabilitation programs, and showed that remorse, he would likely be paroled after three years. Even if his appeal is successful, he may well have served most of that minimum sentence by the time the process is concluded. But it's clear he feels that the appeals gamble is worth risking failure and a longer incarceration—that restoring his reputation and claiming innocence are more important than accepting responsibility.

Despite my resolve not to worry about the future or spend any more time in Cosby's world, I do want him to serve his full sentence. Mercy should be reserved for those who show remorse. Cosby's incarceration is a powerful signal to the world that there are consequences for wrongdoing—even for the most powerful among us. It's an important reminder that money doesn't insulate people from the demands of justice. And perhaps most important of all, his incarceration may give a sense of safety to all those women who are haunted by memories of him. It won't lead to healing—healing always comes from the inside—but it may bring peace.

Cosby will always have a voice—even in jail. Camille Cosby, Andrew Wyatt, Ebonee Benson, and his lawyers continue to tell his story. (As the appeals process makes evident, Cosby's narrative will continue to shadow me and my family.) While my account of the assault was shared in court, my larger story has been told by others, and often with great sympathy and understanding. Yet after so many years of not being able to talk to anyone about what happened to me and my family, it felt important to reclaim my history and my voice.

Just as I suspected when I listened to my parents' victim impact statements, their recovery has been tougher than my own. They have both struggled with health issues, and my father has been hardened by a bitterness he can't seem to escape. So I want people to understand the struggles and the sacrifices my family made—and to see how their love supported me over the years. I want people to understand how they shaped me, and how their example so beautifully illustrates the power of love to conquer all and the power of truth to triumph over darkness. I hope that our story will provide comfort, understanding, and inspiration for people who are facing trying times, and for those who love them.

And now that I have written my story and have spent months and months looking back over my past, I am ready to put all my energy into making a better future. I look forward to continuing my work as a healer, to helping other survivors, to experiencing new adventures. And much to Donna Motsinger's delight, I now look forward to love. I finally feel as if I might have the emotional strength to allow others in again, to make room for vulnerability, affection, intimacy, and passion. After many long years, my world is opening up once more, and the future appears bursting with possibility.

This past winter, I was up at my parents' home in the countryside, spending the weekend with my family. It was a beautiful day, and my niece Melanie and I decided to go for a walk in the woods.

As I bounded through the clean, crisp snow, I heard Melanie call out, "Hey, Auntie Dre. Wait up!"

I turned around. My niece, shorter than me, was struggling in the snow. It was deep, almost up to my knees but past hers.

"I don't think I'm going to be able to make it through," she said.

The sun was sparkling across a fresh white expanse that was broken only by the soft shadows where my boots had compressed the snow.

"Follow me," I said. "Walk in my footsteps!" I would shorten my stride to match hers; I would break a path that she could use.

Marching through the snow on that bright and magical afternoon reminded me of what a joy, a blessing, a *privilege* it can be to blaze trails for other people, to lead the way. I would hardly call my experience with Bill Cosby lucky, yet I recognize the luck I had in it. To be able to be the voice of others, to pursue justice when so many women couldn't. To give victims a sense of vindication and perhaps a bit more hope that their own fights for justice might also bear fruit. To fight the good fight and, against the odds, achieve something profoundly important.

I will be forever grateful that I was given that chance.

———

I wrote the sentence above in April 2021. Two months later, on June 30th, my journey for truth and justice took a sharp turn. It was a little before noon, and I had just come back from a long, sun-soaked walk with my now fifteen-year-old poodle Maddy, when my phone rang. It was Kate Delano, director of communications for the Montgomery County DA's office. She was calling to tell me that the Pennsylvania Supreme Court was about to announce its decision regarding Bill Cosby's appeal.

The next hour or so trickled by as I did my best to stay calm and centred. But when my phone rang again, I pounced on it. A chill went through me as I heard the heavy, rushed tone of Kate's voice.

"Andrea," she said, "the Supreme Court has vacated his conviction."

I was stunned. The judges had not declared a mistrial or simply overturned the jury's verdict. They had rejected the charges against Cosby altogether, accepting the idea that the former district attorney, Bruce Castor, had given Cosby immunity. That meant Bill Cosby could never again be brought to trial for my assault. He would, in fact, walk out of the prison shortly after Kate's call.

I had no time to absorb this shocking news. My phone began ringing and beeping incessantly—friends, family, and news outlets, all wanting to hear from me. Almost three years after the most challenging period of my life had concluded, I was back in a media maelstrom.

As call after call came in, I struggled with my growing outrage. But when I saw Bebe Kivitz's name on my phone, I knew that as much as I wanted to cry, now was not the time for tears. It was, instead, time for action. Indeed, Bebe was calling to discuss the statement that she, Dolores, and I would release later that day:

> *Today's majority decision regarding Bill Cosby is not only disappointing but of concern in that it may discourage those who seek justice for sexual assault in the criminal justice system from reporting or participating in the prosecution of the assailant or may force a victim to choose between filing either a criminal or civil action.*
>
> *On the one hand, the Court acknowledged that the former District Attorney's decision not to prosecute Mr. Cosby was not a formal immunity agreement and constituted at best a unilateral exercise of prosecutorial discretion not to prosecute at the time. The Court also acknowledged that it agreed with the lower court's*

credibility determinations, but nevertheless precluded a future prosecution, which included additional evidence developed in the civil case. The Supreme Court acknowledged that it was bound by the lower court's credibility findings, including that Andrea Constand and her civil counsel, Dolores Troiani and Bebe Kivitz, were not privy to any discussions between the former prosecutor and Mr. Cosby or his then criminal counsel, let alone signatories to any agreement of any kind. We were not consulted or asked our thoughts by Mr. Castor concerning any agreements concerning immunity or anything, and we were not made aware if there were any such discussions. The press release had no meaning or significance to us in 2005 other than being a press release circulated by the then District Attorney.

Once again, we remain grateful to those women who came forward to tell their stories, to DA Kevin Steele and the excellent prosecutors who achieved a conviction at trial, despite the ultimate outcome which resulted from a procedural technicality, and we urge all victims to have their voices heard. We do not intend to make any further comment.

While that last line may be true for Bebe and Dolores, I do have further comment. Now that I have weathered yet another strange turn in this long saga, I realize that I cannot let reversals like the Supreme Court decision defeat me. Life is unpredictable. Much is beyond our control. In the end, happiness is all that matters—and I am determined to live a happy, purposeful life. Part of that bright future will be the work I am doing to support sexual assault victims and to help other voices be heard. We cannot let moments of injustice quiet us.

We must speak up again and again and again—until we arrive at a moment of real change.

HOPE, HEALING, AND TRANSFORMATION

The Cosby trials and everything that happened around them—all those women coming forward with their stories, all those voices being raised—made me realize, once the verdict was in, that I was being given an opportunity to help in another way as well. In the spring of 2019 I contacted Delaney Henderson of PAVE and Geri Lynn Matthews, a longtime advocate for sexual assault survivors. I told them I wanted to create a way for survivors to access support and resources that would help them recover and transform their trauma into purposeful living and healing. I wanted to share what I had learned through my own journey by providing a trauma-informed, holistic healing program. Ultimately, I had found extraordinary people and invaluable tools that helped me address both my personal and my legal struggles. But I wasn't aware of those resources in the early days after my assault. And even in 2015, it took years to find all the resources that helped me through. I wanted to make that process much easier and more timely for other victims.

The conversations and work that grew from there produced Hope Healing and Transformation (HHT), a non-profit organization that I founded in 2019. Delaney and Geri Lynn are board members, along with the wonderful Michelle Francis-Smith, my former massage therapy teacher, healer, and fellow survivor. And we have a small team of talented and dedicated staff. Our online hub provides community support and connections to online resources. In June 2020, we launched the SAFEAPP (for Survivors Achieving Freedom and Empowerment), a set of digital platform modules. Available in the Apple and Google app stores, it offers valuable information about surviving sexual assault, links to various legal and mental and physical health resources, and a mind/body/spirit holistic program focused on trauma-informed healing. Part of the inspiration for writing this book was to support the work we're doing at HHT. A portion of the author's proceeds will go directly to the foundation.

SOURCES

Sources included but were not limited to the following:

"Cosby Tops Forbes List of Richest Entertainers," by James M. Kennedy, *APNews*, September 6, 1987

"Police Investigate Allegation Made Against Bill Cosby," *The Associated Press*, January 21, 2005

"Toronto-Area Woman Accuses Cosby of Sex Assault: NBC," by Scott Stinson, *National Post*, January 21, 2005

"Cosby Claim's Timing Called Bizarre," by Maryclaire Dale, *The Associated Press*, January 22, 2005

"Cosby Hires Lawyer After Groping Allegations," *Knight Ridder News Service*, January 22, 2005

"Unfunny Business," by Carol Beggy and Mark Shanahan, *The Boston Globe*, January 24, 2005

"Prosecutor Cites Flaws in Allegation Against Cosby," *The Associated Press*, January 27, 2005

"Shocking Charges: Cosby Drugged Two Women for Sex," *National Enquirer*, February 1, 2005

"He Did Exactly the Same Thing to Me," by Nicole Weisensee Egan,
   Philadelphia Daily News, February 8, 2005

"Bill Cosby Speaks Out to the National Enquirer," *National Enquirer*,
   March 2, 2005

"Cos Discusses Scandal," by Nicole Weisensee Egan, *Philadelphia
   Daily News*, March 3, 2005

"Bill Cosby Civil Case Files," https://documento.mx/documents/bill-
   cosby-civil-case-files-5c11050d21c88

"I Paid Off Bill Cosby's Girls," by Chelsia Rose Marcius,
   Brian Niemietz, and Larry McShane, *New York Daily News*,
   November 23, 2014

"Gloria Allred: Cosby Should Have $100 Million Ready for Victims,"
   by Kate Mather and Richard Winton, *Los Angeles Times*,
   December 3, 2014

"Phylicia Rashad and the Awful Power of 'Forget These Women,'"
   by Spencer Kornhaber, *The Atlantic*, January 7, 2015

"3 More on Cosby Sex-Accuser List," by Nancy Dillon, *New York
   Daily News*, April 24, 2015

"Document in Cosby Case," www.nytimes.com/interactive/2015/07/07/
   business/media/document-cosby-case.html, July 7, 2015

"Bill Cosby, in Deposition, Said Drugs and Fame Helped Him Seduce
   Women," by Graham Bowley and Sydney Ember, *The New York Times*,
   July 18, 2015

"Highlights from Bill Cosby's 2005-2006 Deposition," *www.cnn.com*, July 23, 2015

"Damon Wayans Defends Bill Cosby, Calls Accusers 'Un-rape-able,'" by Arlene Washington, *The Hollywood Reporter*, September 7, 2015

"PA. Cosby Case May Be Viable Still," by Jeremy Roebuck and Laura McCrystal, *The Philadelphia Inquirer*, September 13, 2015

"Constand Lawyer Rips Remarks by Castor," by Jeremy Roebuck and Laura McCrystal, *The Philadelphia Inquirer*, September 18, 2015

"Cosby Seeking Lawyer for Montco Probe," by Maryclaire Dale, *The Associated Press*, September 24, 2015

"Bill Cosby's Lawyer Signals Defense Strategy: It's Politics," by Maria Puente, *USA Today*, January 1, 2016

"DA: No Deal to Protect the Cos," by Jeremy Roebuck and Laura McCrystal, *Philadelphia Daily News*, January 13, 2016

"Cosby's Lawyers Say DA Violating Deal," by Jeremy Roebuck and Laura McCrystal, *The Philadelphia Inquirer*, January 30, 2016

"Interview with Dick Gregory," *The Breakfast Club Power*, FM 105.1, March 28, 2016

"Read Excerpts from Cosby's 2005-2006 Quaalude Deposition," *The Associated Press*, May 23, 2016

"Bill Cosby Ordered to Stand Trial in Decade-Old Case," by Maryclaire Dale and Michel R. Sisek, *The Associated Press*, May 24, 2016

"Bill Cosby Sexual Assault Trial Can Proceed, Judge Rules," by Graham
    Bowley, *The New York Times*, May 24, 2016

"Gov. Hickenlooper Signs Bill Extending Rape Statute of Limitations,
    Inspired by Cosby Allegations," by Claire Cleveland, *The Denver Post*,
    June 10, 2016

"Bill Cosby's Lawyer Cites 'Racial Bias and Prejudice' Amid Sex Assault
    Allegations," by Michael Rothman and Andrew Wyatt, *www.abcnews.
    go.com*, September 6, 2016

"Bill Cosby's Legal Team Faults Media, Race Bias," *APNews*, September 6,
    2016, www.youtube.com/watch?v=n6r6s7hXxNs

"Bill Cosby's Lawyers Claim Racial Bias," by Maryclaire Dale,
    The Associated Press, September 9, 2016

"For the First Time, Cosby's Lawyers Claim Racism," by Maryclaire Dale,
    The Associated Press, September 9, 2016

"At the Bill Cosby Trial, 'Canada's Mom' Slays 'America's Dad,'"
    by Anne Kingston, *Maclean's*, June 8, 2017

"Cosby Lawyer Seeks to Show a Romantic Tie," by Steven Zeitchik,
    Los Angeles Times, June 8, 2017

"Cosby Jury Breaks with No Verdict," by Laura McCrystal, Michaelle Bond,
    and Aubrey Whelan, *The Philadelphia Inquirer*, June 14, 2017

"Jurors End Second Day of Cosby Deliberations," by Maryclaire Dale
    and Henry R. Sisak, *The Associated Press*, June 14, 2017

"Deliberations Wear on Cosby Jury," by Jeremy Roebuck and Laura McCrystal, *Philly.com* and *The Morning Call* (Allentown, Pennsylvania), June 15, 2017

"Judge Tells Deadlocked Jurors to Keep Trying," by Jeremy Roebuck, Laura McCrystal, and Michaelle Bond, *The Philadelphia Inquirer*, June 16, 2017

"Bill Cosby Sexual Assault Trial Ends in Mistrial," by Hannah Rappleye and Tracy Conner, *NBCnews.com*, June 17, 2017

"Cosby Side Declares Victory, Goes on Attack," AP Archives, June 27, 2017, www.youtube.com/watch?v=7EycualulNA

"Bill Cosby Performs in First Show Since 2015," by Michael Sisek, *The Associated Press*, January 24, 2018

"Cosby's Lawyers Seek to Replace Judge Because of His Wife's Advocacy for Sex Assault Victims," by Debra Cassens Weiss, *ABA Journal*, March 23, 2018

"The Bill Cosby Judge Just Gave a Powerful, Emotional Defense of His Marriage," by Eric Levenson and Aaron Cooper, *cnn.com*, March 30, 2018

"Topless Protester Arrested at First Day of Cosby Retrial Used to Be on *The Cosby Show*," by Natalie Hope McDonald, *Vulture.com*, April 9, 2018

"Catalyzed by Cosby, Advocates Aim to End Time Limits on Reporting Sexual Assault," by Dana DiFilippo, *www.whyy.org (PBS)*, April 11, 2018

"New Cosby Victim Emerges in Light of Conviction — 'I Was Just 16 Years Old,'" by Chris Epting, *www.medium.com*, May 1, 2018

"Should Statutes of Limitations for Rape Be Abolished?" by Ruth Padawer, *The New York Times Magazine*, June 19, 2018

"Bill Cosby: Cops Swarm Mansion on His 81st Bday," *www.tmz.com*, July 12, 2018

"Cosby Faces the Music: Cops Called to Disgraced Comedian's Mansion on His 81st Birthday Over 'Loud Jazz' Celebration as He Remains Under House Arrest," by Hannah Parry, *DailyMail.com*, July 12, 2018

"60 Bill Cosby Accusers: Complete Breakdown of the Accusation," by Wrap Staff and Brian Welk, *www.thewrap.com*, September 25, 2018

"A Complete List of the 60 Bill Cosby Accusers and Their Reactions to His Prison Sentence," by Carly Mallenbaum, Patrick Ryan, and Maria Puente, *USA Today*, April 27, 2018, updated September 26, 2018

"Commonwealth v. William Henry Cosby, Jr." (criminal trial transcripts), www.montcopa.org/2312/Commonwealth-v-William-Henry-Cosby-Jr

"AIG to Settle Defamation Lawsuits with Seven Bill Cosby Accusers," by Joanna Walters, *The Guardian*, April 5, 2019

"Bill Cosby Settles Defamation Lawsuit Brought by Seven Women," by Barbara Goldberg, *Reuters*, April 5, 2019

"Bill Cosby Drops Defamation Case Against Sexual Assault Accusers," by Guardian staff and agencies, *The Guardian*, May 31, 2019

"Model Janice Dickinson Settles Defamation Suit Against Bill Cosby," *losangeles.cbslocal.com*, July 25, 2019

"'They're Not Going to Hear Me Say That I Have Remorse': Bill Cosby Prepared to Serve 10-Year Max Sentence for Sex Assault," CBS/AP, *www.philadelphia.cbslocal.com*, November 25, 2019

Chasing Cosby: The Downfall of America's Dad, by Nicole Weisensee Egan, Seal Press, Berkeley, California, 2019

"Bill Cosby Is Granted the Right to Appeal His Conviction on Sexual Assault Charges," by Eric Levenson and Steve Forrest, *www.cnn.com*, June 23, 2020

"Bill Cosby Sexual Assault Cases," en.wikipedia.org/wiki/Bill_Cosby_sexual_assault_cases#:~:text=Cosby's%20first%20trial%20in%20June,cost%20of%20the%20prosecution%2C%20%2443%2C611

"Bill Cosby Sexual Assault Cases," www.wikiwand.com/en/Bill_Cosby_sexual_assault_cases

ACKNOWLEDGMENTS

First, I want to thank my mother, Gianna, and father, Andrew. They have had such an immense impact on my life, and this book would not have been possible without them. Their love, encouragement, and support allowed me to dig deep to find my voice and tell my story. I am also grateful to my sister, Diana, for her loyalty and friendship, to my nieces, Melanie and Andrea, for knowing when I needed a hug and smiles, and to my brother-in-law, Stuart Parsons, for all the amazing meals he prepared for us to enjoy together. My extended relatives and family members were also a wonderful source of strength and support.

Thanks to my friends both near and far who stood by me through thick and thin—you know who you are. Also to the teachers, coaches, and survivors around the world who supported me often by reaching out through email and social media during the trials.

My legal team, Bebe Kivitz and Dolores Troiani, were my rocks. Prosecutors Kevin Steele, Stewart Ryan, and Kristen Feden were brilliant, tireless, and inspiring champions for justice. My case was also made possible by the hard work and dedication of the Cheltenham Township police detectives. I couldn't have survived the two trials without the love and care of Erin Slight, Kiersten McDonald, Angela Rose, Delaney Henderson, and everyone at PAVE. I will be forever grateful that all of you were there.

Thanks to everyone on the Penguin Random House team: publishing director Diane Turbide, for believing in me and giving me the opportunity to share my story; copy editor Janice Weaver, for her keen eye; editorial assistant Alanna McMullen, for her assistance with photos. Much thanks to my agent, Jackie Kaiser, for taking my hand and walking me through the ins and outs of becoming a first-time author and to Meg Masters, for helping me get my story down on the page.

I owe a huge debt of gratitude to the Cosby survivors who rose up when the world was ready to listen; I stand in truth and solidarity with you all. Activist Bird Milliken, thank you for your friendship, passion, and energy and for bringing survivors together to heal and connect.

Finally I would like to thank God for his divine love, and the Self-Realization Fellowship community for its guidance and support. My guru, Paramahansa Yogananda, and his Kriya yoga, with its timeless wisdom and lineage of masters, have changed my life.